ACID
POWER!

David E. Franks

ACID Power!

Credits: Cover and interior design, Michelle Frey, Stephanie Japs, Cathie Tibbetts, and Kevin Vollrath, *DOV Graphics*; technical editors, Jared Held, Richard Morgan, and Lori Denning; copy editor, Hope Stephan; proofreader, Rodney Wilson; index, Kevin Broccoli, *Broccoli Information Management*.

Publisher: Andy Shafran

Technology and the Internet are constantly changing, and by necessity of the lapse of time between the writing and distribution of this book, some aspects might be out of date. Accordingly, the author and publisher assume no responsibility for actions taken by readers based upon the contents of this book.

Library of Congress Catalog Number: 2001091349

ISBN 1-929685-49-1

5 4 3 2 1

Educational facilities, companies, and organizations interested in multiple copies or licensing of this book should contact the publisher for quantity discount information. Training manuals, CD-ROMs, and portions of this book are also available individually or can be tailored for specific needs.

MUSKA&LIPMAN

Muska & Lipman Publishing
2645 Erie Avenue, Suite 41
Cincinnati, Ohio 45208
www.muskalipman.com
publisher@muskalipman.com

About the Author

David E. Franks

A multimedia artist specializing in digital video production and scoring, David has authored four major books on multimedia software that have been translated into nine languages on six continents. As a freelance composer, he has sold music created in ACID to major software developers for use in widely distributed Flash presentations, product demonstrations, and training materials.

David supports his loop-library addiction by working as the technical editor at a leading video magazine. After hours, he has been collaborating electronically with a producer half-way around the world, scoring an edgy documentary for a cut of any eventual revenues, which no one but the producer actually believes will ever materialize. He currently resides in Chico, CA, and can be virtually visited at maxent.org/acidpower.html.

Dedication

Trite but never truer: to my parents who let me go where the winds may call and my sister who always remembered to ask how the book was progressing. Without their unconditional support, I would not have had the security to follow my bliss. And to ChiaFang, Heidi, and Cherico at Ulead for purchasing my music back when I was an ACID 1.0 novice. It may not have been a big paycheck and the songs are a bit embarrassing to listen to today, but this book would not exist without that little light bulb that blinked on in my head saying, "Hey, I can make money doing this."

Acknowledgments

This book was a collaborative effort from Day One and there are a handful of people I would like to thank. At Muska & Lipman, I'd like to single out Andy "is that chapter done yet" Shafran, Hope "nothing gets past me" Stephan, and Rodney A. Wilson. Almost certainly underpaid and overworked, without their encouragement, advice, and careful editing, this book would be significantly less clear and would contain many more errors. I'd also like to identify a much under appreciated and elite group of folks who went through this book looking for technical errors: Jared Held, Richard Morgan, and Lori Denning (not to mention Rodney again and Allen Wyatt at Muska & Lipman). Their dedication has immeasurably improved this book. Any errors that remain are not to be laid at their doorstep but must ultimately be traced back to their source.

Contents

5–Recording Vocals and Solos 99

6–Mastering the Mix 117

7–FX 135

8–FX Dictionary 149

12–Publishing   251

13–Loose Ends   277

Appendix Shortcuts   287

Index   293

Introduction

Sophisticated yet simple, the process of creating professional sounding music using just about any computer is now in the hands of the masses. ACID is, first and foremost, fun; you can produce something that sounds pretty good the very first time you fire ACID up. This masks the fact that ACID is a powerful and professional level tool ideally suited to song creation and film scoring, among other uses. This book intends to comprehensively cover these higher-level features and show you how to use ACID in real world situations. Whether you are a new wave multimedia designer creating engrossing content for the 'Net or an old school producer in a traditional audio studio, these pages aim to show you how to take full advantage of ACID.

ACID is a musician's tool, and song creation and multi-track mixing are the primary focus of the program. ACID is ideally suited for multimedia professionals who need to create original music for Director presentations and Flash animations. Video and film professionals will find no tool better suited to scoring. DJs and mixmasters can use ACID to remix songs in amazing new ways. And of course studios and musicians will find the multi-track mixing and recording features second to none. The powerful effects sitting behind ACID's apparent simplicity enable you to create truly professional material.

One of the most amazing aspects of ACID is its apparent simplicity. Don't let that fool you—there's a lot going on under the hood. Beat matching, tempo adjustment, key matching, and mixing are only a few of the things that you may never notice as you use ACID. Once you've explored the program for a while, get ready for the next level with complex effects, digital video, MIDI, cutting edge compression algorithms, CD burning, and Internet publishing. That's what this book is about.

How This Book is Organized

ACID Power! is divided into thirteen chapters:

▶ Chapter 1, "ACID Basics: Getting Around"—A short but comprehensive tour of the workspace. This chapter is a one-stop reference to all of the pieces and parts that make up ACID.

▶ Chapter 2, "A Song is Born"—A solid grounding in the fundamentals is a necessary first step to getting the most out of ACID.

▶ Chapter 3, "Composition"—Most ACID songs start as a random collection of ideas and loops. This chapter details how to take an ACID rough draft and turn it into an artistic composition. No previous musical knowledge required!

▶ Chapter 4, "Polishing Up"—The compositional ideas presented in this chapter are the icing on the cake and can be the difference between a good song and a great one.

▶ Chapter 5, "Recording Vocals and Solos"—The first of the more advanced technical sections, this chapter serves as an introduction to sound recording with ACID in a home studio with modest equipment.

▶ Chapter 6, "Mastering the Mix"—A sadly neglected art, mixing is a crucial element of any ACID composition. A bad mix can ruin a good song and this is not a chapter to skip over.

▶ Chapter 7, "FX"—The effects (FX) included with ACID can be infinitely tweaked and combined to create an infinite soundscape. This chapter covers the nuts-and-bolts of FX use, with important signposts identifying potential pitfalls and problems.

▶ Chapter 8, "FX Dictionary"—From Amplitude Modulation to Vibrato, this chapter comprehensively defines all of the effects found in ACID Pro, including detailed explanations of some of the more perplexing controls and parameters.

▶ Chapter 9, "Loops"—Media loops are the atoms from which ACID songs are built and an understanding of how they work is essential to mastering ACID. Loop creation, modification, acquisition, and copyright laws are just a few of the topics covered here.

▶ Chapter 10, "The Secret Life of ACID MIDI"—New to ACID 3.0, including MIDI songs in ACID is a dream come true for many artists. This chapter introduces this potentially complex area of digital music creation in a clear and simple manner.

▶ Chapter 11, "Video"—Also new to ACID 3.0, the inclusion of a simple yet robust video track turns ACID into a powerful scoring tool.

▶ Chapter 12, "Publishing"—Unless you use ACID for purely personal pleasure (and there's nothing wrong with that), distributing and publishing your songs is an obvious last step. Everything from digital compression to protecting your work with copyrights is included here.

▶ Chapter 13, "Loose Ends"—Anything that didn't logically fit in another chapter is here, but that doesn't mean this isn't an important chapter, which includes sections on loop management and a comprehensive treatment of the many preferences found in ACID.

▶ Appendix—Don't overlook this invaluable reference to the stunningly extensive set of shortcuts that Sonic Foundry has programmed into ACID. Even a cursory knowledge will improve your efficiency and will clearly identify you as an ACID guru.

This book takes you beyond the basics and into guru level procedures that utilize ACID 3.0 to its fullest potential. ACID is more than a toy, although it can be more fun that a video game. This book is targeted towards the intelligent user who is ready to use ACID as a serious artistic tool or on the job as a multimedia professional. The clear and solid examples will quickly allow the non-technically inclined reader to express their creativity more fully. On the other hand, technically savvy non-musicians will find the chapters on introductory music theory invaluable in moving beyond casually playing with ACID and into serious music composition. And for those of you who are both techno-wizards in computers and the studio, this book is going to show you the most efficient techniques to maximize ACID's power.

This book is going to start with the fun stuff. As mentioned above, you can definitely be pumping out some pretty amazing tunes within minutes of popping the ACID CD into your computer. And you really should play for a bit immediately after you install the program (and before your read another word). The first goal of this book is to familiarize you with the nuts and bolts of ACID. Thanks to the well thought out workspace and program workflow, ACID can be mastered fairly quickly.

The second goal of this book is to go beyond the basics and into true music creation. Most people never create a song that is more than a bunch of music clips (loops) that sound good together layered track onto track. This simplicity is deceptive, however. Just as a good story or novel has an arresting introduction, a dynamic exposition, a shocking conclusion, and a satisfying denouement, so a good song also has structure. To use another analogy, just because you can type doesn't mean you can write a great novel. The middle section of this book focuses on music and music theory, with a heavy emphasis on how to effortlessly express your musical ideas using ACID.

The final goal of this book is to get into some of the more technical aspects of ACID. From burning industry standard CDs to highly compressed MP3 files with nearly lossless quality, publishing and sharing your music is the ultimate goal. In the process, this book will cover everything you need to know about maximizing the quality of your music after the creative process is over. In addition, it will show you how to polish your masterpieces using effects processing. There are also a hundred other fascinating topics that you can dive into, from amazing MIDI technology to recording your own vocals and solo jams. This book is all you need to get you on your way.

There are a few things that may make using this book easier. The first is a NOTE. NOTES usually contain additional information that is particularly important to understand. Anything critical to understand but likely to be lost in the hundreds of thousands of words that compose this book might be set off as a NOTE.

NOTE
Do not taunt Happy Fun Ball.

A TIP, on the other hand, are not so critical. A TIP typically contains information and ideas to make your life easier or enhance ACID's performance. Sometimes an entire procedure can be executed with a single keyboard shortcut, and such a shortcut will frequently be highlighted in a TIP.

TIP
ACID is most enjoyable when the volume is turned up to 11.

Which ACID is Which?

Sonic Foundry has released a number of different versions of ACID, from a free version that may be included on a CD-ROM that came with a new computer or another piece of hardware up to an expensive professional version. As you might expect, you get what you pay for.

ACID XPress is the free version of the program used as a promotional introduction to the ACID family by Sonic Foundry. You will certainly get a taste of the application and be able to create some pretty cool stuff, but you are otherwise quite limited. Sonic Foundry may offer some good deals on upgrading to a higher version from the Express version.

ACID "Style" (DJ, Techno, and so on) describes a broad category of products, all of which include the ACID Style version of the program and a collection of loops from a specific genre (e.g. ACID Techno is a collection of electronic loops and the ACID Style version of the application). While ACID Style is a bit more capable than ACID XPress, these versions of the program are still truly introductory in nature and lack some of the features you will need to take ACID beyond the novice stage. Again, check with Sonic Foundry for special upgrade prices.

ACID Music is the base level of application that this book covers. If you are even mildly serious about producing quality music, there is no question that you need to own at least this version of ACID. Full-featured and powerful, ACID Music is reasonably priced to fit the budget of the interested amateur musician and composer, yet it can still produce professional level output. ACID Music also comes with a CD of basic loops.

ACID Pro is the high-end version of ACID that is appropriate for studios, professionals, and prosumers. As with other versions, stepping up to this version when you are ready is a simple matter. Uncompromising quality and the technical tools you need to get the job done make this an awesome addition to any multimedia professional's audio rack. ACID Pro also comes with a CD of basic loops and includes an extensive set of audio effects plug-ins.

Getting Additional Help

Readers of this book should not forget (nor underestimate) the quality of the documentation that came with the program from Sonic Foundry. This text should be seen as a supplement to these primary references and not as a substitute. Read the manual, pause the mouse cursor over unfamiliar items in the UI to get ToolTips, watch the Status Bar at the bottom of the program, and don't forget to use F1 for specific context sensitive Help on just about anything. Finally, check out Sonic Foundry's Web site and user forums. The discussions that occur on ACIDPlanet can often be nearly as interesting as the music that shows up there.

http://www.sonicfoundry.com

http://www.acidplanet.com

1

ACID Basics: Getting Around

As you undoubtedly have already noticed from using ACID, the program is well laid out and easy to use. This may lull you into thinking that ACID is a simple program, when, in fact, it is a very sophisticated and powerful tool. Familiarity with ACID's various windows, dialog boxes, and menus is critical to getting the most out of this software. The ACID workspace is laid out in a logical and efficient manner, designed with a specific workflow in mind. Understanding this workflow will maximize your ACID experience.

Fortunately, learning the workspace is a simple process. This chapter starts by noting some of the different ways you can use ACID. The remainder serves as a full introduction and reference to all of the various parts of ACID. Individual controls and windows are explained more fully in later chapters as they become relevant. Although the focus of this book is on more advanced topics, musical composition, and taking ACID to the next level, a solid grounding in the fundamentals is the necessary first step.

ACID Loops

ACID is a loop-based music composition tool, which raises the more basic question: What are loops? Loops are typically short segments of music that are combined to form larger works. The word "loop" comes from the original concept of taking a short piece of magnetic audiotape and connecting the start and finish to form a circle that would play back endlessly. Using tape loops and samples from other songs (and other sources) became a very popular technique in the mid-1980s. Arguably, the most sampled material came from older James Brown songs sampled and looped into dance tracks. Many original artists rejected the appropriation of their work and criticized the new music as being, at the very least, derivative and possibly even copyright violations for using material without permission. Other artists, notably George Clinton, embraced the new music and encouraged others to sample their work freely.

Modern electronics and computers have eliminated the magnetic audiotape from the equation. Loops are now created on computers and sold on CD-ROMs. While loops are most obviously used in repetitive electronic dance music, widely available acoustic and even orchestral loops mean that loop-based composition has invaded just about every genre of music. A three-piece guitar/bass/drum band might want a tabla percussion line in a song and use a commercial loop library instead of trying to find a tabla player. Or an ad agency might need an orchestral swell to build into the studio-recorded soundtrack to a commercial, but might not have the budget to rent out a symphony for an afternoon.

Today, they can turn to commercially produced loops. A tabla player was originally paid by a loop-production company (perhaps Sonic Foundry) that now owns the copyright and grants the end user (you) legal permission to use the recording in your own work. Musicians can also create their own original loops in addition to buying commercial loops on CD-ROM. As with any multitrack studio, this allows a single (talented) individual to play all of the parts of a song. While it may be a simple matter to pick out a James Brown yell in a modern club mix, the ubiquity of high-quality loops, in all styles of music for any application, makes it very difficult (if not impossible) to identify the use of loops in music today.

ACID is the premiere tool for creating loop-based music. This music might be 100 percent loop-based and created from scratch from within ACID, or it might be music that is 90 percent conventional recorded-by-actual-musicians-in-a-studio music with the addition of a loop or two. ACID functions as a virtual multitrack recording studio, laying down loops into individual tracks just as a musician might lay down a track in a real-world studio. More than this, ACID is a specialized tool that specifically targets looped media, identifying pitch and tempo characteristics of looped media files saved in a particular ACID format. This allows ACID to automatically line up the beats in various loops, seamlessly loop media end-to-end, and match the key or pitch. This specialization allows ACID to be used as a standalone tool or in combination with other multimedia tools, both hardware and software based.

For example, while ACID has some pretty impressive features that allow you to manipulate audio files on your computer, Sonic Foundry's Sound Forge is better suited for heavy duty audio file editing. Likewise, although ACID functions as a multitrack environment, it is still geared towards loop-based music; Sonic Foundry's Vegas is a much more capable virtual multitrack studio. New MIDI features expand ACID's potential greatly to include music generated by your sound card's music synthesizer, but ACID is not a MIDI editing tool, like Cakewalk SONAR. ACID is the ideal musical companion to a host of multimedia tools, allowing you to create soundtracks for video projects in video editors; produce small music files for Flash presentations on the Web; and compose original music for Director projects. Critical to all of this is that the music created in ACID can be high-quality original music, free of copyright restrictions and available for publication and broadcast.

A Visual Tour

The ACID 3.0 workspace is broken up into three major sections, as illustrated in Figure 1.1. Significant portions are taken directly from Microsoft Windows design principals. By using the Windows interface you're already familiar with—for example, menu commands and buttons— ACID creates a comfortable environment that is not novel or strange. Getting to know the overall layout will make using ACID (and reading this book) easier and is the key to really uncovering the features that make ACID special.

Figure 1.1
An overview of the
ACID workspace.

Menus

Toolbar

Timeline

Window
Docking Area

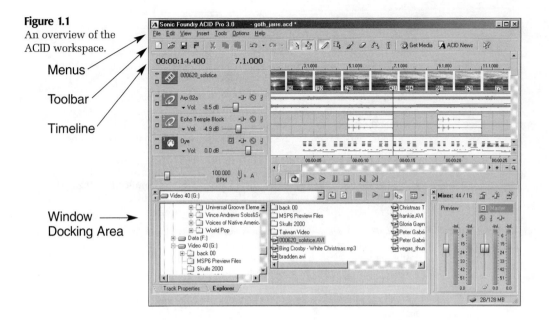

CHAPTER 1

The three major sections of the workspace are:

▶ **Menu** and **Toolbar**—These are standard Windows features that you are probably comfortable using. The menus contain very nearly all of the commands that control ACID. The toolbar contains a smaller subset of more frequently used commands and can be customized to display your choice of buttons.

▶ **Timeline**—Some sort of timeline is frequently a part of many multimedia programs, such as Macromedia Director or Adobe Premiere. Time increases as you progress towards the right down the timeline, allowing you to visually align events in a project. One important aspect of ACID's timeline area is the Track Header, located at the far left of the timeline. While not a part of the timeline proper, the Track Header contains many special controls.

▶ **Window Docking Area**—Below the timeline is the Window Docking Area. This is a broad catchall area that can contain all of the smaller sub-windows that do the real work in ACID. These sub-windows do not need to remain in this lower region but can be dragged anywhere on the screen or returned and docked in the Window Docking Area.

These three areas are discussed in more detail later in this section.

TIP

Many of the menu and toolbar items are standard features of any good Windows application. The main menus at the top of the program are the most comprehensive list of available commands in ACID.

ACID makes extensive use of shortcuts to speed up commands. Many of these shortcuts follow standard Windows conventions—for example, the Copy command can be quickly executed by pressing Ctrl + C on your keyboard simultaneously. Likewise, a Save command may be executed by pressing Ctrl + S.

Beyond the standard Windows commands, ACID menu shortcuts are identified to the right of the specific command. For example, all of the various windows in ACID can be instantly displayed or hidden by using the commands on the View menu or by using the associated keyboard shortcuts.

Figure 1.2 shows the View menu. To view the Explorer Window, for example, press Alt + 1 simultaneously. If you look at the View > Show Envelopes > Volume menu item, you'll notice the V next to it indicating that all you need to do is press V as the hotkey shortcut to do the same thing. While most menus can be navigated in ACID using keyboard shortcuts, only a limited subset of commands have hotkeys that can be executed without navigating menus.

Figure 1.2

Press Alt + V, E, and then V to toggle the Volume envelopes or press V at any time.

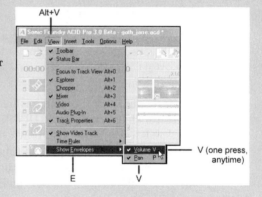

Timeline

The timeline forms the bulk of the ACID workspace. This is the area where the project is laid out, left to right, in chronological order. The various sounds or loops that are used to create a song are mixed together in tracks from top to bottom. There is no hierarchy to the tracks; all loops that overlap vertically are mixed together to form the audio that is played back from ACID. Track order is therefore left entirely up to you and is for your own benefit. The timeline is made up of many separate parts (see Figure 1.3).

Figure 1.3
The various parts of the Timeline.

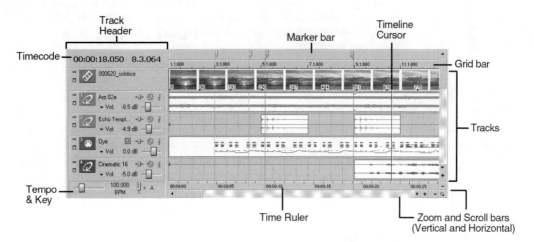

ACID **tracks** correspond to audio tracks in the real world. A traditional recording studio has equipment that allows the recording engineer to record multiple parts in a studio session to different tracks on a tape. For example, some drums might be recorded on one track, a saxamaphone on a second, a bass guitar on a third, and a piano on a fourth. Since each track is independent of the others, the engineer can then modify and mix these tracks individually. ACID tracks operate in a similar way, but they are actually much more versatile, since a track might have an audio recording, a MIDI composition, or a video component.

The **Timecode** at the upper left of the program specifies the current position of the timeline cursor (Time at Cursor) in a selected format and the measure and beat. The timeline cursor is a vertical line that runs from the top of the timeline to the bottom and moves when the project is played back. It may be thought of as being analogous to the playback head on a tape recorder.

The **Tempo** and **Key** of the project can be adjusted just below the track header. Both the Tempo, which defines the speed of the song, and the Key, which helps to generate the harmonics, are fundamental parts of any composition.

The **Maker bar**, **Grid bar**, and **Time Ruler** are all used to help you align and organize a song. The units displayed can be changed to your preference.

The **Zoom** and **Scroll** bars are important and easy to use, allowing you to see more detail in a project or navigate quickly to a new location.

NOTE

There are two basic cursors in ACID. One is the standard Windows mouse cursor, which most frequently appears as an arrow. In ACID, the straight vertical line that runs from the top to the bottom of the timeline is also a cursor, always referred to as the timeline cursor.

Navigating the Timeline

Moving forward and back on the timeline moves you forward and back through time in your project. The timeline cursor marks the position in time of the project and is the focus of any actions that you take. For example, when you press the Play button, the project begins playing back the project from the timeline cursor's position. If you paste a loop into a project, it will be pasted at the timeline cursor's position. Clicking anywhere in the timeline area moves the timeline cursor to that position.

Horizontal Scrolling (through time)

You can navigate the timeline by using the horizontal scroll bar at the bottom of the timeline. This allows you to view different parts of the project and is independent of the timeline cursor (that is, the timeline cursor does not always need to be on the screen).

▶ Use the arrow buttons on either end of the scroll bar to move left or right through a project.

▶ Drag the scroll bar to move left or right.

▶ Press and hold the Shift key on your keyboard and use your mouse wheel to move left or right.

NOTE

The wheel in the center of a Windows mouse is referred to as the mouse wheel, wheel button, or scroll wheel. Many Windows applications now take advantage of the mouse wheel for scrolling and zooming. While I don't want to seem like a mouse salesman, I must say that once you've used a mouse with a wheel, you'll wonder how you ever lived without it. This is doubly true for ACID 3.0.

Vertical Scrolling (through stacked tracks)

Eventually, a project will have enough tracks stacked up so that it will be difficult to conveniently view all of them at once. In this situation, you will also need to move up and down through the various tracks in a project.

▶ Use the arrow buttons at the top and bottom of the vertical scroll bar.

▶ Drag the vertical scroll bar up and down.

▶ Press and hold the Ctrl key on your keyboard and use your mouse wheel to move up and down.

Zooming

Zooming in and out on the timeline is one of the most fundamental skills needed to master ACID. Fortunately, zooming is very easy, especially if you have a mouse with a wheel button.

Project Zooming

Zooming controls the accuracy of your editing in ACID. While the final goal of ACID—and the ultimate measure of a project's success—is in what you hear, much of the brilliance of creating with ACID is that editing is done visually on your computer monitor. When loops are inserted into a project on the timeline, the audio is represented with a squiggly line. Loud sounds are represented with large squiggles and silent sections of an audio file are represented with flat horizontal lines. These lines are known as the *waveform* of the audio. Zooming in on a project allows you to see greater detail in an event's waveform or perform edits within very small fractions of a second. Zooming out gives you a better feel for a project overall and allows for much faster navigation. You will constantly be zooming out to move about a project and then immediately zooming back in to make a precision edit. Figures 1.4a and 1.4b show two different zoom levels of the same project.

Figure 1.4a
Zooming out allows you to see the entire project.

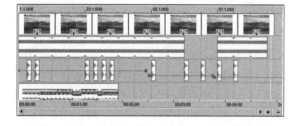

Figure 1.4b
A much closer look at the same project. Zooming in can allow editing at the millisecond level.

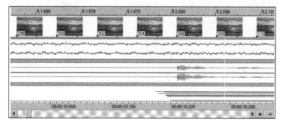

There are three ways to zoom in and out of a project:

- ▶ Use the + or − buttons on the horizontal scroll bar.
- ▶ Drag the edge of the horizontal scroll bar.
- ▶ Use the mouse wheel button.

http://www.muskalipman.com

CHAPTER 1

Track Zooming

Less important than project or timeline zooming is track level zooming. This simply controls the height of the tracks in ACID (see Figure 1.5), allowing you to see more tracks at one time (zoomed out) or to see more detail in a track (zoomed in). There are three ways to change the height of all of the tracks:

▶ Use the + or − buttons on the vertical scroll bar.

▶ Drag the small bar between the + and 1 buttons on the vertical scroll bar.

▶ Individual track heights can be adjusted by dragging the bottom edge in the track header.

Figure 1.5
Zooming out using the
Vertical Zoom/Scroll
bar makes the tracks
shorter and allows
more tracks to be
viewed at the same
time.

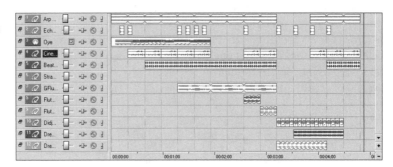

Transport Controls

The Transport Controls (see Figure 1.6) operate like standard media file playback or VCR controls. These buttons are used to move the timeline cursor around on the timeline and to control playback and recording in a project. A few transport controls are also available in the Explorer and Chopper windows (defined later).

Figure 1.6
The Transport Controls
are used to playback
and navigate around
media files.

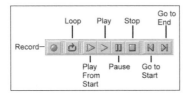

Tracks

Tracks are the equivalent of an audio track in a multitrack recording environment, as used by professionals in a studio. Each track is associated with a particular media file or loop on your computer, whether audio, video, or MIDI, just as a particular instrument might be associated with a particular instrument in a studio. Tracks can control effects, volume, panning, and other important aspects of how a media file is mixed into a project. Each track is divided into two major parts: the Track Header on the left and the timeline portion of the track on the right (see Figure 1.7). The Track Header serves as the control panel for the track with volume faders and FX controls and is analogous to the track controls on a physical mixer board in a studio. The main timeline portion of the track is where the song is displayed visually and most editing takes place.

Figure 1.7
Tracks are stacked on the timeline and are divided into two parts: the Track Header and the main body of the track on the timeline.

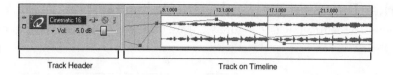

Track Header   Track on Timeline

CHAPTER 1

Events

Events are the most fundamental objects in ACID. Events can be thought of as containers for media files or windows into a media file. A single event can contain multiple repetitions of a media file or only a small portion of a much larger file. Events are drawn or painted onto the timeline and visually represent the project's output. Depending on the zoom level, events also display the sound in a media file with a waveform drawing (see Figure 1.8). The waveform shows the amplitude (loudness) of the sound waves over time, making visual edits possible.

Figure 1.8
Events contain media files and control exactly how they occur in a project. This event contains four repetitions of a loop.

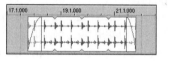

The most important distinction that you need to remember is that the occurrence of a loop or audio files in ACID is called an event. All editing and positioning is done on events and not on the original media file. All editing is completely non-destructive, meaning that changes you make to events on the timeline do not change the original source file in any way.

Envelopes

Envelopes overlay events in a track, controlling the volume and panning aspects in real time. Envelopes allow you to fade in and out of a loop or pan across stereo channels. For example, a red volume envelope that starts at the bottom of a track and moves up towards the center indicates a volume that gradually increases over time or fades in (see Figure 1.9). While envelopes are technically track-level objects, they operate on events and typically correspond to specific events in a track. For this reason, envelopes can be locked to events (they move as the events move) by making sure the Lock Envelopes to Events button is depressed.

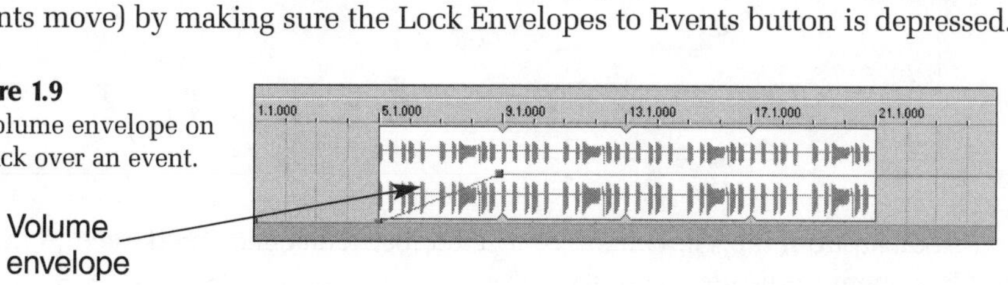

Figure 1.9
A volume envelope on a track over an event.

Volume envelope

Marker Bar, Grid Bar, and Time Ruler Bar

Surrounding the timeline (see Figure 1.10) are three bars that help you organize and subdivide your project.

Figure 1.10
Three bars help
organize a project.

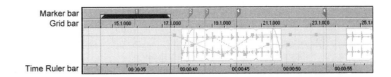

▶ **Maker bar**—This contains all markers and regions that you can use to organize and quickly navigate around a project. Markers serve as snapping points for the cursor and events in a project.

▶ **Grid bar**—This is divided up into measures, beats, and time in the following format: measure.beat.time or 00.00.000. Grid spacing can be changed. The detail visible in a grid depends on the zoom level in a project. Grid lines serve as snapping points for the cursor and events in a project.

▶ **Time Ruler**—This appears along the bottom of the timeline and is independent of the Grid. It serves only as a reference to time and can display time in a number of different formats (for example, SMPTE timecode of HH:MM:SS:FF).

Toolbar

The toolbar (see Figure 1.11) contains a small subset of the total number of commands available in ACID. The idea is that these buttons should be the commands that you use the most frequently, giving you faster access to them. The ACID toolbar defaults to twenty or so common buttons:

Figure 1.11
The default buttons
on the toolbar.

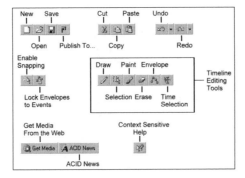

To Show or Hide the Toolbar, from the View menu, select Toolbar. The check mark next to the Toolbar item on the View menu indicates visibility.

The name of a button (and the command it executes) can be displayed by holding the mouse cursor over any button. The ToolTip that pops up over the toolbar buttons also appears over many objects in ACID and often displays the associated shortcut keys.

The default toolbar is Sonic Foundry's best guess as to what the user might want to do most frequently. ACID also allows a significant amount of customization to fit your personal work habits. This being the case, the particular command buttons that appear on the toolbar can be specified by the user. To customize the Toolbar:

1. From the Options menu, select Customize Toolbar.
2. In the Customize Toolbar dialog (see Figure 1.12):
    –Select a button from the Available toolbar buttons list and click Add to add a new button.
    –Select a button from the Current toolbar buttons list and click Remove to remove a button.
3. Click the Close button when finished.

Figure 1.12
Customizing
the toolbar.

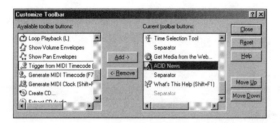

The order that the buttons appear on the toolbar can be changed by selecting individual buttons on the Current toolbar buttons list in the Customize Toolbar dialog and then clicking the Move Up or Move Down buttons.

Window Docking Area

The Window Docking area at the bottom of the ACID window is a catchall area designed to conveniently organize many of the smaller windows in ACID. By default, two of the most important windows are visible: the Explorer window and the Mixer window. The full list of windows that are associated with the Window Docking area can be found on the View menu. A checkmark next to a window's name indicates visibility; clicking a window name on this menu changes whether it is visible or not.

TIP
Use shortcuts to make the various windows visible: Press and hold the Alt key while also pressing the number keys 1-6 along the top of your keyboard.

Docking Windows

The "Docking" part of the Window Docking area means that the various windows can be locked into place and organized at the bottom of the program. This implies that there must be an undocked state for all of these windows, and indeed, there is. All of these windows can be dragged to and from the Window Docking area and can be positioned and resized anywhere on the screen (see Figure 1.13). This allows you to customize the look and feel of ACID to suit your working style.

Figure 1.13
The Chopper window in its docked and undocked (or floating) states.

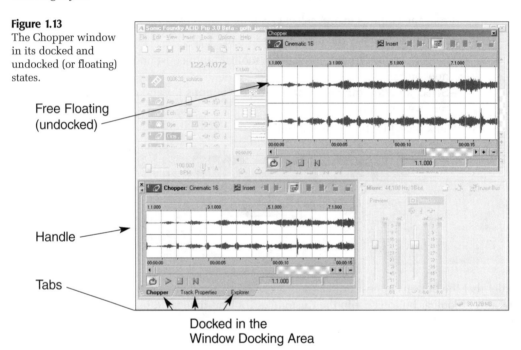

Free Floating (undocked)

Handle

Tabs

Docked in the
Window Docking Area

> To drag a window off the docking area, click on the handle on the left side of the window and drag it out of the docking area (typically towards the top of the application).

> To return a window to the docking area, click the title bar and drag it back to the docking area until it snaps into place.

Organizing the Window Docking Area

The purpose of having a docking area is organization. The docking area organizes the various windows in two distinct ways. First, the docking area itself can be subdivided into a number of different regions. Second, each region in the docking area can contain any or all of the various windows, stacked in a tabbed arrangement. Typically, the docking area is divided into two (or sometimes three) regions, and each region then contains one or two windows. The Window Docking area in Figure 1.14 is divided into three regions, allowing all of the possible windows to be conveniently accessed.

Figure 1.14
The Window Docking area in this example is divided into three regions.

Notice that the Video Preview and the Mixer windows are in their own regions by themselves. This allows these windows to remain visible at all times for important previewing and monitoring of project playback. Windows in the docking area can be rearranged by dragging them by the handle on the left side of the window.

▶ To stack windows in the same region, drop a window's handle directly on another windows handle.

▶ To place a window in its own region in the docking area, drop the window's handle anywhere in the docking area away from any other windows.

While it is possible to have all of the windows in separate regions or all in a single region, it is probably best to stack some less frequently used windows in the same region.

TIP
Layout considerations include frequency of use and available screen real estate. While the exact layout is entirely up to you, a good layout is one where you rarely ever need to resize or move any of the windows.

Resizing Windows

The various windows can be resized by dragging the edges of the window in and out. Windows can be resized in either a docked state or in a free-floating state. The entire docking region can be made taller or shorter by dragging the bar that separates the timeline from the Windows Docking area. In all cases, watch for the mouse cursor to change to a resize cursor when you are over the correct location for resizing.

NOTE
ACID saves the window layout that you have customized and will restart remembering all of the changes you have made.

CHAPTER 1

Defining the Windows

Each of the windows in ACID serves a very particular function. The operation of each of these windows is briefly outlined in the last part of this chapter. Detailed use is explained in later chapters as each window becomes relevant to your project.

Explorer (Alt+1)

The Explorer window functions almost exactly like Windows Explorer and allows you to locate and manage media files on your computer. ACID's Explorer, however, allows you to preview a selected media file (click the Auto Preview button—see Figure 1.15) and also gives you additional information about the selected file in the Summary View at the bottom of the window. This works only when a loop is selected: If nothing is selected, nothing is previewed and no information is displayed. Media files are added to new tracks in a project by double-clicking the files or by dragging them to the timeline from ACID Explorer.

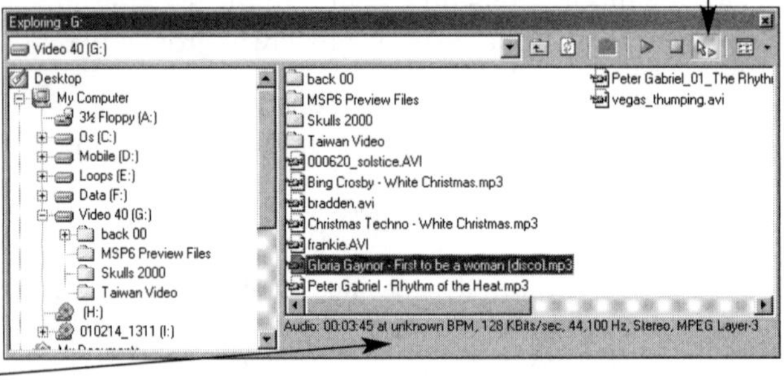

Figure 1.15
The Explorer window highlighting the Auto Preview button and the Summary View.

Auto Preview Button

Summary View Bar

Chopper (Alt+2)

The Chopper window (see Figure 1.16) is almost a miniature audio editing tool that allows you to trim audio files. It is completely non-destructive, meaning that changes you make in the Chopper do not change the original source file in any way. The Chopper allows you to quickly and accurately select shorter sections of a media file and then insert these sections into a track as events.

Figure 1.16
The Chopper window displaying an audio file.

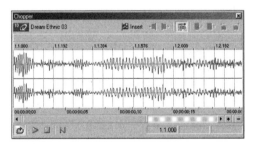

Mixer (Alt+3)

The Mixer window is a critical window that allows you to monitor your project and route audio signals to various channels and effects. ACID's virtual Mixer is analogous to a real world mixing board and contains many of the same features and controls. Preview volumes, output volume, and FX routing are a few of the operations that are controlled in the Mixer window (see Figure 1.17).

Figure 1.17
The Mixer window. Usually, this window is more simply displayed, but it can be a powerful tool controlling complex hardware bus arrangements and effects sends, as shown.

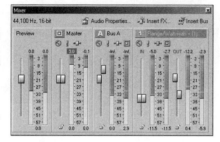

Video (Alt+4)

The Video window (see Figure 1.18) is a simple window that allows you to monitor (preview) the video component of a project. With the appropriate hardware, the output from this window can be sent to another television monitor. There are no editing controls in this window.

Figure 1.18
The Video window.

Audio Plug-in (Alt+5)

Audio Plug-ins and FX are used to modify the sound of a project. They can be used to fix, clean up, sweeten, or otherwise improve the audio or they can more used more artistically to radically change a sound. Each audio plug-in or effect has its own individual array of controls (see Figure 1.19) and is displayed in the Audio Plug-in window. The Audio Plug-in window is used for track and project level FX control and can be accessed by pressing the FX button wherever it is found in the workspace.

Figure 1.19
One set of possible
controls that can
appear in the Audio
Plug-in window.

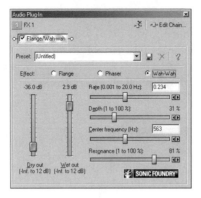

Track Properties (Alt+6)

The Track Properties window displays all of the relevant information about the media file
contents of a track. Since there are a few different kinds of tracks in ACID, the information
displayed is dependent upon the type of track selected. Many of the properties that are
displayed can be modified in this window (see Figure 1.20). While a media file (especially a
loop file from Sonic Foundry) may already contain the extra information to specify a track's
properties, these properties are independent of the actual file. In other words, a media file's
ACID properties often correspond to a track's properties, but this is not necessary (an intended
one-shot media file can be placed in a loop track). Video tracks do not have any properties that
are displayed in this window.

Figure 1.20
The Track Properties
window displaying
information about a
loop track.

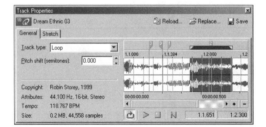

Top Ten Shortcuts

While it is not necessary (nor even possible for normal humans) to memorize the entire list of
available shortcuts in ACID, you should always remember that ACID utilizes keyboard shortcuts
extensively. If you find yourself using the mouse to push buttons or navigating the same set of
menus and submenus again and again, it is probably a good guess that there is some type of
shortcut associated with these actions. Especially useful are the mouse wheel navigational
shortcuts (although from the exhaustive use of keyboard shortcuts in ACID, you might get the
impression that the folks at Sonic Foundry have an irrational fear of mice). Please see Appendix
A for a complete listing. Table 1.1 is a short-shortcuts list. I find myself using these shortcuts
literally every single time I use ACID:

Table 1.1
Top-ten ACID shortcuts.

Press these keys	In order to
Mouse Wheel	Zoom in and out on a project (also Up and Down Arrow keys)
Shift + Mouse Wheel	Horizontally scroll through a project
Ctrl + Drag an event (or events)	Duplicate selected events and move them to a new location
Space	Play—start/stop playback, restarts playback
F8	Turn Snapping on and off (or even better, temporarily disable snapping with the Shift key)
D	Change edit tool (frequently used by pressing D to switch to the Selection Edit tool and then Ctrl+D to switch back to the Draw tool)
K	Insert Key change (or even Tempo change)
M	Insert Marker
S	Split an event (or events) at timeline cursor position
V	Insert Volume envelope (or view/hide Volume envelopes)

* This list could be topped by the standard Windows commands Ctrl+Z and Ctrl+Y (Undo and Redo) as well as Ctrl+C (Copy), Ctrl+X (Cut), and Ctrl+V (Paste). Of course holding the Ctrl key (or Shift key) while selecting events allows you to select multiple events. And don't forget the Windows motto—"Save early, save often": Ctrl+S.

2

A Song Is Born

The goal of this chapter is to introduce the basic features of ACID and how they function in actual use. The procedures described here are the fundamentals: Cutting, trimming, moving, and mixing are just a few of the operations detailed. Along the way, I will define terms and give many examples. The best way to use this chapter is to turn on your computer, run ACID, put this book in your lap, and try the procedures as you read. You will start a project, lay down a few tracks, and mix sounds together. The final section explains how to save a song so that you can publish it and share it with others. From start to finish, this chapter shows you how to begin a project and output a final song.

Building Blocks

ACID uses specific terms to convey specific ideas. It is important to understand what the program, the manual, and the Help files mean when they refer to program-specific terms, the meaning of which might be quite different from the way the word is used in the real world (although real-world meanings often offer a clue). Here are a few fundamental ideas that need to be discussed.

Projects

The first step in composing a song with ACID is to create a project. When you first run ACID, it automatically begins a new project. Every time you use ACID, you are working on a project. Projects are saved on your computer and contain all of the information about your composition, such as key, tempo, and audio files used. Project files control every aspect of your song: which sounds are used, how they are mixed together, and what effects modify the sound. ACID project files have the *.acd extension and are only recognized by ACID—they cannot be opened or played back in any other applications. While a project saves information about your composition and the sounds that make it up, a project file is not a song and cannot be played back as such on a media player, over the Internet, or on a CD player.

The great thing about working with projects (instead of actually editing audio files on your computer) is that when you edit, you are not actually changing any media files on your computer. This is called non-destructive editing, and it lets you edit and experiment with sounds without fear of changing the original files. In ACID, you edit ACID project files, not loops or media files. When you are done with your project (which is made up of loops and media files), it can be saved to another format that can be burned to a CD or published on the Internet. This is called *rendering* and is the process of creating an actual song. Actually, since ACID is also a video scoring tool, the final render might even create a new movie file.

Media Files and Loops

Files are the most basic unit a typical computer user works with. Files could be text documents (*.txt), pictures (*.bmp), or songs (*.mp3). Media files (see Figure 2.1) are just files that contain audio, video, digital music, or pictures. In the context of ACID, media files that can be used are video, audio, or MIDI in nature. Audio files are paramount, however (see Figure 2.1). Some typical file formats for audio that can be used in ACID are *.wav or *.mp3.

Figure 2.1
Windows Explorer showing a file folder that contains Windows audio files in the WAV (*.wav) file format.

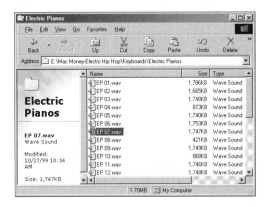

Loops are specially recorded audio files that are usually fairly short in duration. Loops are standard audio files that can be played back using just about any Windows-compatible media player (even the Windows Media Player). What makes a loop a loop is that it is recorded and structured so that when it is played back twice in a row, the end of the loop immediately and seamlessly leads back into the beginning of the loop. This means that most loops can be played over and over again infinitely, sounding as if it were a much longer continuous recording. Loops are normal *.wav audio files and are commercially available from multimedia companies for use in loop-based music tools. ACID loops from Sonic Foundry contain a little more information than a typical *.wav file (such as key and tempo information) that make them particularly easy to use in ACID. Sonic Foundry loop libraries can be used with many other multimedia applications (for example, video editing applications or Flash animation tools) and loops from other companies' loop libraries can also be used in ACID.

The definition of a loop has expanded from its original meaning over the years to include non-repeating material (often called One-Shots in ACID). Solo sections and vocal quotations from old movies are not designed to loop, but they are still broadly referred to as loops when used in loop-based music creation tools. In the same way that we no longer "dial" a telephone number, loops may not always "loop" infinitely. In any case, loops are still short audio files on a computer that can be put together to make longer, more complex songs.

Tracks

In a bricks-and-mortar studio, the audio of a song is recorded into separate tracks. Physically, tracks are narrow bands on an audiotape that run parallel to each other for the length of the tape. By recording the various parts of the song to separate tracks on the same piece of tape, perfect synchronization can be achieved and a tape with recorded material can be played back while a new part is recorded to one to of the blank tracks. Another feature of this method is that the individual tracks can be adjusted and mixed individually to another tape. Musically, a track corresponds to an individual part or performance in a song; for example, the guitar, drums, and vocals can all be recorded to separate tracks.

Tracks in ACID (see Figure 2.2) are analogous to tracks in a studio or on an audiotape. A track in ACID contains one media file or part. The controls on an ACID track can be used to adjust, mix, and otherwise modify an audio loop with special effects. In the ACID world, the number of tracks is unlimited and can contain MIDI songs or even video.

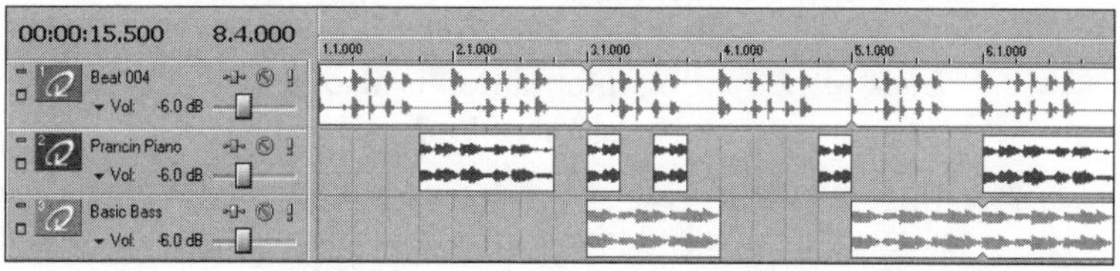

Figure 2.2
Three loop tracks with a drum beat in Track 1 ("Beat 004"), a piano part in Track 2 ("Prancin Piano"), and a bass line in Track 3 ("Basic Bass").

Every track has a number of important controls (see Figure 2.3) on the Track Header portion of the track on the left side. Many of these controls correspond to faders and knobs typically found on a mixer board in a conventional studio. (See the Chapter 7 for more on mixers and mixing in ACID).

Figure 2.3
The controls available in the Track Header.

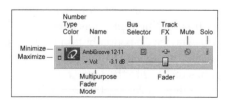

▶ **Minimize/Maximize/Restore buttons**—Changes the vertical size (height) of the track between three preset values. Many aspects of a track's appearance can be customized. Track size can be controlled by using the track size buttons (Minimize, Maximize, and Restore) in the Track Header. The lower edge of the track in the Track Header can also be dragged to change the size manually. Finally, the vertical scroll bar on the right side of the timeline can be used to zoom in and out of the timeline, changing the vertical height of all tracks. Tracks can be all different sizes. The width of the Track Header can be changed by dragging the narrow bar that separates the Track Header from the timeline.

▶ **Track Number/Type/Color/Pitch**—Track number is the order of the track from the top and is located in the top-left corner of this area. The track number is simply a numerical indication of the tracks' order from top to bottom. Track order, and thus track number, does not affect the mix or sound of a project. Track color can be changed by right-clicking the colored square in the Track Header, selecting Color from the context menu, and then choosing a color from the sub-menu. The color of the waveform of the events inserted into the timeline is determined this way as well. The color is used for your reference only. One possibility is to make all bass tracks the same color, all percussion tracks another, keyboard tracks another, and so on.

The type of track is largely determined by the kind of media file being used (for example, *.wav or *.mid), but it can be independently set in certain situations. Loop tracks are represented by a looped arrow, One Shot tracks a straight arrow, MIDI tracks with a painter's palette, and Video tracks with a film strip icon. Track pitch shifting information is also displayed in this area of the track. (See Chapter 9 for a discussion of loop and track types.)

▶ **Track Name**—Defaults to the name of the media file but can be changed. The name of a track is derived from the name of the source media file by default. This name can be changed by double-clicking the track's name and entering a new one.

▶ **Bus/Device Selection button**—This sets the routing for the track to one of the busses or devices. The audio signal in ACID can be sent through any number of real devices (such as multiple sound cards), virtual devices (busses in ACID), or effects (FX), just as an audio signal can be sent through a device in a real studio (for example, a guitar through a phaser pedal). While this can seem a bit confusing at first, all of this routing represents a lot of flexibility and power to control the mix. The Bus/Device Selection button is not visible on the track unless you have more than one device (sound card) on your computer or have inserted an additional bus or FX into the project. (See Chapter 7 on Mixing for more information on grouping tracks together into a bus.)

▶ **Track FX button**—Click this button to add effects that operate on the track level. Clicking this button opens a dialog box that lets you add effects to a track. (See Chapter 8 on FX for more information on adding and modifying a project with effects.)

▶ **Mute and Solo buttons**—Mutually exclusive buttons that silence a track or make it the only track playing. Multiple Solo buttons can be pressed to have more tracks playing "solo" at a time. Click the Solo button on one track to hear only that track. Click another Solo button on another track to hear both of those tracks. Likewise, click the Mute button on a track to silence it. Multiple tracks can also be muted at the same time.

▶ **Fader (multi-purpose)**—By default, the Fader (see Figure 2.4) controls the volume (Vol) of a track in the mix. Click the Multipurpose fader mode button to change the function of the Fader to panning (Pan) or to assign the track to a bus (Bus A) or Assignable FX (FX 1). (Assignable FX are discussed in greater detail in Chapter 8 on FX.)

Figure 2.4
The multipurpose
Fader is used to control
volume, panning, and
FX level.

Events

Occurrences of a media file in a project are known as *events*. Media files appear in the Explorer window, and when a media file is inserted into a project, it is added as a new track.

Events are containers in a track on the timeline and are the most basic unit of editing in ACID. They contain media files or loops and can be moved, mixed, and modified in ACID. Events control the mixing and occurrence of sounds in your project. Events can be thought of as windows into a media file and are not to be confused with the media files themselves. In Figure 2.5, the media file "Synco Shuffle 3b.wav" in the Explorer window was use to create Track 1. The event in the track represents the sound of the media file visually with a waveform and controls how the media file is used in the project, setting which part of the entire file is played, the number of repetitions, and when the sound occurs (among other things).

Nothing that you do to an event, neither distortion nor deletion, will ever change the actual media files stored on your computer. Instead, events are used to control every aspect of how a sound file is played back and mixed into a project and a final song. Trimming an event does not trim the media file as saved on your computer. This is known as non-destructive editing and is an open license for you to create aural mayhem on your machine, safe in the knowledge that your original source media files (loops) are not being modified.

Figure 2.5
A media file in the Explorer window was used to create the track on the timeline that, in turn, has an event on it that controls how the media file is mixed into the project.

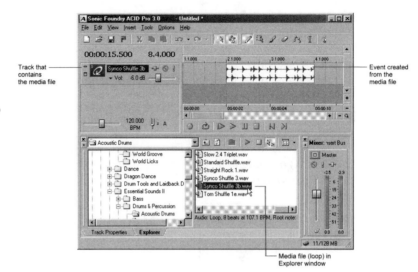

Track that contains the media file

Event created from the media file

Media file (loop) in Explorer window

An event can be shorter than the media file it contains, in which case only a portion of the loop is mixed into the project. An event can be longer than the loop it contains, in which case multiple repetitions of the loop are mixed into the project. Figure 2.6 shows a number of different events created from the same media file. Track 1 (top track) contains an event that is exactly the same length as the loop file (only one repetition). Track 2 uses the same source loop file, but the events in it use only short sections of the total file. Track 3 again uses the same source loop file, but the event in it is three times longer than the original file and therefore contains three repetitions (it is looped three times).

Figure 2.6
Three tracks with a number of different events that all use the same media file.

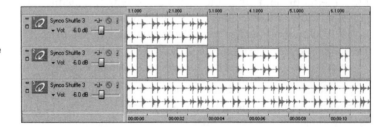

Projects

When you edit in ACID, you are editing a project with the goal of creating (rendering) a song from the final project. The creating, opening, and saving of projects is discussed in detail in the following pages.

Creating a Project

After you've launched ACID, from the File menu, select New (or press Ctrl+N). In the New Project dialog box (see Figure 2.7), click the OK button. You are presented with the ACID workspace or user interface (UI) with an empty timeline and no tracks.

Figure 2.7
The Project Properties
dialog box. All of the
information on this
tab of the dialog box
is optional.

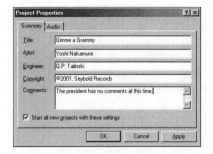

All of the information on the Summary tab is optional. The Audio tab contains properties that
affect the quality of the project's output (see Figure 2.8).

Figure 2.8
The Audio tab.

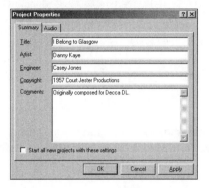

CHAPTER 2

▶ **Number of additional stereo busses**—Determines how many busses are available
to group tracks together or for Assignable FX. This number depends on your
hardware setup (such as the number of sound cards) and on how many groups
of tracks you'd typically like to create. Don't worry if any of this is mysterious at
this point; additional busses are easy to create and can be added at any time.
(More information on busses and why you might want to use them is available
in Chapter 7 on Mixing. More information on Assignable FX and how they work
is available in Chapter 8 on FX.)

▶ **Sample rate**—One of the two fundamental parameters that control the final
objective quality of the audio file that you render from your project. The sample
rate is measured in number of samples per second (Hz); 44,100 Hz (44.1 kHz) is
the same quality as a music CD and is the default setting in ACID. Higher
numbers mean higher quality and larger final file sizes, while lower numbers
make smaller files that may be more suitable for distribution on the Internet.
While it is convenient to set up a project sample rate in this dialog box, it is not
necessary. The final song's sample rate can be independently set when you
render the final song after a project is finished.

▶ **Bit-depth**—The other fundamental parameter that determines the quality of a song, measured in number of bits per sample. Having more bits per sample allows more information about a sample to be saved, yielding a higher-quality file; 8-bit-depth represents each sound pressure measurement (on a microphone or out of a speaker) with only 256 possible values (2 to the 8th power), while 16-bit-depth samples have a much greater resolution, with 65,536 possible values ($2\wedge16$). Bit-depth is important to both file size and quality. (This is discussed in greater detail in Chapter 12.)

NOTE

From the Bit-depth and Sample rate, you can calculate the final file size on your computer. For 1 second of uncompressed CD-quality audio:

$$(44,100 \text{ Hz} \times 16 \text{ bit}) \times 2 \text{ stereo channels} = 1,411,200 \text{ bits}$$

or, since there are 8 bits in a byte:

$$(1,411,200 \text{ bits} / 8) = {\sim}176,400 \text{ bytes}$$

For a number of reasons (including the actual size of a byte), this is only an estimate. The file created has a small amount of additional information saved in the header, so the actual number is slightly larger.

If you always want your project to use the same settings, and these settings are different from ACID's default settings, on the Summary tab choose the option Start all new projects with these settings.

Saving Your Project

Immediately after you create a new project, you can save it as a project file to your computer's disk drive. Until the project is saved, no information or changes you make will be permanent. To save a project:

1. From the File menu, select Save (or press Ctrl + S).
2. The first time this is done, the Save As dialog box opens. Browse for a location on your computer's hard disk drive (HDD) and enter a name for the new project. The name will have the format of MYPROJECT.ACD, where MYPROJECT is any name you want. The *.acd extension is required for ACID project files.
3. Click the Save button when finished.

After a project has been saved, future saves can be accomplished by pressing Ctrl + S. It is a good idea to get into the habit of reflexively hitting Ctrl + S whenever you've made a change that you like or as frequently as possible. To create a copy of a project, from the File menu, select Save As and enter a new name. This is a great way to create different versions of the same song.

NOTE

The Save and Save As commands are used only to save proprietary ACID project files (*.acd). When you are ready to create a song for general playback on any media player, to burn to a CD, or to publish on the Internet, use the Render As command.

Change Project Properties

Although you can set up the project properties when you first create a new project, these settings can be changed at any time. Furthermore, you can always change the settings on the Audio tab at the time that you make the final render.

1. From the File menu, select Properties (or press Alt+Enter). You could also click the Project Properties button on the Mixer window.

2. On the Summary tab, enter the optional song composition, engineering, and copyright information. Some audio file formats you create for publication will save this information along with the song. Otherwise, this information is for your personal reference.

3. On the Audio tab, enter the Number of additional stereo busses. This is important if you have multiple audio outputs (that is, multiple sound cards) on your computer.

4. Also on the Audio tab, set up the quality of the song. The default settings for the Sample rate (Hz) and Bit-depth are 44,100 Hz (44.1 kHz) and 16-bit, which is CD quality. These settings can all be changed when you create the final version of the song for publication.

5. For future convenience, select the Start all new projects with these settings item to always load new projects with these changes.

6. Click the OK button when finished.

Exploring Loops and Previewing

After you have started a new project, you are presented with the ACID workspace and a completely empty timeline with no tracks on it. Since events are what are mixed into a final song and events are created from media files (loops) on your computer, locating loops is the first step in creating a song.

Locating loops for a project is most easily done using ACID's Explorer (see Figure 2.9). This window looks and operates just like Windows Explorer and is just as easy to use. The left side of the window contains the Tree View that allows you to browse through drives and folders, while the right side contains the List View that displays folders and media files. By default, the Explorer window is located in the Window Docking area located at the bottom of the ACID workspace. If it is not, from the View menu, select Explorer or press Alt+1.

Figure 2.9
Media files appear in
the Explorer window.

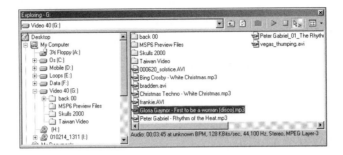

While you can drag media files directly into the ACID workspace from Windows Explorer, the
Explorer window in ACID displays more loop-related information and also allows you to
automatically preview loops. The preview process can be done while playing back a project, so
loops can be auditioned to see if they fit your creative vision for your song. There is a small
group of buttons along the top right of the Explorer window, shown in Figure 2.10, that aid in
previewing.

> ▶ To display information about a selected loop, make sure the **Summary View**
> item is selected on the menu that appears when the arrow next to the Display
> button is clicked in the Explorer window.

> ▶ To automatically preview the selected loop file, click the **Auto Preview** button in
> the Explorer window, making sure it is depressed. You can manually preview
> loop files using the **Start Preview** and **Stop Preview** buttons if you prefer.

> ▶ When you have a folder of loops that you particularly like or that you frequently
> use, click the folder to select it (in either the left or right panel) and click the
> **Add to Favorites** button. This creates a shortcut to that folder in the special My
> Favorites folder found in the root of the Tree View.

The basic routine when adding media to a project is to play back the project (or loop play a
smaller portion of the project) and preview media files in the Explorer window one at a time
(possibly using the arrow keys on your keyboard to move, pause, and preview through the files
in a folder) until you find suitable loops. Of course, this isn't an entirely random process. As
you become more familiar with your loop library, you'll be able to zero in on what you need
much more quickly.

Figure 2.10
The Explorer window
toolbar. The Auto
Preview button is an
On/Off toggle button.
Clicking the View
button cycles through
the different view
options while clicking
the arrow next to the
button displays a menu
of options.

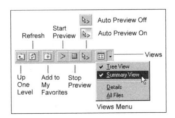

NOTE

Most loop libraries come on CD-ROM disks. The ACID Explorer window allows you to browse for and preview media files in any location on your computer, including on floppy disks. CD-ROM drives are not typically as fast as your computer's hard disk drives, however, and since you will frequently be previewing loops in the course of using ACID, it is highly recommended that you copy your loop libraries to your hard drive. Although media files such as loops can take up a lot of space, the time savings of having these files on your hard drive is significant, in addition to not having to swap CD-ROMs in and out of your CD-ROM drive.

Event Basics

Events are the bricks from which songs are built in ACID, so creating events is the most important ACID skill to master. Fortunately, it isn't very difficult. For one reason or another, Sonic Foundry decided that a drawing or painting metaphor was appropriate for describing event creation in ACID. This is why the two primary tools used to create events are the Draw and Paint tools. The rest of this section covers all of the basic event operations, such as copying, pasting, and moving them around a project.

Creating a Track

All audio events, video events, and MIDI events are contained in tracks on the timeline. Therefore, you need to create a new track before you can create an event. To create a track, browse for and preview media files (loops) in ACID Explorer and then double-click one to create a track.

The new track is added to the project as the last track (see Figure 2.11). Media files can also be dragged to the timeline, creating a new track wherever it is dropped. Once a track has been created and is visible on the ACID timeline, it is ready to have events inserted into it.

Figure 2.11
Double-click Strings 3.wav in the Explorer window to create a track that contains that event on the timeline.

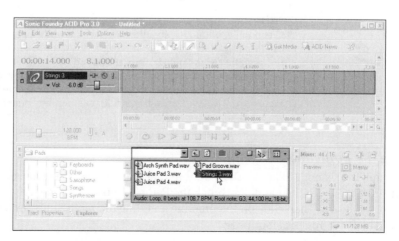

CHAPTER 2

Creating an Event with the Draw Tool

Finally, we get to the meat-and-potatoes of ACID music composition: the creation of events. The easiest tool to use is the Draw Tool, which is selected by default when ACID is first run.

To draw an event, click the Draw Tool button on the toolbar to select it (or press Ctrl + D). This is the default tool, so it may already be selected. Then click on the timeline and drag the mouse cursor horizontally to draw an event, as shown in Figure 2.12.

Figure 2.12
Using the Draw Tool
to draw an event on
the timeline.

Events can be any length at all. Most events in a project are typically based on loops that can be repeated and are, therefore, contained in tracks that are loop tracks. Loop tracks are identified by the loop icon in the Track Header. In short, to create an event to be mixed into your project, double-click a media file in ACID Explorer to create a track and then draw the event on the timeline.

Events that are created in a loop track automatically repeat (loop) when the event extends beyond the length of the original media file. A small notch in the top and bottom of the looped event divides each repetition (see Figure 2.13).

Figure 2.13
This event contains
three repetitions
(meaning, it is looped
three times) of a media
file. A notch in the
top and bottom of
the event indicates
each repetition.

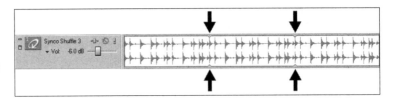

NOTE

One thing you'll notice about drawing events almost immediately is that you can't exactly draw events anywhere you want. Instead, when you begin drawing, the event tends to want to begin drawing on one of the Grid lines and also tends to want to end on one as well. This behavior is called *snapping* and it is designed to make sure events line up with the project's beat (see Figure 2.13). Snapping can be toggled on and off by pressing F8 on your keyboard.

Using the Paint Tool

The Paint Tool is not unlike the Draw Tool in that you still drag the mouse on the timeline to create events. To use the Paint Tool, click the Paint Tool button on the toolbar or press the D key on your keyboard. Then click on the timeline and drag the mouse cursor horizontally to paint an event. The Paint Tool has four uses:

▶ **Painting across tracks**—While the Draw Tool works only horizontally within a single track, the Paint Tool works across all tracks. This can be a time saver in some situations, but mostly it is just incredibly fun to doodle around with the Paint Tool, instantly creating a song. Try this out in a live performance, painting events just-in-time before the playback timeline cursor arrives.

▶ **Creating multiple events with a single stroke**—Typically, this is useful with a short one-shot media file, such as a single kick drumbeat. When you drag the mouse on the timeline while using the Draw Tool, a single instance of the loop is drawn no matter how far the mouse is dragged. When the Paint Tool is used, a single event is created for every Grid line that is crossed when dragging. By zooming in and out on the project, you can set the Grid spacing to be every measure, once every two beats, every beat, or some other spacing. Then, to use the kick drum beat example, you could use the Paint Tool to quickly insert a kick on beat 1 of every measure, on beat 1 and 3, or on every beat or periodically at any Grid spacing you zoom to.

▶ **Erasing**—Right-click an event using the Paint Tool to erase sections of the event. The amount of the event that is erased is equal to the space between two Grid lines and is, therefore, dependent on Grid spacing and zoom level. Snapping must be turned on for this to work.

▶ **Joining events**—Events that are split or that are in separate pieces can be rejoined by painting across the split or gap between them.

Snapping

Snapping is a default behavior in ACID. It is quite intentional and a huge time saver because it automatically synchronizes loops in a project to the beat. Snapping applies not only to moving events but also to event creation and trimming (see Figure 2.14). There are many times that you may not want an event to snap to the particular Grid lines that are visible, however, and there are two main solutions to this: turn off snapping or zoom in on the project. There are three ways to turn off snapping:

▶ Click the Enable Snapping button on the Toolbar to toggle snapping on and off. Snapping is on when the button is depressed.

▶ Press the F8 key on your keyboard. This is a shortcut for the Enable Snapping button and toggles this function on and off.

▶ To temporarily disable snapping, click on an event and then (without releasing the mouse button) press the Shift key. Now you can drag the event with snapping temporarily disabled. When you release the Shift key, snapping will be re-enabled.

CHAPTER 2

Figure 2.14
Events line up with the
vertical Grid lines on
the timeline. Also notice
that the beats in the
drum part tend to line
up with the Grid lines
as well. This is all
automatic as long as
snapping is turned on.

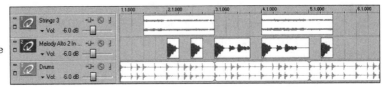

Moving and Trimming Events

Events can easily be moved around on a track by dragging them. Since each track is associated
with a single media file, events must remain within the original track they were created in (in
other words, events can be dragged only horizontally). Once again, the leading edge of the event
snaps back and forth to Grid lines as they are dragged. Events can be dragged over other events
that already exist on the timeline, thus covering them up. The covered-up portion is not mixed
into the project and is essentially trimmed, but if you drag the covering event off the covered
event, you will find that it is still there and will be restored to the mix.

Trimming events is about as easy as moving them. Move the mouse cursor over an event edge.
When the cursor changes from an edit tool icon (such as the pencil for the Draw Tool) to the
trim cursor, drag the edge of the event towards the center of the event to shorten it or away from
the event to lengthen it. Again, the edge you are trimming snaps to the Grid lines. The mouse
cursor changes to a trim cursor when it is over either edge of an event. Events that are being
trimmed are always selected, which is indicated by an event background that is colored instead
of white.

Waveforms

A waveform is a visual representation of a sound file. Waveforms are visible in ACID in events,
in the Chopper window, and in the Track Properties window, among other places. Ultimately,
editing in ACID is done by ear, but you can make very precise cuts, splits, and trims simply by
looking at the peaks and valleys of the waveform picture of a media file or event.

- ▶ The size of the peaks is determined by the amplitude (loudness) of the sound.
- ▶ Stereo media files have two parallel waveforms that represent the two stereo
  channels. The top waveform is the left channel and the bottom waveform is the
  right channel.
- ▶ The color of the waveform as displayed in ACID is determined by the associated
  track's color.

Waveforms can also be used to identify where the beat falls in rhythmic music. The two events
in Figure 2.15 display the waveforms of two different media files. The top track has a spoken-
word media file. The bottom track contains a drum part and displays clear periodic peaks in the
waveform that line up with the beat marks along the top of the timeline. By zooming in and out
on the timeline or in another window, you can see more detail in the waveform and make more
accurate edits.

Figure 2.15
Two events that display
stereo waveforms.

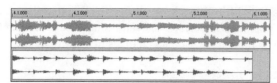

NOTE

ACID calculates and draws the waveforms of media files as they are inserted.
For short media files (like most loop files), this can be done extremely quickly.
The waveform for longer media files—typically, entire songs or the sound
track to a video file—take much longer to draw. In these situations, ACID
stores the waveform drawing for future reference on your hard disk as an *.sfk
file. For example, if you inserted suppers_ready.mp3 into a project, ACID
would calculate the waveform and save it to suppers_ready.sfk. You can
delete these small *.sfk files at any time; ACID will redraw them as necessary.

Slip Trimming

When trimming an event, the event edge moves to cover or reveal a media file. For example,
when a drum part with a kick beat on 1 is trimmed, the kick remains on beat 1, even though the
event gets longer or shorter. Slip trimming is a type of trimming where the relative distance of
the media in the file remains the same from the edge being trimmed. In other words, the media
within the event moves along with the trim and changes relative to the project, the timeline, and
the beat. Take a look at Figure 2.16 for a visual explanation. The top event is the original. Track
2 shows what happens if you drag the edge of the event (trim) to measure 5.1. Track 3 shows the
results of a slip trim to the same position. The event is the same length as the one in track 2, but
the media within the event is in a different position. Notice that the loop notch is also in a
different position and that the mouse cursor is a slip trim cursor.

Figure 2.16
Track 3 shows the
results of a slip trim
to the same position.

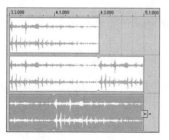

Slip trimming is performed by pressing the Alt key on your keyboard while dragging the edge of
an event. Watch for the mouse cursor to change from the regular Draw or Paint tool cursor to the
special slip trim cursor when the Alt key is pressed.

Shifting the Media within an Event

The media within an event can also be shifted and moved relative to the project while the event
itself remains stationary. In Figure 2.17, Track 1 has a single event in it. Track 2 below it has an

identical event, but the media within it has been shifted. Notice that the waveform of the event in Track 2 is in a different position from Track 1, even though the event remains in the same position on the timeline. The mouse cursor also changes to a shift cursor.

Figure 2.17
The waveform of the second event is shifted to the right while the event remains in the same position when pressing the Alt key while dragging inside of an event.

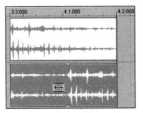

The media within an event can be shifted by pressing the Alt key on your keyboard while dragging inside of an event. The mouse cursor changes to the shift cursor when the Alt key is pressed.

Chopper Window

The Chopper window is a special tool that is used to perform precise trims of media files and insert the trimmed portion into the timeline. The advantage to using the Chopper to trim events is that you can trim an event in more detail in the Chopper window without zooming in on the project timeline. There are also a number of other tools in the Chopper window that make trimming easier.

To view the Chopper window, from the View menu, select Chopper or press Alt+2. The Chopper window displays the entire media file of the selected track. Click on a different track to load a different media file into the Chopper. To trim and insert events into the timeline using the Chopper:

1. Drag the mouse on the waveform in the Chopper window. A selection region is created and highlighted.

2. Position the timeline cursor on the main timeline where you would like the new event to be inserted.

3. In the Chopper window, click the insert button.

You can see in Figure 2.18 that the selection area in the Chopper window is also highlighted on the main timeline, representing the location of the event to be inserted.

Figure 2.18
The selected area in the Chopper window is inserted into the timeline at the timeline cursor's position.

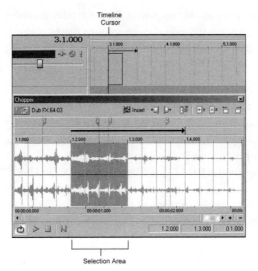

There are many more features to the Chopper, including (but not limited to) markers, regions, and spacing out events at regular intervals. See Chapter 5 for more information on trimming events using the Chopper to create interesting variations on a media file by creatively splitting it up.

Zooming

Zooming is a fundamental skill that is easy to master. The purpose of zooming in is to work with the timing of your project in more detail. At extreme levels, zooming allows you to make micro-second changes in event placement and trimming. Zooming also subdivides the project into finer Grid lines (see Figure 2.19), giving you more control over event placement and trimming, yet continues to offer snapping to existing song structure.

Figure 2.19
The Grid lines in the top example are at every measure. The second example is zoomed in a bit and the Grid lines fall on each beat. The final example is zoomed in much further and shows even more detail in the pictured event.

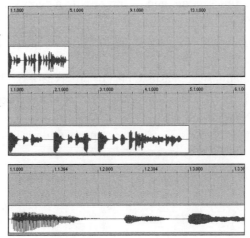

There are a number of different methods for zooming. Horizontally zooming in on the timeline means that less time is visible, but more detail can be seen in the waveforms. Zooming out horizontally shows more of a project and gives you an overview of the song. Vertical zooming changes the track height. More information on zooming is found in Chapter 1.

Copying, Cutting, and Pasting Events

The standard Windows functions Copy, Cut, and Paste all work as you might expect them to in ACID. As with Windows, copying or cutting events places the data from the event temporarily on the Windows Clipboard. Copy, Cut, and Paste are all available from the Edit menu. The standard Windows shortcuts apply (CTRL+C for Copy, CTRL+X for Cut, CTRL+V for Paste). Copying leaves the original event on the track, while cutting removes the original event from the track. You could also right-click an event and select Copy or Paste from the context menu (see Figure 2.20). Once you have some data saved to the Windows Clipboard, it can be pasted into a new location.

When pasting an event, click on the timeline to move the timeline cursor to the location where you want the pasted event to begin. The cursor snaps to the nearest Grid line, meaning that pasted events are automatically snapped into synchronization with the project. Snapping can be turned off or you can move the cursor using the Left and Right Arrow keys on your keyboard for more precise placement.

Figure 2.20
Right-click an event
to display a context
menu that contains
the Copy, Cut, and
Paste commands
(among others).

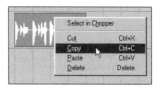

Another way of pasting in ACID is Paste Repeat (see Figure 2.21). This command allows you to quickly paste an event multiple times, either end to end or with a defined interval between repetitions. To Paste Repeat an event (from the Clipboard):

1. Click on the timeline to move the timeline cursor to the location where you want the pasted event to begin.

2. From the Edit menu, select Paste Repeat or press Ctrl+B.

3. In the Paste Repeat dialog box, enter the number of times you want the event repeated in the Number of times to paste box.

4. Select a Paste spacing option and enter a spacing interval in the Paste every box, if applicable.

Figure 2.21
This event was Paste Repeated eight times, evenly spaced, once each measure.

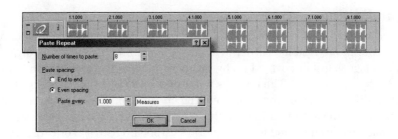

One final pasting technique is the Paste Insert command. This command is very powerful, but it can be a bit intimidating because it shifts events in every track in your project. In short, Paste Insert pastes the Clipboard data into a project at the cursor position, moving every event in every project out of the way and down the timeline (to the right). Events that are bisected by the timeline cursor are split. To Paste Insert an event (from the Clipboard), click on the timeline to move the timeline cursor to the location where you want the pasted event to begin. Then, from the Edit menu, select Paste Insert or press Ctrl + Shift + V.

In a regular Paste operation, the event is pasted directly over anything that is underneath it. In a Paste Insert operation, everything is moved out of the way and nothing is overwritten (see Figure 2.22a and 2.22b). Paste Insert is related to Ripple Editing (discussed in more detail in the next section) but is unaffected by whether Ripple Editing is turned on or off.

Figure 2.22a
Before the Paste Insert operation is executed. The event that has been copied is highlighted.

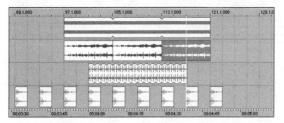

Figure 2.22b
The effects of a Paste Insert on the events on the timeline. The insertion point is marked and all of the other events in the project have been moved down the timeline.

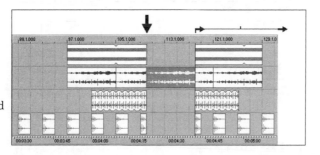

NOTE
Ripple Editing and the Insert Time commands also move events down the timeline and out of the way.

CHAPTER 2

Ripple Editing

Ripple editing is a term taken from the world of film and refers to moving clips out of the way when new clips are inserted earlier in a movie. Sometimes called a film-style insert, this means that no footage is lost or covered up by the inserted clip. The total length of the project is increased by this process. The result is not unlike executing the Paste Insert command, with the important difference being that ripple editing operates only on a single selected track and Paste Insert works on the entire project, as illustrated in Figure 2.23. Both operations work from events that have been copied to the Windows Clipboard (Ctrl+C or Ctrl+X).

Figure 2.23

A comparison of normal Paste, Ripple Editing Paste, and Paste Insert operations.

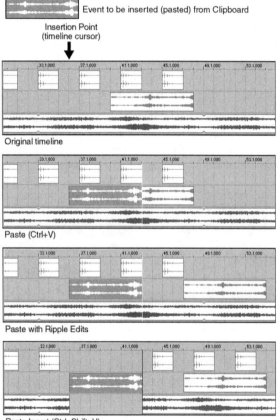

Selecting Multiple Events

There are three basic ways to select more than one event at a time. Selected events have a colored background. The first two are standard Windows operations:

▶ Press and hold the Shift key to select a range of events. In this operation, you first click on one event, press the Shift key, and then click on another event. Both events are selected as well as any events that fall between them. This includes events on the same track or events on different tracks. Imagine drawing a rectangle with the two clicked locations defining two of the corners; every event that is covered by the imaginary rectangle is selected when the Shift key is pressed.

▶ Press and hold the Ctrl key while clicking on multiple events. Every event that you click on is selected individually and added to the selected group when the Ctrl key is pressed. Clicking a selected event again will de-select it.

▶ The Selection Tool on the toolbar in ACID can also be used to select multiple events. Click the Selection Tool button on the toolbar or press the D key on your keyboard to cycle through the various editing tools. To select multiple events, click and draw a rectangle on the timeline (as shown in Figure 2.24).

Events are selected as the boundaries of the rectangle touch them anywhere in the project. When using the Draw Tool, you merely need to click and drag to move an event. When using the Selection Tool, you need to click once to select it, then click again and drag to move it. This also works when selecting multiple events: Click and draw a selection area, release the mouse button, click one of the selected events, and drag to move all of them.

Figure 2.24
Holding the Shift key and then clicking two events selects all of the events in between. The rectangle outlined by the dashed line shows which events are selected. Selected events have a colored background.

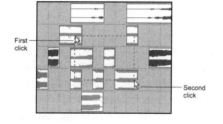

First click

Second click

TIP

Use a combination of these operations to select the events you want most effectively. For example, use the Selection Tool to select a broad range of events, switch to the regular Draw or Paint tool, and press and hold the Ctrl key while going back through the events, clicking on the ones you do not want to select.

Duplicating Events

A close relative of the Copy-Paste operation, duplicating events (in combination with selecting multiple events) is one of the most useful ACID skills you can acquire. Not only is it useful for a repetitive copy-and-paste task involving a single event, but you can duplicate entire sections of a project. Repetition in a song is an important structural element that cannot be ignored.

To duplicate an event, select the event you want to duplicate by clicking on it. Press and hold the Ctrl key and drag the event to a new location. The original event remains in place, while a new event is created and moved to a new location. This is essentially a Copy-Paste operation all in one quick action. The events in the top part of Figure 2.25 were all selected using one of the multiple selection methods previously discussed. Then the Ctrl key was pressed as the events were dragged to the right down the timeline. This instantly power duplicated all of the events and repeated them, leaving the original events as they were.

Figure 2.25

All of the events in the top example were selected. Then the Ctrl key was pressed while dragging one of the events. This instantly duplicated all of the events.

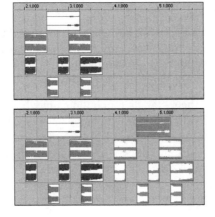

Playback and Mixing

Playing a project or part of a project back is something that will quickly become second nature as you work with ACID. Mixing, on the other hand, is a surprisingly complex concept that cannot be overlooked in any project. It is pretty important to work with volume and panning to control the mix early in a project, but mixing is also probably the last and most important variable to finalize before a song is published or committed to a CD.

Project Playback

Previewing a project and playing it back is accomplished by using the Transport controls (see Figure 2.26) just below the timeline. What you hear when you play a project back is the sum total of all of the events as mixed together by ACID. The position of the playback is indicated both by the timeline cursor and by the position numbers at the top of the Track Header. Since this is such a common operation, there are a number of important shortcuts that make this process easier.

Figure 2.26

Project Transport controls are found just below the timeline.

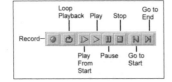

- ▶ Press the Spacebar on the keyboard to start and stop playback at the timeline cursor position.

- ▶ Press Enter to pause playback. The difference between stopping and pausing is that stopping returns the playback to the original timeline cursor position, while pausing freezes (and, therefore, allows you to resume) playback at the current playback position.

▶ Use looping playback to isolate smaller sections of the project.

Looping Playback

Looping playback is repetitively playing back the same short region of a project. Being able to do this becomes especially important once a project gets longer than ten seconds or so. While the short section of project is playing back repeatedly, you can simultaneously make small changes to the project and immediately hear the results of such changes without delay. Looping playback is activated by clicking the Loop Playback button on the Transport bar. Press the L key to toggle looping playback on and off. The portion of the project that is looped is indicated by the Loop Region bar on the top of the timeline. To create a Loop Region (see Figure 2.27), drag the mouse on the Marker bar. To loop play a section of a project, click the Loop Playback button on the Transport bar. This is a toggle button: Looping is on when this button is depressed. Click the Play button on the Transport bar when the timeline cursor is inside of the Loop Region.

Figure 2.27
The Loop Region bar is gray when looping is turned off and dark blue when turned on.

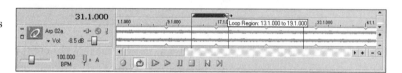

NOTE
The loop region plays back only if playback begins from within the Loop Region or earlier. Playback that begins before the Loop Region eventually enters the Loop Region and, when playback reaches the end of the region, looping will occur. Playback that begins after the Loop Region never enters the region and, therefore, never loops.

Monitoring the Mix

It is also important to monitor the mixing of all of the events and tracks in a project in an objective way by watching the Mixer window as a project is played back or as events are previewed. By visually monitoring the project in the Mixer window, you can prevent clipping errors that may ruin a song. The Mixer window (see Figure 2.28) is one of two windows that is visible by default when ACID is first run (the Explorer window is the other). If it is not visible, from the View menu, select Mixer or press Alt+3.

CHAPTER 2

Figure 2.28
This is an exploded view of the Mixer.

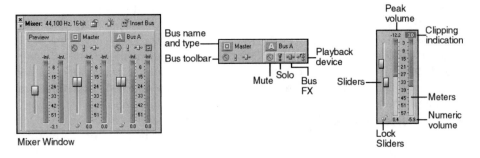

The Mixer window is subdivided into a number of master control panels, each of which has a fader and a small number of other controls. These control panels are used to control the mix and the routing of the audio signal through ACID. The controls correspond to similar controls found on physical mixers in the real world (see Chapter 7 on Mixers). By default, the Mixer window displays a Preview and Master control panel.

► The **Preview control panel** sets only the volume for media files as they are previewed from the ACID Explorer window. While this does not affect the mix of the project, the initial volume for a track is determined by the Preview volume. As with the other faders in the Mixer window, a numeric value for the volume is displayed below the fader. The Preview control displays both stereo channels, but you cannot divide the fader to control the volume of the channels independently.

► The **Master control panel** controls the final volume of the project overall. FX can be added to this control panel to affect the whole project.

► **Busses** are different routes the audio signal from ACID can take through your computer. The Preview bus and the Master bus are available by default. If you have multiple sound cards, you can create additional busses to route signals through. For example, you could have the entire project routed out one sound card through the Master bus and have one of the solo tracks route out through another sound card, perhaps to a pair of headphones used to monitor that track. FX and audio plug-ins can also be routed through their own busses. The actual routing of the bus to specific hardware is done by clicking the Playback Device button on the Bus toolbar. Busses can also be routed through other busses. (More information on configuring busses is available in Chapter 7.)

Individual tracks can be assigned to a bus. This is especially useful when you want to group tracks together to apply the same FX scheme to them as a unit.

Busses are automatically named, but they can be renamed by double-clicking the bus name and entering a new one. Hardware busses are typically named using the letters of the alphabet. FX busses are named according to the effect used. The number of FXs used on a single bus is indicated by a number at the top of the panel.

Clipping

Clipping is a term used to describe the condition that occurs when the volume is too high. This happens when the total volume of all of the events in a mix combine to make the volume greater than 0 dB. The problem with this isn't that the volume is too loud but that it has exceeded the possible range for the data; data above the range is lost, or "clipped," generally resulting in a poor quality mix. Clipping is considered to be a mistake or error and should be avoided at all costs. Clipping produces distortion in a signal and can actually intentionally be used as a distortion effect, especially on guitar parts.

NOTE

The maximum useable volume is a contentious issue. Suffice it to say that any volume less than 0 dB is technically acceptable, but pushing the mix all the way to 0 dB doesn't leave any room for future additions to a project. Keeping it below −10.0 dB always gives you a safety margin, but there is no real reason to use that number as opposed to any other reasonable value.

Clipping is displayed on the Mixer's Master Meters as a red decibel warning just above the meter (see Figure 2.28). Normally, the decibel rating displayed in this area is not highlighted in red and serves as a peak volume indicator. The decibel values are reset every time playback is stopped and restarted. To reset these values during playback, click on the peak volume indicator.

Master Volume

The simplest way to solve clipping problems is to lower the Master Volume fader. The fader is divided into two halves, left and right, which control the volume to the left and right stereo channels. Here is how to do this:

▶ Click and drag the middle of the slider to move the sliders together.

▶ Double-click either slider control to align them (if apart).

▶ Use the Lock at the bottom of the slider to lock the two halves together relative to one another.

▶ The Up and Down Arrow keys on the keyboard can be used to control the volume as well. Shift+Up or Down Arrow controls the left slider and Ctrl+Up or Down Arrow controls the right slider separately.

The Master Volume is not usually the best way to solve clipping problems, although it is certainly the easiest way. Clipping can often be an indication that a song needs to be remixed. Since the Master Volume levels reflect the entire frequency spread of a project, clipping (and poor mixes) can happen because a project has too much bass or treble. In other words, clipping can happen even if the project doesn't sound too loud. Volume, panning, and equalization should all be considered as potential solutions to clipping problems. Regardless of whether or not you think the mix sounds too loud or distorted, clipping should always be fixed.

Track Volume

The way tracks are mixed together is determined by the combined volume of all of the tracks in a project. Each track has a fader called the Multipurpose Fader that controls the volume by default (see Figure 2.29). Dragging the slider left and right controls the volume (gain) of the track. The precise volume is indicated numerically to the left of the Fader. Since this is a Multipurpose Fader, it can be used to control not only the volume but also the panning and FX volume of the track.

NOTE

The initial volume of a track is determined by the volume of the Preview fader in the Mixer window at the time the track is created.

Figure 2.29
The Faders on these tracks all control the volume.

Panning

Panning is the balance between the two stereo channels. Panning 100 percent left means that the audio comes out of the left speaker only. Panning is an important, and often overlooked, aspect of ACID mixes. Blasting every loop out both stereo channels at 50 percent through each can result in not only boring mixes but can also cause clipping problems. Moving a saxophone solo track 70 percent to the right, for example, can also make a mix sound more realistic, as if the performers are actually arranged on a real stage. Careful track panning can also add space to a song, making it seem bigger in a room (although you don't want it to sound like you have a piano that is fifty feet wide either). All in all, panning can be a subtle yet important way to improve a song. Click the Multipurpose Fader mode button to change to a Pan Fader (see Figure 2.30).

Figure 2.30
Click the Multipurpose Fader mode button to change to a Pan slider.

Fading Events

You can fade in or out from individual events by using the fade envelopes found on either side of any event. Sometimes referred to as ASR (Attack Sustain Release) envelopes, this is the easiest way to smoothly fade continuous events. To use Fade envelopes, move the mouse cursor over either upper corner of an event. When the cursor changes to the Fade envelope icon (see

Figure 2.31), drag the envelope towards the center of the event. The blue curved line represents the fade visually, and the duration of the fade is indicated by hash mark across the end of the event. Right-click the Fade envelope and, from the context menu, select Fade Type and then select a shape from the submenu. These shapes can also be accessed by right-clicking the upper corner of the Fade envelope.

Figure 2.31
Click and drag the top corners of an event to create fades.

Envelopes

Envelopes are used in ACID to animate volume and panning in real time. This can be done to gradually fade a track in and out or it can be used to move a sound across stereo channels, from left to right, for example. Effects (FX) can also be faded in and out using envelopes. Finally, envelopes can be used to fix localized clipping without adjusting the entire track's volume and panning. Envelopes are track-level objects and control the volume and panning of an entire track, but track output is controlled by the placement of events within the track. Envelopes, therefore, are closely associated to the occurrence of events in a track.

Envelopes appear in tracks on the timeline as colored lines (see Figure 2.32). A flat line indicates an unchanging volume or panning. Lines that lie at an angle indicate a rising or falling volume or a pan from left to right (left = top; right = bottom). By default, all ACID projects can use Volume and Pan envelopes. FX envelopes can be used only if FX (audio plug-ins) are added to the Mixer as Assignable FX busses. FX envelope automation is a powerful reason to use FX as Assignable FX (as opposed to the other ways FX can be used). See Chapter 8 on FX for more information.

Figure 2.32
Four possible envelopes on a track. Hold the mouse cursor over a node to see a ToolTip that identifies the envelope.

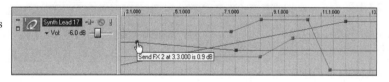

TIP
Envelopes are color-coded in ACID: red = volume, purple = pan, and blue = FX.

In Figure 2.32, to make the illustration more clear, no events are visible in the track. In an actual project, an event would also be inserted somewhere in this track to take advantage of this rather artificially complex tangle of envelopes. Without an event, there is no output from a track and therefore no reason to automate the volume, panning, or FX with envelopes. To use envelopes, right-click on a track and, from the context menu, select Insert/Remove Envelope. Then select the type of envelope to insert or remove (e.g. Volume).

CHAPTER 2

To remove envelopes from a track, right-click a track with envelopes and, from the context menu, select Insert/Remove Envelope. Then, from the submenu, select the envelope that you want to remove. Envelopes that are active have check marks next to them on the submenu.

Envelopes can remain active (that is, they will affect a track's output) and still not be visible. To show/hide envelopes, from the View menu, select Show Envelopes. From the submenu, select the particular envelopes you would like to show/hide. Volume and Pan envelopes can be instantly shown/hidden by pressing the V or P key on the keyboard. These shortcut keys insert new envelopes if a track does not already have an active envelope of the corresponding type. It does not ever remove an envelope, however.

NOTE

Removing an envelope essentially deletes the envelope and all of the nodes and adjustments you have made. This is not the same as showing/hiding envelopes, which allows you to hide envelopes when you are not working on them. Hidden envelopes continue to affect the project, but they are out of view and protected from unintentional changes.

The small square boxes on an envelope are called nodes and are used as animation key points. An envelope is always a straight line between two nodes, indicating a smooth animation of the volume or panning (see Figure 2.33).

▶ Double-click an envelope to add a node.

▶ Drag nodes up or down to change the volume or panning. You can also drag the line between two nodes to move both simultaneously.

▶ Drag nodes left or right to reposition them.

Figure 2.33
The event in this example pans from left to right (Pan envelope goes from top to bottom) as the volume gradually fades in (Volume envelope starts on the bottom and rises to the center). Each of the envelopes has two visible nodes with a straight envelope line between them.

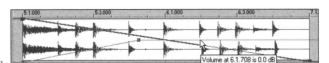

NOTE

Although envelopes and nodes are used to control the volume and panning of events in a track, they are, in fact, track-level objects. This means that when events are moved within a track, the envelopes and nodes do not necessarily move with them. To make sure envelopes move with events, click the Lock Envelopes to Events button (active when the button is depressed).

Creating MP3 Files

The final step in any ACID project is the creation of a song. Up to this point, the project has been saved only as an ACID project file (*.acd). For this reason, the only way to hear the song is to play it back from within ACID. In order to make the song more universally available, it needs to be saved into a standard multimedia file format. The process of creating a multimedia file from a project file is called rendering. The format that you choose to render your project to is an important decision that affects the size of the media file, the quality, and how accessible it is to others. Your choices are pretty clear cut:

▶ If you want to create an audio CD that others can play on their home stereo or car CD players, the standard Windows Wav (*.wav) format is a good choice. The quality is very high, but these files are far too large to e-mail to friends or post on the Internet.

▶ If you want to publish your song on the Internet, the Windows Media Audio (*.wma) or MP3 Audio formats are good choices. Small file sizes at the price of some quality make these formats ideal for e-mail as well.

Currently, one of the most popular formats is the MPEG-3 format, commonly referred to as MP3. This is certainly not the only format you can use, nor is it necessarily the best. It is very widespread, however, and is an excellent format to use if you want to share your song with others on the Internet. To render an MP3 file, follow these steps:

1. From the File menu, select Render As to bring up the Render As dialog box (see Figure 2.34).

CHAPTER 2

Figure 2.34
The Render As
dialog box.

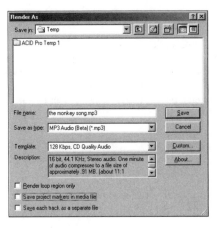

2. Choose a format from the Save as type list. In this case, choose MP3 Audio (*.mp3).

3. Enter a name for the song in this format: mysong.mp3. The project's name is used as the default name.

4. From the Template list, choose a compression template. This is a complex balancing act between quality and file size, with size increasing with the quality selected. For now, 128 Kbps, CD Quality Audio is a good choice, yielding a fairly small file with acceptable quality.

5. Browse for a location to save the file and click the Save button.

Render times can vary, depending on the length and complexity of the project, but they typically do not exceed a few seconds (video renders can be significantly longer).

Rendering formats, maximizing quality versus compression, and tweaking all of the various settings for rendering are covered in much more detail in Chapter 12.

3
Composition

A well-composed song is more than a collection of sounds and loops haphazardly thrown together on a whim. And it is more than just a beat, a bass, and a beautiful melody. Good songs, like good stories, have structure—and ACID has the tools to help you create this structure. Although you should, of course, feel free to violate any and all rules in the name of Art, even the most abstract avant-garde composers can benefit from a basic knowledge of music theory and composition.

A story may be broadly divided into a beginning, middle, and end. Structurally, it can be seen to be composed of words, sentences, and paragraphs. Songs may also be viewed structurally in terms of components: beats, measures, and phrases. Of course, this is a technical book, so only the barest surface of the topic is covered here, and I encourage you to broaden your musical composition skills with a book dedicated to that topic. By examining a few music fundamentals, this chapter details some of the more interesting features of ACID and shows you how to create the structure of a song in a number of different genres. As you work through the examples, the finished projects can be used as templates for your own creations.

Song Structure

Just as a good story has a beginning, an exposition, and a satisfying conclusion, so too are many genres of music based on some type of structure. At the largest level, a song might be broken up into verses and refrains. Verses and sections might be subdivided into smaller musical phrases and ideas. At the most basic level are individual measures, which are in turn composed of notes and beats. Each level of organization is important in telling a complete story.

The highest level of structure can very easily be seen in the parts of a standard pop song, which center around the verse and refrain pattern. Throw in an introduction and maybe a short solo break and you have a complete song. The next few pages are going to demonstrate how to use markers to annotate a song and give it an underlying structure. Through clever use of duplication, a pop song can emerge from only two or three musical phrases.

The most common large-scale structure heard in popular music today is the Verse-Refrain-Repeat structure. This is also very common in any sing-along type of song, such as church music or Christmas carols. The verses usually tell some sort of story, either individually or as a group, and each verse is different from the others. The refrain (or chorus) usually contains the main point of the song, often using the words in the title, and is repeated word for word (more or less) at every occurrence. Although composers typically avoid intentionally boring the listener, the predictability of this simple structure makes popular music more accessible, easier to understand, and allows the listener to hum or sing along with the refrain very quickly. Repetition also makes a song more memorable and makes a tune catchy.

From simple children's songs to church music, the Verse-Refrain-Repeat structure allows us to sing along with a song, since everyone can quickly pick up the repeated refrain. Letters can be assigned to the various parts of a song to identify them. Verses can be labeled "A" and the Refrain can be labeled "B," for example. A typical song might be summarized as follows:

Verse   Refrain   Verse   Refrain   Verse   Refrain

A   B   A   B   A   B

Popular music as heard on the radio is rarely composed of only a few verses and a refrain. Instead, almost all songs add a third element to spice up the mix, which can be labeled "C." The band Genesis had an eponymous hit song and album in the 1980s that followed this pattern:

A B A C A B

In words, ABACAB worked something like this: Verse-Refrain-Verse-**Break**-Verse-Refrain. The break, or C section, signaled a major shift in the music and allowed the band to perform extended solos during live performances. Returning to the verse (A section) and then finishing with the refrain (B section) gives the song a very satisfying resolution. Of course, Genesis did not invent this ancient and simple pattern, but its widespread use in music from acid jazz to zydeco cannot be overstated.

Songs often have more than just three parts. Logically extending the structure of a song is as simple as adding more letters. The point of using this type of notation is to quickly demarcate structure and to clearly highlight repetition. In improvisational music, especially jazz, a band leader can unobtrusively mouth the letter "F" to the band to let them know that the next section is going to be the F section of the song, which helps to maintain the structure while still giving each performance freedom of form (he could have said "D" or anything else). Repetition, when used correctly, does not automatically mean a boring song, and it is the first step towards turning ACID from a toy used for play into a tool used to create songs.

ACID allows you to divide the timeline into rough sections in the very early stages of a project using timeline Markers. The structure created at this point serves as a sketch or outline for the song and gives you visual clues about where a song is going and how it is coming together. It isn't necessary to do this, but you should consider using these features to help you create well-constructed and satisfying compositions.

Creating Structure with Markers and Regions

Creating a visual structure for a song in ACID can be accomplished through the use of markers. Markers allow you to outline a song and plan for future sections. Markers can also serve as quick navigation tools to move about the timeline. As temporary features, markers can be used to identify places and sounds that you want to work on. Regions are like markers, but instead of marking a single point in time, they identify periods of time. Both regions and markers are important in the early stages for planning structure and visually identifying the structure of a song, as well as identifying specific occurrences of sounds and events.

Working with Markers

Markers can also be used to note anything useful in a song. Another common use for markers is to mark cues or transitions in a song. Since markers can be deleted by selecting the marker and pressing the Delete key on your keyboard, markers can easily be temporary placeholders in a composition. You can instantly jump to the location of a marker by pressing the associated number key on your keyboard. This type of navigation is limited, however, because you can set only ten markers that you can jump to, 0 through 9 (although the total number of markers is unlimited). Markers are automatically assigned numbers in the order of their creation. This allows a renamed marker to assume double duty, serving as a numerical navigational element and as a structural marker as renamed by the composer.

Creating Markers

To add a Marker, right-click the Marker bar above the timeline and, from the context menu, select Markers/Regions. Then, from the submenu, select Insert Marker (see Figure 3.1). Markers can be added instantly by pressing the M key on your keyboard. Markers are automatically numbered 1-9 and finally 0 as they are added to a project. You can continue to add more markers, but they are not numbered after the tenth (0) marker is added.

Figure 3.1
Right-click the Marker
bar to insert a marker.

Marker bar

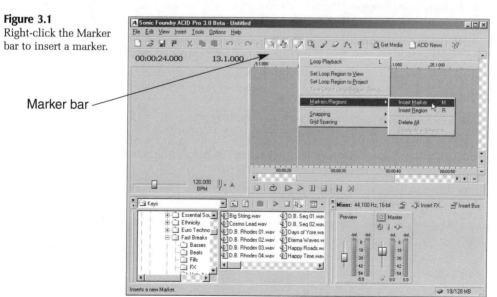

TIP

The simplest method of adding markers is to position the timeline cursors at the place where you want to insert a marker and then press the M key on your keyboard.

To instantly navigate to a marker, press one of the number keys at the top of your keyboard (not on the number pad). Markers can be quickly named (and renamed) with a short note or name more clearly identifying its purpose. Right-click a marker and, from the context menu, select Rename or double-click the marker. Then you can type or edit the name. Click away from the marker or press the Enter key to finish. Names are for your reference only. Figure 3.2 shows a number of markers used to identify the Verse-Refrain structure in a song.

Figure 3.2

Named markers define the structure of a song.

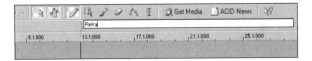

TIP

Markers are, of course, general-purpose flags that can be used to identify anything. Markers can be added on the fly during playback by pressing the M key. You can then go back and name these markers during editing and use them to snap and line up events.

Moving and Deleting Markers

Markers can be moved by dragging them to any location. By default, markers are numbered according to the order they are added. Since you can drag a marker to any location, it is possible (and even likely) that markers with lower numbers may appear later on the timeline and seem out of order. Markers will snap to grid lines when snapping is turned on. Remember—to temporarily disable snapping, press and hold the Shift key on your keyboard while you drag.

There are three methods of deleting markers in ACID:

▶ Right-click a marker and, from the context menu, select Delete.

▶ Create a selection area (by dragging the Selection Edit Tool on the Marker bar) and then right-click a marker and select Delete All In Selection Area from the context menu to delete multiple markers.

▶ Right-click a marker and, from the context menu, select Delete All to remove all markers in a project.

TIP

A loop region can be created instantly between two markers by double-clicking the marker bar between any two markers. This applies to all markers including Key, Tempo, Region, and Time markers.

Working with Regions

Regions are related to markers in that they are used to create structure and instantly recreate loop regions. Region markers are green and come in pairs (regular markers are orange). Regions are automatically numbered along with markers. Pressing the number key that corresponds with a region automatically selects that region. The two green markers that identify a region are ultimately used to instantly recreate the Loop Region in a project (see Figure 3.3) that is used to control looping playback or to identify a shorter section of a project to be rendered (that is, saved as a song).

To Add a Region, drag on the Marker bar to create a Loop Region of the desired size of the region. Then, right-click the Loop Region and, from the context menu, select Insert Region.

Figure 3.3
Right-click the Marker bar to insert a region. Regions are identified by two green markers. The Loop Region (visible in the lower image) is dark blue and is used to repeatedly loop project playback.

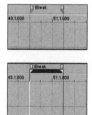

TIP

The easiest way to create a region is to create a loop region (by dragging on the Marker bar) and then press R on the keyboard.

Regions share many properties with markers, such as renaming, automatic numbering, and deleting. Working with Regions is not unlike working with markers, except that they come in pairs.

▶ **Name a region**—Right-click the left region marker of a pair and select Rename.

▶ **Delete a region**—Right-click either region marker of a pair and select Delete.

▶ **Create a Loop Region**—Double-clicking the Marker bar between any two markers, a region marker and a regular marker, or two regular markers.

CHAPTER 3

> ▶ **Preview**—Double-clicking the beginning or ending Region marker creates a loop region between the two region markers. You must have looping turned on for playback to loop. This allows you to repeatedly preview a shorter section of your project while simultaneously making adjustments to the project.

> ▶ **Move a region**—Hold the Alt key while dragging either Region marker to move the entire region (both region markers with the same spacing between them) intact to a new location.

Time Markers

Time markers are another, very different kind of marker that can be used to create or define structure in a song. The reason they are so different is that time markers can be completely unrelated to the parts of the song itself. Time markers are based on real-world measurements of time in minutes and seconds, while a song is measured in measures and beat, with the beats in turn being determined by the tempo (number of beats per minute), which can vary wildly. Time markers appear in purple or mauve on a dedicated Time Marker bar below the timeline. Since Time markers are true to the measurement of time in the real world, they are ideal for syncing audio events in a project with video events. Time markers snap to units of time and not to the Grid marks from the top or the timeline (see Figure 3.4).

Figure 3.4
The Time Marker bar with associated Time Markers at the bottom of the timeline.

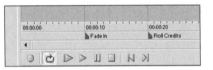

To add a Time marker, position the timeline cursor at the location where you want to drop a marker. Then, from the Insert menu, select Time Marker. You can also press the H key as a keyboard shortcut.

As with other kinds of markers, you can rename and delete Time markers by right-clicking them to access the context menu. Time markers can be dragged to a new location and can be used for navigational purposes as well (again from the context menu).

Musical Phrasing

How long should a verse or refrain be? As with all discussion of structure in this and the next chapter, there are some widely followed guidelines that are common in much of today's popular music. Of course, you should feel free to violate these guidelines at will for your own projects, but a basic understanding of these principles can be important to the creative process.

Beats

When you count along with a song, you are usually counting the beats. Beats are not related to the drums or rhythm section of a song. A beat can be strong or weak and does not need to be explicitly heard. A beat is more formally defined in musical notation and time signature, where it has a very precise meaning. The tempo of a song can be expressed in terms of the number of beats that occur in a minute. The speed or tempo of a song can be specified in terms of the number of beats per minute (bpm). The bpm of most popular songs can range from a slow 80 bpm in a sad ballad to more than 200 bpm in frenetic dance music. Just about any style of music can be played at just about any tempo (see Figure 3.5), so it is a great overgeneralization to say that disco music is 120 bpm (although it frequently is). Beats can often be seen as sharp peaks in the waveform of events in percussion parts on the timeline.

Figure 3.5
The tempo of some popular musical styles. This represents only a rough guide; each style covers a range of possible tempos.

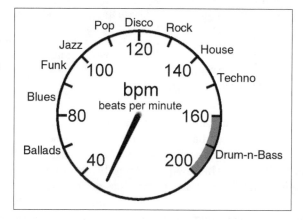

Measures

Beats are most frequently grouped together into measures in groups of four in Western popular music. Or, to put it another way, a song is divided into measures, which are further subdivided into beats. The most popular grouping is four beats in a measure. This arrangement is so ubiquitous that this time signature is called common time. This is the default time signature in ACID and is represented by a 4/4 in the lower part of the Track Header (see the following section on time signature). Most loops from Sonic Foundry (and, indeed, from most loop content companies) are also recorded in 4/4 (or less frequently in 6/8). Measures are sometimes referred to as bars. The ACID timeline is also divided into measures and beats. If you were looking at the sheet music, or staff, it would look like the top of Figure 3.6, while the bottom of the figure shows how it is represented in ACID.

Figure 3.6
Measures are typically separated by lines in a score. The ruler at the top of the timeline in ACID divides time into measures and thousandths of a second.

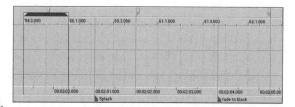

CHAPTER 3

Time Signature

The bottom number in a time signature represents the type of note that gets one beat in a measure: 1 = whole note, 2 = half note, 4 = quarter note, and 8 = eighth note. The top number in the time signature denotes the number of beats in the measure. So 4/4, or common time, means that there are four beats in a measure and the quarter note gets the beat. A time signature of 6/8 means that there are six beats in a measure and eighth notes get a single beat.

The time signature of a piece of music is completely unrelated to the speed of the music (tempo) and is a relatively unimportant concept in ACID. However, it is important in more traditional compositional techniques and occasionally affects ACID, especially at the loop level.

NOTE

ACID projects do not really have a time signature, although the Grid bar divides a project up into beats and measures. Loops, on the other hand, are almost always recorded in some time signature, which affects how a loop plays and how it mixes with other loops that may have been recorded in different time signatures. See Chapter 9 for more information on using and changing the way beats are measured in loops.

Time signature can be used for organizational purposes in ACID. The Grid on the timeline can be divided to visually aid composition based on a time signature (see Figure 3.7). Since you can snap event edges to Grid lines, this can also make placing events on the beat much easier. Changing the Grid spacing does not alter the project audibly in any way and, of course, the inherent time signature in which a loop was created does not change. The relationship between the time signature and various loops in a project can be important and also can be modified to some extent. See the section on setting the number of beats in a loop in Chapter 9 for more information. Changing the Grid will help with composition and organization and sets the snapping behavior of events on the timeline. To Change the Grid Spacing, from the Options menu, select Grid Spacing. Then, from the submenu, select the note that gets a single beat in the time signature.

Figure 3.7
Some time signatures
and how the Grid
Spacing might represent
them. A single measure
is displayed. Grid marks
are visible only if the
zoom level is high
enough to reveal them.

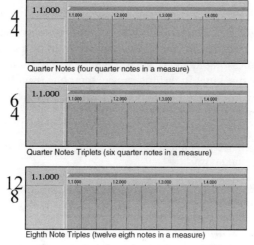

$\dfrac{4}{4}$

Quarter Notes (four quarter notes in a measure)

$\dfrac{6}{4}$

Quarter Notes Triplets (six quarter notes in a measure)

$\dfrac{12}{8}$

Eighth Note Triples (twelve eigth notes in a measure)

NOTE

Notice that the grid marks do not necessarily line up with the Ruler (as
illustrated by setting the Grid Spacing to Triplets), which divides the project
into measures with four beats subdivided into thousands of a second: 1.3.937.

Phrases

Measures may be loosely joined together into less formal groupings known as *phrases*. A phrase
may be as large as an entire section (such as section A in ABACAB) or a verse, or it can be as
small as a few measures. There is no strict rule about the length of a phrase, but once again, the
number four frequently turns up in phrases composed of four, eight, twelve, or more measures.
Additionally, shorter phrases can be combined to create longer phrases. And phrases fit together
to form the larger sections A, B, and C, which are combined into complete songs. In summary,
songs are broadly divided into sections, which may be split into less formal phrases, which are
in turn composed of measures made up of beats.

One example of a phrase is the twelve-bar blues phrase, which is very common in popular
music. This is the grouping of twelve measures into a single complete phrase. You will almost
certainly recognize this structure if you have ever listened to blues, jazz, or rock music, and you
can probably predict where the phrase is going and where it will end as you listen to it. Again,
this predictability is part of the appeal of using this simple structure. Setting the listener up to
expect the next bar in the phrase and then creatively surprising the ear could not be done if this
phrasing were not so prevalent. See Chapter 4 for more information on creating a twelve-bar
blues phrase in ACID.

CHAPTER 3

Tempo

Tempo is the speed of a song and is completely unrelated to the time signature. Tempo is expressed in beats per minute (bpm) and can be easily changed to fit the mood of a song. The tempo can also be changed mid-song in ACID. ACID defaults to 120 bpm, which is fairly typical for popular music. Generally speaking, in written music, tempo is usually indicated by the number of quarter notes in a minute (see Figure 3.8), so estimating the tempo of a song from a score is a straightforward conversion.

Figure 3.8
Tempo can be indicated in quarter notes per minute in written music, which frequently can be directly interpreted as beats per minute (bpm) in ACID.

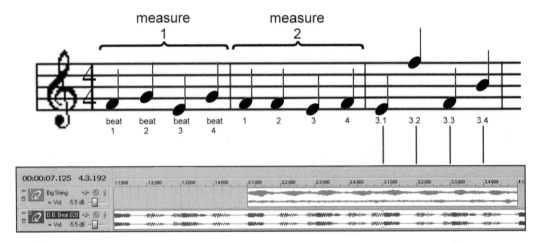

Project-Level Tempo Changes

Changing the initial tempo of the project can be done at any time, but it is best to plan your song out as much as possible at the start. As illustrated in Figure 3.6, tempo is important to the type of song you are creating and can set the overall mood of a piece. The default tempo for any new project in ACID is 120 bpm. To change the tempo of a project, double-click the tempo indicator at the bottom of the Track Header. A box appears around the tempo and the cursor flashes. Enter the new tempo (see Figure 3.9). The tempo also can be changed by dragging the tempo slider next to the numerical indication of tempo. As with many other sliders in ACID, holding down the Ctrl key will make the slider move with more precision.

Figure 3.9
Manually entering a new project tempo.

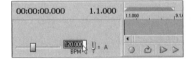

NOTE

The Tempo indicator displays the tempo at the timeline cursor position. It does not necessarily indicate the tempo of the project unless the cursor is positioned at the very beginning of the project.

Changing the Tempo on the Timeline

The tempo can also be changed on the fly at any time in a project. Mid-song tempo changes are represented by blue markers at the top of the timeline (along with key changes). To change the tempo in mid-song, move the timeline cursor to the position where you want the tempo change to occur and, from the Insert menu, select Tempo/Key Change. Enter the tempo you want to change to in the Tempo/Key Change dialog box (see Figure 3.10).

Figure 3.10
Changing the tempo in mid-song.

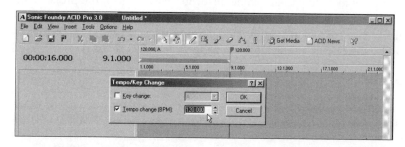

TIP

Clustering a larger number of tempo markers allows you to gradually decrease or increase the speed of a song.

The Tempo/Key Change bar may not be visible until the first time you change the tempo or key from the Insert menu. Once the Tempo/Key Change bar is visible, you may make changes directly on the bar.

To change the tempo in mid-song from the Tempo/Key Change bar, right-click the Tempo/Key Change bar at the point where you want the key to change and, from the context menu, select Insert Tempo Change. Enter the Tempo you want to change to in the Tempo/Key Change dialog box.

CHAPTER 3

The tempo of the project at a specific marker also can be changed using the Tempo slider at the bottom of the track header. To change the tempo using the tempo slider, click on an existing tempo/key change marker to select it (or move the timeline cursor to the marker's position) and then drag the Tempo slider. If no tempo changes have been made anywhere in the project, the slider alters the project's initial tempo.

TIP

The simplest and fastest way to change the tempo is to move the cursor to the position where you want the tempo to change and then press the T key on your keyboard.

Changing the tempo does not alter the pitch or key of a song or loops, within reason. There are limits to this technology, and some distortion may occur if the project tempo is radically different from the original tempo of the loop. This can be heard most easily in vocal loops. The original tempo of a loop from Sonic Foundry in beats per minute is displayed in the information bar along the bottom of the Explorer window (see Figure 3.11).

Figure 3.11
The original tempo of the selected loop is displayed at the bottom of the Explorer window.

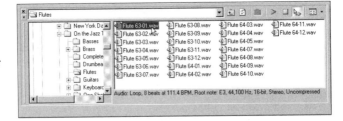

Matching Project Key to a Loop

If there is one dominant loop in your project that must be 100 percent undistorted in any way (for example, a solo vocal track), you can match the tempo of the project to that loop. This is best planned out well in advance and done as early in a project as possible. To match the project tempo to a loop's tempo, right-click the track header for the loop that you want to use the tempo from and, from the context menu, select Use Original Tempo. The tempo of the loop is also displayed as a part of the menu item (see Figure 3.12).

Figure 3.12
Matching the project tempo to a loop's tempo.

Tempo/Key change bar

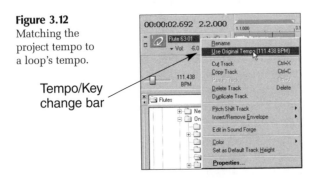

Adjust the Tempo to Fill a Length of Time

There is one other extremely clever method of setting up the tempo of a project. Say you've composed the perfect background music for a thirty-second commercial spot. The only problem is that the music runs for thirty-five seconds at 120 bpm. Speeding up the tempo will make it run faster, but how much do you need to increase the tempo? Guessing and experimenting will eventually get you the right answer, but ACID has a feature that lets you automatically adjust the tempo using just one marker.

To match the project tempo to a length of time, do the following:

1. Add a marker to the end of the music.
2. Position the timeline cursor at the desired length of time.
3. Right-click the marker and select Adjust Tempo to Match Cursor to Marker.

If the cursor is positioned before the marker (see Figure 3.13), the tempo is increased and the total length of the music is shortened. If the cursor is positioned after the marker, the tempo is slowed and the total length of the music is lengthened.

Figure 3.13
In this example, a 15-second project is shortened to be of the same duration as a 12-second piece of video.

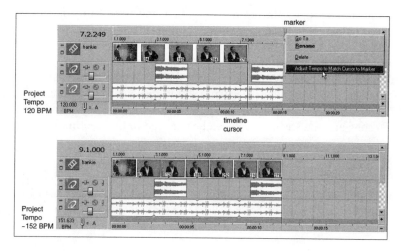

This procedure is most effective when the change in duration of the project is relatively small, yielding a correspondingly small change in the tempo. Although total project duration is always changed by this procedure, it can be used anywhere in a project. This means that you can use it to synchronize musical changes with video action by placing a marker at the musical change, placing the cursor at the location of the video action, and then using the Adjust Tempo to Match Cursor to Marker function to synchronize.

CHAPTER 3

Key

Most people never move beyond playing with ACID as a simple toy (which is, of course, perfectly fine), but if you're ready to make serious music, what follows is vital. Again, as with the previous chapter, the musical ideas discussed here are simple and should be seen as an introduction to music theory in light of ACID technology. None of these concepts should be viewed as a rule that must be followed—but you can't break the rules unless you first understand them. You certainly don't need to be a musician to work with ACID, but some knowledge of musical notation is necessary to use ACID to its fullest potential.

The key of a song is sometimes described as the root note that a song is based on. The key of a note determines its pitch or how high or low it is. The key of a song sets which notes of a scale are going to be used, depending on the harmonics of the piece. For example, a C.P.E. Bach piece in C major would use a certain subset of all of the possible notes in a scale. The harmonics largely determine whether the song sounds pleasing (or not) to the ear, which, in turn, is strongly influenced by culture. An harmonic European scale is completely different from an Indonesian one, as just one example.

When you start a project, the entire song is in a single key (A by default), and this is the root note of the song. The root note defines the key of the song, but, interestingly, that note might never be used in the song. The key (in Western music, at least) determines what notes of the scale will sound good together and how chords are formed. Loops are necessarily recorded in a specific key, or root note. Generally speaking, loops that sound good together are in the same key, and loops that are of different keys clash and sound dissonant. ACID does a lot of background work that is transparent to the user converting loops of different keys to match in a project. Both the key of a song and the key of a loop can be changed in their entirety or in mid-song/loop.

NOTE

It is important to note that the key of a song and the key of a loop do not necessarily need to match in order to sound good together. While ACID automatically tries to change the key of a loop to match a project, this can be manually controlled and over-ridden. See Chapter 9 for more information.

The key of a phrase or song can be any note from A to G. This is most easily seen on a piano keyboard (see Figure 3.14).

Figure 3.14
Keys on a piano.

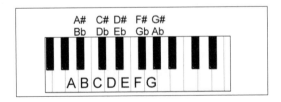

The tonal distance between two adjacent keys may be a whole step, as it is between A and B, or it can be a half step, such as between E and F (see the next section, "Chords and Intervals," for more information). The key can also be modified by sharps and flats. Flats (b) are a half step lower and sharps (#) are a half step higher. It may be easiest to think of the black notes on the keyboard as the sharp and flat notes. Therefore, a song could be in the key of B or a half step lower, in the key of Bb. The key of Bb can also be accurately described as the key of A#. You can see that there is no black note between B and C. While it is not incorrect to talk about B# or Cb, it is often easier to refer to B# as C, since they are equivalent notations.

In ACID, the key can be changed at the loop (media file), event, mid-project, and project level. Changing the key is sometimes referred to a shifting the pitch (or pitch shifting).

Chords and Intervals

Chords are composed of two or more notes played simultaneously and are responsible for much of the emotional feel of a song. For example, major chords tend to sound happy and minor chords sound sad, to a Western ear, at least. Chords are actually not related to key, but key is important in determining the structure of a chord. In ACID, the creation of chords is rather limited, although it is a good idea to know a little about chords and structure since some loops are based on chords. These loops are usually explicitly named after the chord or structure, for example "Pad Dmaj 02.wav" is composed of a D major chord. Strummed and even plucked guitar parts are often described in terms of chords and are also sometimes indicated in the name of the loop. Arpeggios are another variation of a chord, with the notes being spread out in time instead of being played simultaneously.

There are twelve keys on a piano keyboard from A to G#, and this represents twelve half steps, or intervals. The distance between two notes can be described in terms of steps. The distance between E and F is one half step (one semitone), while the distance between D and E is one full step (one tone or two semitones). Chords can simply be described in terms of intervals, or the distance between the various notes that make up the chord. For example, a chord called a C major triad could be described as a C root note, a second note four semitones higher, and another note seven semitones above the root. Expressed numerically, a major triad might be described as a 0-4-7 chord. Unfortunately, life is not so simple.

Intervals

Intervals are not typically expressed in terms of the number of semitones distant from the root note. Instead, musicians use terms like major third and perfect fifth to describe specific intervals (see Figure 3.15). While not entirely intuitive, the system is logical and well constructed. A perfect fifth is one of the most useful intervals in popular music and is the basis of a power chord when pounded out of a heavy metal guitar. A perfect fifth is really an interval of seven half steps or semitones. The Indigo Girls often harmonize in thirds, meaning one voice is just a bit below/above the other. It sounds nice and harmonic, while a second or a fourth tends to sound harsh.

CHAPTER 3

Figure 3.15
A major third and a
perfect fifth interval.

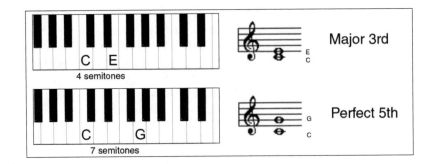

Intervals Table

Table 3.1 describes the names of all of the possible intervals. Notice that an interval of six semitones has two names, depending on how it is written on the staff. There are many cases where it is possible to represent a given interval in two ways. For example, an interval of eight semitones could be C to Ab or C to G#. These two representations are harmonically equivalent.

Table 3.1
How intervals are defined and named.

Semitones	Interval Name	Example in C
1	Minor second	C and Db
2	Major second	C and D
3	Minor third	C and Eb
4	Major third	C and E
5	Perfect fourth	C and F
6	Augmented fourth	C and F#
	Diminished fifth	C and Gb
7	Perfect fifth	C and G
8	Minor sixth	C and Ab
9	Major sixth	C and A
10	Minor seventh	C and Bb
11	Major seventh	C and B
12	Octave	C and C

Major Triad

A major triad is a simple chord created from a perfect fifth interval and a major third interval. It has a happy sound and may be abbreviated as C major, Cmaj, or even just C (see Figure 3.16).

Figure 3.16
Two different
major triads.

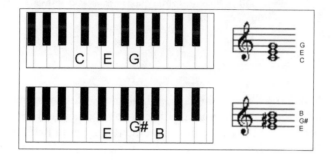

Minor Triad

A minor triad is a major chord with the second note raised a half step (sharpened). This means that the second note is three semitones higher than the root, also known as a minor third. This chord sounds sad or depressing and a C minor third is abbreviated C minor, Cmin, or, most simply, Cm (see Figure 3.17).

Figure 3.17
A C minor triad.

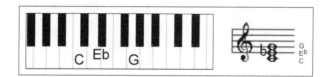

Key Progression

The key of a piece of music is the root note in which it is written. Usually, the key of a song will change occasionally. The sequence of key changes may be called a key progression. For example, a typical blues progression might start in C for four measures, switch to F for two measures, return to C for two, G for one, F for one, and finally go back to C for two measures. As mentioned earlier, this twelve-bar blues pattern is very common and can be represented as pictured in Figure 3.18. Moving the key up in a song can often step up the emotional intensity, while lowering the key can have the opposite effect.

Figure 3.18
A typical twelve-bar
blues key progression.

CHAPTER 3

NOTE

In this book, key progressions are distinct from chord progressions (which are discussed later in this chapter). Key progressions involve only changes from C to Eb to F# and so on, while chord progressions involve changes from major to minor (among other harmonics).

Limits

ACID does an excellent job with changing the original tempo and key of media files without distortion, but there are limits to how much a file can be stretched and changed. Without compensating for speeding up the tempo of a loop, the pitch would naturally shift up, making vocals sound like singing chipmunks. Likewise, lowering the pitch would naturally make a media file play slower. ACID takes care of this. It can maintain the pitch while the duration is being stretched or maintain the duration while the pitch is being shifted. There are limits, however, and beyond a certain point, every loop will begin to sound strange and distorted. Vocal loops seem to be especially prone to these distortions, since we are so used to hearing voices every day. Remember that this limit also applies to media files as they are inserted into a project with a different key. For example, when the project key is in C and you want to use a media file with a root note of A, the loop will automatically be transposed to match the project, resulting in a pitch shift of +3. ACID 3.0 has a + or −24 semitone pitch shift limit, but distortion usually occurs well before you reach it.

There are four levels at which the key can be altered in ACID: project, track, event, and loop.

Project-Level Key Changes

Changing the fundamental key of the project can be done at any time, but it is best to plan your song out as much as possible at the start. The default key for any new project in ACID is A, but this is easily changed (see Figure 3.19). To change the key of a project, click the Key button at the bottom of the Track Header and, from the context menu, select the key you would like to use.

Figure 3.19
Changing the project's key from A to D.

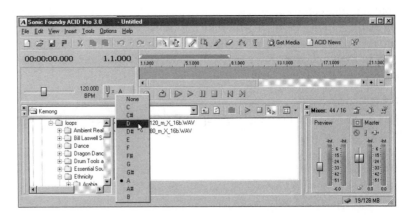

Mid-Song Key Changes

The key can also be changed on the fly at any point in time in a project. Mid-song key changes are represented by blue markers at the top of the timeline (along with tempo changes—see Figure 3.20). To change the key in mid-song, move the timeline cursor to the position where you want the key change to occur. Click the Insert menu and, from the submenu, select Tempo/Key Change. Enter the Key you want to change to in the Tempo/Key Change dialog.

Figure 3.20
Changing the key
in mid-song.

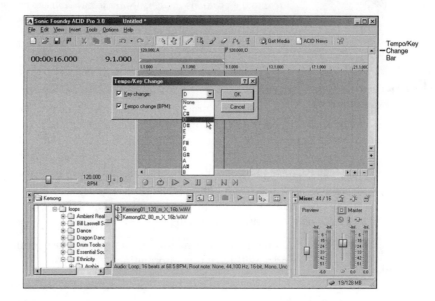

The Tempo/Key Change bar may not be visible until the first time you change the tempo or key from the Insert menu. Once the Tempo/Key Change bar is visible, you may make changes directly on the bar (see Figure 3.21). To change the key in mid-song from the Tempo/Key Change Bar, right-click the Tempo/Key Change bar at the point where you want the key to change. Then, from the context menu, select Insert Key Change and enter the key you want to change to in the Tempo/Key Change dialog. The key can also be changed after the key change marker is inserted by clicking the Key Change button at the bottom of the Track Header. The key changes at the current position of the Timeline Cursor. You can also use the Key Change button on the Track Header. Click on an existing key change marker to select it (or move the timeline cursor to the marker's position). Then, click the Key Change button and, from the context menu, select the key you would like to use.

Figure 3.21
Tempo/Key change bar.

CHAPTER 3

Add a simple tonal loop (not a drum loop) to the timeline and paint a brief section across the key change to hear the results of the change. Key Change markers can be dragged with the mouse to reposition them.

TIP

The simplest and fastest way to insert a key change is to move the timeline cursor to the position where you want to have the key change occur and press the K key on your keyboard, followed by the key that you want to change to—for example, press K and then G to change the key to G.

Loop-Level Key Changes

Commercial loops from Sonic Foundry (or any loops that have been ACIDized—see Chapter 9) contain key (sometimes called pitch) information and are automatically adjusted to match a project's key when it is inserted into a project. Changing the key or root note of a loop as it occurs in a project can be accomplished by modifying the properties of the loop after it has been inserted into a project. This change affects only the loop in the project—it is non-destructive, meaning it does not change the audio file on your computer. Again, the root note of a loop allows ACID to automatically adjust the pitch to match a project, but this can be over-ridden. To change the root note of a loop, do the following:

1. Insert a loop with key information into a project. Most commercial loops from Sonic Foundry will have this information.

2. Right-click the track that contains the loop and, from the context menu, select Properties.

3. In the Track Properties dialog box, click the Stretch tab.

4. From the Root note list, select the new key for the loop.

While all of the methods for changing the pitch are fundamentally the same, changing the root note of a loop as it occurs in a project is probably the last method you should use. The default root note information saved with an ACIDized loop was saved there by the artist who recorded the loop and provides important information both to you, the composer, and to ACID itself about the inherent key of the audio file. In most cases, it is probably better to change the key of the track that contains the loop instead of changing the root note of the loop in the properties dialog box, even though the results are identical. See Chapter 10 for more information about the root notes of loops.

Pop Music Progression

One of the most basic key progressions in popular music (and one which you would surely recognize if you heard it) starts from a root (project) key of C and looks something like Figure 3.22.

Figure 3.22
A very basic pop music
key progression.

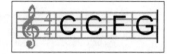

The keys of C, F, and G are the three "Pillars of Pop" and have been used extensively since the birth of rock and roll. As such, you probably don't want to overuse these key progressions, but they make for an excellent learning example in ACID. They are great for setting up listener expectations, which you can then smash with your own unique stylings. To create a pop progression in ACID:

1.   Start a new project.

2.   Change the key of the entire project to C by clicking the tuning fork Key button at the bottom of the Track List and selecting C from the pop-up menu.

3.   Right-click the Time Ruler at Beat 1 of Measure 3, represented by 3.1 on the timeline, and, from the context menu, select Key.

4.   Select F to change the key to F.

5.   Move the playback cursor to Measure 4, Beat 1 (4.1) and change the key to G.

6.   Change the key at the 5.1 point back to C.

Set the loop bar to encompass the first four measures and draw an event from a simple bass line in a track in the project. The more simple the bass line is, the easier it is to hear the key changes. At this point, if you also add a basic beat and a piano, the song sounds nearly complete, if a bit boring. Even at this very simple level, you can already hear the familiar pop pattern. The project ends up looking like the one illustrated in Figure 3.23.

Figure 3.23
A simple pop
progression as it
appears in ACID.

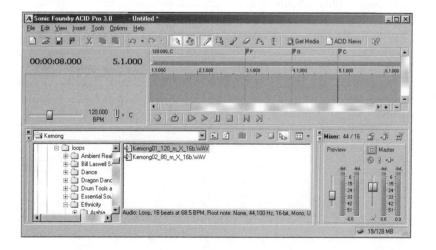

CHAPTER 3

Remember the dominance of the number four I talked about in the Structure section: four beats in a measure (bar) with four measures in a phrase? One of the most common phrases in pop music is twelve bars, or measures, long. To extend the simple C/F/G/C phrase previously created into a full-blown pop music song is a simple matter (see Figure 3.24).

Figure 3.24
A full twelve-bar pop progression C/C/C/C–F/F/C/C–G/F/C/C in ACID. A simple bass line loop (8thnotesimple1.wav) has been added to the project so the results of these key changes can be heard clearly.

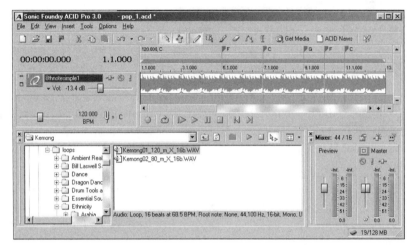

NOTE

Loops that are being previewed in the Explorer window change key as the project is playing back, making it possible to assess the harmonics of the new loop in relation to the project.

Blues

The twelve-bar phrase outlined in the previous section sounds so familiar because of its venerable roots, which extend well back to the blues. The blues is one of the most fundamental and characteristically American forms of music. The great thing about studying the blues is that its basic form is not hard to understand, yet it can serve as a springboard into jazz and many other kinds of music. This is not to suggest that the blues is in any way simple or unsophisticated. In fact, the blues is one of the most expressive and emotionally rich genres and can be a great foundation for your own instrumental and vocal solo improvisations. A basic blues key (chord) progression might look like Figure 3.25 in a root (project) key of F.

Figure 3.25
A full twelve-bar pop
progression
F7/F7/F7/F7–
Bb7/Bb7/F7/F7–
C7/Bb7/F7/C7/ in
ACID. Notice that
when changing the
key to Bb, you actually
need to select A# in
ACID, which is tonally
equivalent.

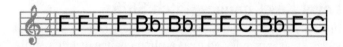

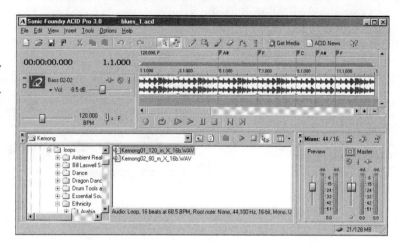

The pattern illustrated in Figure 3.26 is frequently referred to as a blues chord progression, but in reality it is only a key progression: The chord structure remains a constant dominant seventh. ACID does not automatically allow you to select the type of chord used, but if you throw in some loops (especially a good bass line) from a blues loop CD or bass lines with "blues" in the file name, you should get excellent results. The pattern works well with many jazz and pop bass lines as well, so go ahead and experiment. Again, the prevalence of this phrase (and even its inclusion in this book) may suggest that it is not the most creative blues pattern in the world, so feel free to funk it up.

Track-Level Key Changes (Pitch Shift)

Track-level key changes alter the basic key of every event that occurs in a track (see Figure 3.26). A key change can also be referred to as a pitch change or pitch shift. Events in the track still respond to event-level pitch shifting and to project-level key changes. To pitch shift a track, right-click the track and, from the context menu, select Pitch Shift Track. Then, from the submenu, select Up Semitone or Down Semitone.

Figure 3.26
Pitch-shifting a track
(changing its key).
The +5 on the Track
Header reveals that this
track has already had
its pitch shifted up five
semitones.

+5 Pitch Shift
on track header —

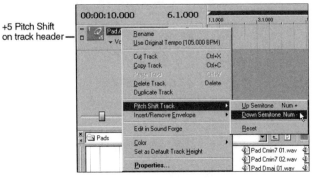

TIP
Obviously, it would be a bit tedious to click through the menus, one semitone at a time, until the desired pitch is achieved. An easier method of changing the pitch of a track quickly is to click on the Track Header to select it and then press the + or – keys on your keyboard's number pad repeatedly. For example, pressing the + key twice raises the pitch of the track a full step.

Event-Level Key Changes (Pitch Shift)

Changing the key of individual events in a project (see Figure 3.27) adds a new creative level to song composition within ACID. In ACID, changing the key of an event is called pitch shifting; the effects on an individual loop are identical to using a project-level key change. To pitch-shift an event, right-click an event on the timeline and, from the context menu, select Pitch Shift. Then, from the submenu, select Up Semitone or Down Semitone.

Figure 3.27
Pitch-shifting an event
(changing its key). The
event shown here has
already been shifted
one semitone up.

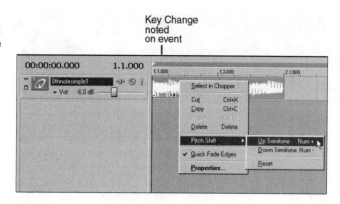

TIP

Click on an event to select it and then press the + or − keys on your
keyboard's number pad repeatedly to quickly pitch shift an event.

Radical Event-Level Key Changes

Through meticulous splitting of a loop into one or two note events, entirely new melodies can
be created with the use of event-level key changes (see Figure 3.28). While the distortion of such
drastic changes may limit this process somewhat, the increased variety that this process
provides makes it possible to avoid the bane of all loop-based music composition—too much
repetition.

To create intra-event key changes, do the following:

1. Draw an event into a project. It may be easier if you limit the event to the length
   of the loop (one loop).

2. Zoom in on the event until individual beats or notes can be seen in the waveform.

3. Press F8 to turn off snapping.

4. Click on the event between two notes. The timeline cursor moves to this position.

5. Press the S key on your keyboard to split the event. The original event is now
   split into two events. The events can be split further for more flexibility.

6. Select the newly created events and change the key by repeatedly pressing the
   + or − keys on the keyboard's number pad.

Figure 3.28
A single event that covers one repetition of a loop split into four events. Some of the events have been pitch shifted to create the C/F/G/C pattern.

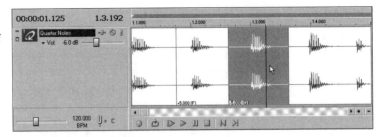

It is not necessary (or even useful) to split the event between every single note. Once the event has been split and modified, you can duplicate the split events as a group to easily repeat the pattern by holding down the Ctrl key as you drag the loops.

TIP

Although unique melodies can be created from scratch by this method, perhaps the best use of this technique is to modify a loop so that it is not so repetitive. To this end, small sections of the event can be altered in simple ways to provide a more natural and interesting sound as the loop is repeated throughout a project.

Chord Progressions

Changing the key and creating key progressions is a simple and powerful technique in ACID. Some of the most interesting progressions also develop and release tension by changing the structure of the musical chord itself while at the same time changing the key. Key progressions are distinct from chord progressions, however, and creating complex chord progressions in ACID is not possible. This is not a flaw or limitation in the software, since the chord is typically an inherent part of a loop.

Whether a chord, arpeggio, or melody is major or minor is determined by the loops you choose in ACID. It is impossible to change a loop from major to minor in the same way that you might change the key from F to A. It may be difficult to find loops that will fit into this type of progression. This does not mean that you cannot take creative advantage of the powerful nature of chord progressions in ACID. There are three ways you can create chord progressions in ACID: hunt down loops with the proper chord structure, create your own chords from simple loops, or create your own chords. None of these methods is particularly easy, but the results are well worth the effort.

Chord Progressions from Pre-Existing Loops

Creating chords from pre-existing loops requires only that you have purchased a loop CD with the proper loops. Unfortunately, this severely limits your creativity, because it would be just about impossible to provide even the most basic and popular chords in any quantity on any single loop CD. There are some good pads on some techno and electronica CDs that may contain some useful chords (see Figure 3.29), but, by and large, the selection is far too limited to be useful.

Figure 3.29

The Explorer window displaying some loops that might work in a chord progression. As with other chorded-type loops, the names of the chords are a part of the loop's (media file's) name.

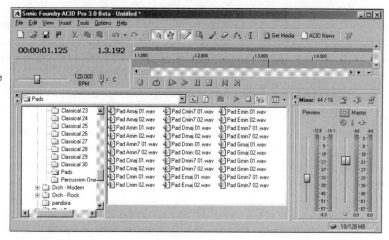

One possibility is to use a major and a minor version of an audio file to create a chord progression. Again, you need to be fortunate enough to find an appealing loop with the appropriate harmonic variations to get this to work, but even a simple major and minor version can produce a satisfying chord progression. For example, take a look at the chord progression shown in Figure 3.30.

Figure 3.30

A simple but effective chord progression.

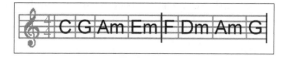

Setting up the key changes is a simple matter. The trick is to insert both the major and minor versions of the audio file into the project in two tracks. Then, the major version is used for the C, F, and G sections, while the A, D, and E sections use the minor version, producing Am, Dm, and Em chords (see Figure 3.31).

CHAPTER 3

Figure 3.31
A simple chord
progression using a
major and a minor
variation of an
audio file.

Chords and harmony are very complex topics that extend well beyond major and minor
descriptions and well beyond the scope of this brief chapter. Although changing a loop from
major to minor is impossible from within ACID, some simple mono-tonal loops can be used to
create chords and these chords can be modified and progressed.

Creating Chords with Simple Loops

It is possible to take certain simple loops and stack them into different tracks to create chords, as
shown in Figure 3.32. This is a very interesting and creative method that allows you to create all
sorts of major and minor chords. It is especially well suited to electronic or dance music, where
strange and rich sounds are highly valued. This technique is limited in more conventional
acoustic projects because of the artificial way the chords are created. While it can also be a
challenging and time-consuming process to find loops suitable for this type of work and then to
layer the events into dynamic chords, chording events can produce unique harmonics. To create
chords from events:

1. Insert a simple event into a new project.

2. Right-click the Track Header and, from the context list, select Duplicate. Repeat
    so that you have three tracks (or however many notes you need in the chord)
    that each use the same loop.

3. Draw in an event in each track.

4. Select each event and use the + and – keys on the number pad to change the
    pitch of the events.

Figure 3.32
Tracks of the same
loop stacked to make a
C major triad and a
C minor triad.

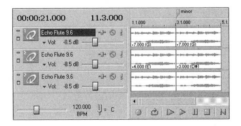

You have quite a lot of flexibility in creating the chord. It may be convenient to arrange the tracks in the order that the notes appear in the chord, with the first track holding the highest pitched note and the last track holding the lowest pitched note, although this is not necessary. Chords also do not need to be stacked to occur simultaneously in time. Instead, you can create arpeggios with this same technique, but it is not really necessary to use multiple tracks if the notes do not overlap in time. See the earlier section on chords and intervals for more information.

NOTE

Once you have created a satisfying chord, it may be useful to mix the multiple tracks that compose the chord down to a single track or even to render the tracks as a new loop file. This allows you to use this chord in other projects and saves RAM and processor cycles.

4

Polishing Up

Previous chapters have covered the basics of song composition. When we remember a song, we usually are thinking about a kind of summary of the song: its melody, bass line, or the words to the refrain. A finished song has more, however, including an introduction, a break section, and of course a conclusion. The compositional ideas presented in this chapter are the icing on the cake and can be the difference between what makes a good song and a great one. This is a short chapter and the concepts covered here are simple, but no song is truly complete without using the techniques that are discussed here. The chapter concludes with some advice on long-term project management that will allow you to revisit "finished" songs at a later date.

Introductions

Like the introduction to a story, the intro to a song should say something about what is ahead and should be a catchy hook to entice the listener to keep listening. On the other hand, a slow fade-in, creating mystery and building tension, can be very effective in some situations. As discussed in the previous chapter, most songs have some type of structure, whether it is a verse-refrain structure or a 12-bar blues pattern. Most songs do not launch directly into these patterns right away, however. Instead, a song frequently opens up with a brief introductory phrase. Like the overture to an opera, the introductory phrase often briefly quotes or references other parts of the song, most frequently the refrain.

Making Space for an Intro

Usually, since the introduction is composed of parts of the main song, it is pretty difficult to know what the introduction is going to sound like in the early stages of composition. Creating an introduction after a song has matured a bit poses a problem, though: How can you add material to the beginning of the project? Of course, you could use the selection tool to select every event in the project and move them as a unit down the timeline, but there are better ways to move complex projects around.

One of the easiest ways to add an introduction is to insert some time at the beginning of a project, moving the rest of the project right down the timeline. This is called a *ripple edit* and is similar to a Paste insert.

To insert time in this way, do the following:

1. Move the timeline cursor to the beginning of the project. The easiest way to do this is to click the Go to Start button on the Transport bar or press Ctrl + Home on your keyboard.

2. From the Insert menu, select Time.

3. In the Insert Time dialog, enter the amount of time to insert.

In most cases, you will want to insert only whole measures of time (for example, 4.0.000—see Figure 4.1). The time is formatted in measures.beats.milliseconds (with beats in 1-4); 12.3.500 would insert twelve measures, three beats, and a half-second of time (500/1000). Since the actual real-world amount of time inserted is based on the tempo of the song in number of beats per minute, a second of time might be any number of beats. Your introduction can be any length, but in most popular music, it will be four, eight, or twelve measures (or some multiple of four). There is no reason you need to follow this convention, but knowing it might be helpful for planning purposes.

Figure 4.1
The Insert Time dialog box and the gap it creates on the timeline.

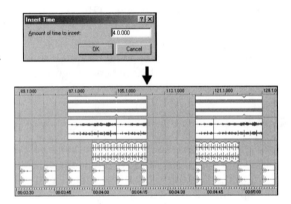

Types of Introductions

There are, of course, many possible types of introductions, including fanfares, overtures, a brief quotation of the refrain (often without vocals), and even a simple fade-in. Since the introduction is usually composed of elements of the song that already exist, the multiple-selection-and-copy techniques discussed in Chapter 2 are ideal for quickly creating an introduction.

▶ Quotation of the refrain or main melody is a very good introduction. As a kind of summary, introducing the theme or *idée fixe* can really add emphasis to a song and even create anticipation.

▶ Adding instruments one at a time is actually a variation of a fade-in. Drums and the bass line are most commonly used to establish a song in the introduction, but solo vocal lines are also effective.

▶ Use FX to mute or muffle the song during the introduction to create an interesting electronic intro. A very slow flange can create an introduction that sounds as if it were being transmitted over a short-wave radio before the song explodes into the main body. The easiest way to do this is to group the tracks you want to use into a single bus and then apply the flange to the bus.

These are just a few ideas to get you started with the introduction; in creative reality, the possibilities are unlimited.

Fading In and Out

A fade-in can be done using a combination of Volume envelopes and slowly adding instruments (tracks) one at a time. Although you could simply add Volume envelopes over the existing beginning of a song (before you create a dedicated introductory section), you will still lose the first verse or refrain, so it is still probably a good idea to insert time and create a dedicated introduction.

Fading with Track Envelopes

Track envelopes (both Volume and Pan) were discussed in Chapter 2. Remember that the volume of a track is unaffected by a Volume envelope that is in the vertical center of the track.

To create a fade-in

1. Click a track to select it.

2. Press the V key on your keyboard.

3. Double-click the Volume envelope at the end of the introductory section to add a node.

4. Drag the first node on the envelope to the bottom of the track.

Dragging a node down decreases the volume, while dragging it up increases it. Hold the mouse cursor over a node to see a ToolTip displaying the numeric value that modifies the track volume. As shown in Figure 4.2, the envelopes can cross multiple events and do not need to begin fading at the beginning of the project. Events that do not begin exactly at the start of the project need to have three envelope nodes to create a proper fade-in or else the fade will not start at zero at the beginning of the event.

Figure 4.2
Multiple Volume envelopes and staggered instrument introductions can create a simple beginning to a song.

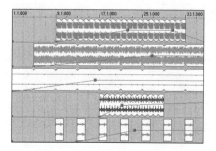

NOTE

Pressing the V key on your keyboard (or P for panning) actually does one of two things. Either it inserts a Volume envelope in a track if one doesn't already exist, or, if a Volume envelope is already inserted into the selected track, it shows or hides all Volume envelopes. For example, if you press V once in a track with no Volume envelopes, a Volume envelope will be inserted AND all other Volume envelopes in the project will be made visible. Pressing the V key again will hide all Volume envelopes.

By default, the line between two nodes on an envelope is straight (linear). The type of fade can be controlled more precisely by changing the shape of this line. To change the shape of the fade, right-click the envelope line on the fade (or either node). Then from the context menu, select Linear Fast, Fast Fade, or Slow Fade (see Figure 4.3).

Figure 4.3
The three types
of fades.

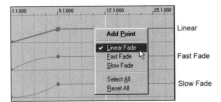

A check mark next to a menu item indicates the type of fade selected. The shape of the horizontal lines (unchanging volume/pan) cannot be set, although you could change the shape of a horizontal line and then later drag the node to create a fade.

Fading using Event Fades (ASR)

Volume and Pan envelopes (as well as FX envelopes) are track-level envelopes—that is, they run across an entire track, affecting every event in that track. Individual events can also be quickly faded in or out using event fade envelopes, otherwise known as Attack-Sustain-Release (ASR) envelopes. To create an event fade, move the mouse cursor over the upper (left or right) corner of an event. The cursor changes to the special event fade cursor (see Figure 4.4). Drag the fade envelope in towards the center of the event.

Figure 4.4
The mouse cursor
changes to a special
cursor when positioned
correctly. The position
of the end of the fade is
displayed in a ToolTip
(where the gain = 0.0
dB) and the faded
portion of the event is
visually faded as well.

By default, the blue envelope line that appears on the event is curved. Like track-level envelopes, the shape of the envelope can be changed. Both types of fades (track and event level) sound the same in the final mix. To change the event fade envelope shape, right-click the envelope and select Fade Type from the context menu. Then, from the submenu, click on the shape of the fade you want (see Figure 4.5). From top to bottom, these correspond to track envelope Fast (default), Linear, and Slow fades. If you right-click when the event fade cursor is visible (see Figure 4.4), the event fade type menu appears immediately as the context menu.

Figure 4.5
Event fade (ASR)
envelope type shapes.

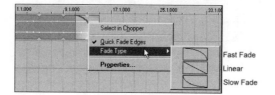

Quick Fade Edges

Quick fade edges are related to the other types of fades in name only. While event fade and track volume envelopes are used to control the mix of events into a project, quick fade edges are used to prevent clicks and pops that might be associated with the edge of an event, which may sharply cut into a loop. The quick fade edge is so short in duration that it is not normally visible on an event unless the zoom level is very high (see Figure 4.6), and it cannot be heard. The clicks and pops it potentially prevents are very audible, however, so it is a good idea to leave this feature toggled on by default. To toggle quick fade edges on or off, right-click an event and, from the context menu, click Quick Fade Edges.

Figure 4.6
A quick fade edge on
the end of an event.
Notice that the timeline
displays only 150/1000
of a second or so and
that this is a very short
fade edge.

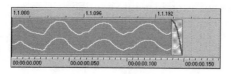

Like other toggled menu items in ACID (for example, snapping), a check mark indicates that quick fade edges are active. The precise duration of the quick fade edge (and whether it is used by default on all events in a project) can be set in the Preferences Dialog box (see Figure 4.7).

To set the quick fade duration:

1. From the Options, select Preferences.

2. In the Preferences dialog box, click the Audio tab.

3. Make sure that quick fade edit edges of audio is chosen.

4. In the Quick fade time (ms) box, enter the duration of the quick fade in milliseconds (thousandths of a second).

Figure 4.7
The Audio tab in the
Preferences dialog
contains the quick
fade options.

Quick fade options ➤

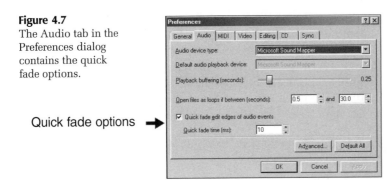

Conclusions

One of the most common conclusions to a song is the fade-out. Fading out is just as easy as fading in (previously discussed) and is accomplished by using envelopes. Although conclusions are generally easier to compose than introductions, it is best to have a dedicated ending to your song. In other words, don't just fade out the final refrain but repeat the refrain one more time (or a short portion of it) and fade it out. There are other types of finales, however, and a simple fade-out may be an indication that the composer just couldn't think of anything else to do.

In the broadest terms, the end of a song should sound like the end. It should be satisfying and have a nice resolution. Since music is such a big part of our lives, the listener can often predict when a song is going to end based on familiar devices used in popular music. With the great flexibility of ACID, another great idea is to seamlessly merge the end of one song into the introduction of another. This becomes an extremely interesting and effective technique once a few of your songs start to come together as an idea into a unified CD or album, and it is especially powerful in electronic music genres. Of course, we don't want to create standard boring tunes, but following a few of the conventional styles can make a song sound complete.

End on Beat 1

It is a little counterintuitive, but one very effective way to end a song is by ending it on Beat 1. As with many of the discussions in this book, it is rather difficult to describe this in words, but if you fire up ACID and try it out, you'll be surprised at how simple and clear this ending is. In order to effectively find Beat 1, you need to zoom in sufficiently close on the project to find the individual beats and split the events. It might also help if you turn snapping off (F8).

To end on beat 1 (on the timeline):

1. Turn off snapping by pressing F8 on your keyboard.

2. Move the timeline cursor to the end of the project. Click the Go to End button on the keyboard or press Ctrl+End on your keyboard. This moves the timeline cursor to the edge of the last event.

3. Zoom in until only one measure (or less) is visible. Use the mouse scroll wheel or the zoom arrows at the bottom of the timeline.

4. Drag the edge of the event(s) that you want to use as the ending to the right until the first beat is visible. You can use the Grid marks as reference, but ultimately you are going to need to estimate where the note on Beat 1 falls by looking at the waveform of the event.

Extending the event further and then splitting the event between notes can frequently be easier than simply extending an event. Click the event to move the timeline cursor to the split position and press S on your keyboard. Use an Event Fade envelope (ASR) to trim the edges of the event more seamlessly, especially if there isn't a clean break between beats 1 and 2. Of course, this particular technique is highly dependent upon finding loops that are suitable, but there are many loops in many different genres that will work.

Big Finale

There are certain key progressions (discussed in Chapter 3) that very clearly signal the end of a song, especially in Western popular music. One of the most classic is a progression that gradually falls by half-steps for a measure and then finally quickly rises back to the root note in two beats to a resolution, used from Day One (and earlier, of course) in rock music in songs like Bill Haley's "Rock Around the Clock." Try setting up a project finale that looks like the one shown in Figure 4.8 to listen to this instantly recognizable pattern.

Figure 4.8
Big finale in a project key of C. Notice how this pattern is organized in the number of measures on the Grid bar as well.

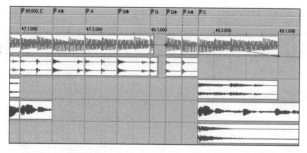

This particular technique is also highly dependent upon finding suitable loops. In the case shown in Figure 4.8, a simple bass line with repeating notes worked particularly well. In some cases, you may be able to isolate a single note in a loop to use with this progression. Chord progressions are also extremely effective in creating a sense of resolution to a song. ACID is not particularly well suited to creating unique chord progressions, however. Also discussed in Chapter 3, you should take advantage of this when you can.

Mixing and Merging Songs

Albums and CDs are sometimes conceived as unified works, much as a symphony is usually composed of a number of individual movements. At times, this large-scale structure is a part of the artist's initial goal. At other times, the big picture is not visible until the components are finished. Whenever the inspiration to group songs together into a larger theme strikes, song order, introductions, and conclusions are all important to creating the whole structure.

ACID is certainly not limited to electronic music creation, and a huge variety of acoustic loops and samples are available to prove this point, but techno, ambient, new age, and other electronica are some of the genres that are particularly well suited to the mixing and merging of songs. Either two at a time or as continuous CD-length, mixing is much more than beatmatching. Mixing is most important in the introduction and conclusion of mixed songs, although a unifying theme or instrumentation is often an important element.

Beatmapping is not the only consideration when mixing, but it is an important one. ACID defaults to 120 bpm for all projects, and, unfortunately, many people use this tempo over and over again, which has the side effect of making beatmapping very easy. Hopefully, your music uses a variety of tempos and tempo changes, but this means that you will need to match tempo and beats (in other words, beatmap) in the conclusions and introductions of mixed songs. Beatmapping is a different process depending on whether you are mixing finished (rendered) songs or ACID projects.

Mixing Rendered Songs

Mixing finished songs has applications well outside of original song creation in ACID. Mixing songs from existing material "ripped" from commercial CDs is an industry unto itself and can be a great way to make spectacular mix CDs for your own use. ACID definitely allows you to do things that you would not be able to do with two turntables, although a live mix using 12-inch platters is much more of a performance art. The first step in mixing two audio files in ACID is to beatmap each of them using the Beatmapper Wizard. Once this is done, both songs can be inserted into an ACID project. The tempo of the project will automatically match the tempo and downbeat of both songs, and mixing is then a matter of mixing the two tracks together. The tempo of the project may be determined by one song or the other (right-click the track header and select Use Original Tempo), or it may be a distinct tempo somewhere between the original tempos of the two. Most effectively, you can use multiple, closely spaced Tempo Change markers (press T on your keyboard) to gradually alter the tempo of the song before and after the overlapping mix section.

The mixed portion of the two songs does not need to be limited to the few measures of the introduction or the conclusion. Splitting the events that contain the songs into smaller parts can allow you to do many creative things with a mix. The Chopper window is especially useful in targeting smaller sections of a long song with regions that can be quickly inserted into the mix. See the section called "Chopper Trimming" later in this chapter for more information.

Mixing Projects

Working at the project level gives you even more creative control in mixing. While it is possible to open two copies of ACID, select all of the events in one project, and paste them into another to create one project from two, this can be a cumbersome way to mix two songs. Instead, it is better to pick a few key tracks or instruments to mix together. Fading pads in and out or introducing the drums from one song into another is very effective. This mixing does not need to take place only at the boundaries between two songs, but it is especially easy to mix throughout a song when mixing projects. This is so easy and effective that you can create an entire CD without discernable song breaks. Again, as with mixing rendered songs, tempo matching is important, but beat matching is automatic with projects. Gradual tempo changes from one song into another are made possible by using multiple, closely spaced Tempo Change markers.

TIP

When burning a continuous mix CD, make sure to eliminate the two-second pause that is usually inserted by default between songs. See your CD authoring software's manual or Help file for more information. This space cannot be removed when using ACID to write songs to CD.

Breaks and Bridges

Breaks and bridges are short sections that divide the main parts of a song. A break may be as simple as a pause in the music, although it is definitely a pregnant pause that builds quite a bit of tension. Bridges can be longer in length and are frequently found in pop songs as instrumental sections between one of the refrains and a verse. Bridges can be used in a live performance to highlight solo instruments and might be formally labeled as a separate section. For example, the C section in ABACAB might be described as a bridge (see Chapter 2). In this discussion, breaks are defined as very short sections lasting two measures or less that build tension and then explosively release it; bridges are longer sections that might include solos but always contain some kind of major change.

Break It Down

One of the most arresting types of breaks is one that involves complete silence followed by a rapid and explosive build back into the main song. In electronic music, the build may be a frenetic snare drum that rises in volume back to the main song. Surprisingly, this is so effective that it sounds like the snare and the song increase in tempo as it proceeds, even though it usually doesn't (although it may double in beat at one point). This is very difficult to describe in words, although it is instantly recognizable in music.

Like the Beat 1 conclusion discussed previously, a break that begins on Beat 1 can be very effective. The pause on beats 2, 3, and 4 is very tense, and the return to the song on Beat 1 of the next measure is quite powerful in the anticipation that it creates in the listener. Variations on this can include silencing all instruments except the drums. Breaks can be much longer, but you may lose the listener beyond two measures or so. On the other hand, a break may also be as short as a half-beat, starting on the AND of Beat 4 (that is, one-and, two-and, three-and, four-BREAK, one-and…). In any case, the return of the song after a break can result in a huge release of tension.

Figure 4.9

A break beginning after Beat 1 in Measure 35 (35.1.000). The break continues for two measures, with the bassline (Track 1) broken up for variety. The song returns on 37.1.000.

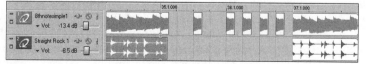

There are a number of different loop styles that are particularly useful as break loops:

▶ **Hits**—Hits are musical blasts or crashes that emphasize the beat very strongly. Sometimes called verbs, hits may be labeled as such in loop names (for example, Horn Hit Loop.wav). Look for one-shot drum loops and crashes as well. You can also create your own hits from a loop file by carefully splitting it to isolate a single note or chord.

▶ **Rolls**—Typically done on the snare drum, a roll is a very rapid sequence of beats that can build into the return of the main song. Using the track envelope to increase the volume through the roll event can significantly increase the tension. As mentioned, the building can be so enthusiastic as to create the illusion of a tempo increase, although this is rarely the case (however, the beat may double). Like hits, rolls are often labeled as such (for example, Snare Roll.wav). Rolls can also be created from existing drum parts. See the following section on using the Chopper for an example.

▶ **Fills**—A roll is actually a repetitive version of the fill. Fills are usually a radical change in the drum pattern and may be labeled as such (for example, 4-4 Fill 39-02.wav).

An important part of a break is the return to Beat 1 in the next measure. Most loop files are designed to loop infinitely and fit together end to beginning. This is ideal for coming out of a break since you can use Beat 4 of one of the loops that was silenced during the break as the lead back into that loop.

Figure 4.10
A full-featured break beginning on Beat 1 (23.1.000), lasting two measures, and returning with a roll (Track 4–Straight Snr Roll), an intro back into the piano part (Track 3– E Grand 02), and a crash (Track 5–BD Crash 2) on Beat 1 (35.1.000).

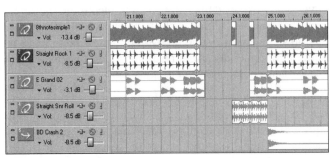

Bridges and Solos

In this text, bridges are longer sections of music that differ from the main part of the song. In popular music, a bridge might explicitly be called an instrumental bridge and can serve as a time for instrumental solo sections between vocal refrains and verses. While a bridge may be radically different from the rest of a song, it still needs to fit together with the overall scheme. A break can often be used to introduce a longer bridge section. Bridges are more diverse than short breaks, and it is difficult to describe any specific techniques to use in creating an effective bridge. You should look for loops that are in solo or one-shot folders.

Spicing Up Solos

The best and most interesting solos are original performances recorded into your ACID project. As mentioned, there are some solo loops of longer-than-average length in some collections of commercial loops. It may also be possible to split a shorter loop into a number of parts, rearrange it, and use key changes to create an entirely new sound.

Solo instrumental sections or vocal rap sections in an otherwise non-rap song are very common. There is no particular secret to creating an effective solo section; treat it as you would any other part of a song's structure (see Chapter 2).

Loops that are well suited to solos are often found in solo folders on loop discs or even on discs composed only of solos. Solo loops are longer and may be in one-shot folders also. While many solos on loop discs are just fine as-is, you can also significantly modify a solo for variety, as shown in Figure 4.11.

To modify a solo loop, you can:

▶ **Split a solo event between notes and rearrange the split pieces**—Press the S key on your keyboard to split the original event.

▶ **Change the pitch of the individual events split from the main loop**—Select an event and press the + or – keys on the number pad to change the pitch.

Figure 4.11
The top image shows the original solo loop. The bottom image shows the same loop file, split into a number of pieces. Many of the pieces have also been pitch shifted up or down to create an entirely new solo.

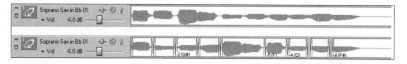

Chopper Trimming

The Chopper is a window that specializes in trimming. In many cases, trimming directly on the timeline may be the easiest way to edit your events. The advantage to using the Chopper is that you can leave your project at a lower zoom level for easier navigation and use the Chopper at a higher zoom level, allowing you to make precise splits and trims on the waveform. There are a number of other features in the Chopper that make certain edits much easier. The Chopper window is a powerful time-saving tool that is largely ignored by most ACID users. Understanding what it is used for and how it is used is definitely one of the marks of an ACID guru. Let's start by looking at the Chopper window layout (see Figure 4.12).

▶ The **timeline** displays the waveform of the entire media file associated with a track and the grid marks that are used for snapping.

▶ Turning **snapping** on and off in the main program also affects snapping in the Chopper.

▶ **Zoom** in and out on the Chopper timeline with the mouse scroll wheel, the + or − buttons on the right of the horizontal scroll bar, or by dragging the edge of the horizontal scroll bar itself.

▶ The **Grid bar** units cannot be changed in the Chopper. The Time Ruler along the bottom can be changed to display your choice of units.

Figure 4.12
The Chopper window has a short timeline that covers the duration of the media file.

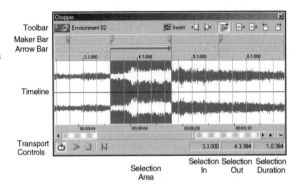

A basic event insert using the Chopper works something like this:

1.   Create a selection area by dragging on the Chopper timeline (see Figure 4.12).

2.   Position the main UI timeline cursor where you want the insert to occur. The selection area and arrow from the Chopper window are represented on the main UI timeline at the timeline cursor position.

3.   Click the Insert Selection button on the Chopper toolbar. An event appears on the timeline corresponding to the selection area in the Chopper.

As mentioned earlier, there are a number of reasons why you might want to insert events this way. One major reason is that you can have a much larger media file and use only a very small portion of an event on the timeline. With larger disk drives widely available and with people saving entire CDs to their hard drives, it is not uncommon to use a whole four- or five-minute song as the source media file for a track. It is likely that in your own creations, you will want to use only small portions of these songs as looping events, however. The power of the Chopper is that you can open an entire song and then create multiple regions for the various smaller parts of the media file.

Here is how to use the Chopper:

▶ **To create a region**—Drag on the Chopper timeline to create a selection area and press the R key on your keyboard.

▶ **To recall a region**—Press the associated number key along the top of your keyboard (not on the number pad).

▶ **To save a region**—Regions are saved when your project is saved and are associated with the track and not the media file (in other words, other tracks using the same event will not have the same region information available).

CHAPTER 4

Regions and markers added in the Chopper also show up in the Track Properties dialog (and vice versa). You can save regions (and markers) to the media file so that they can be accessed in other projects by clicking the Save File button in the Track Properties window.

The Chopper toolbar contains a number of tools to make selection modification and timeline cursor movement possible (see Figure 4.13).

Figure 4.13
The Chopper toolbar.

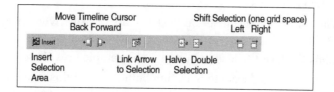

The Arrow bar and arrow in the Chopper represent the total length of time that is inserted into the timeline, regardless of the selection area. By default, the arrow and the selection area are always the same length. Click the Link Arrow to Selection button on the toolbar to toggle between whether the arrow and the selection area are independent or not. The reason for doing this is shown in Figure 4.14.

Figure 4.14
The effects of the arrow on inserting events from the Chopper. Four events were inserted and a fifth is ready to go, as displayed on the main timeline.

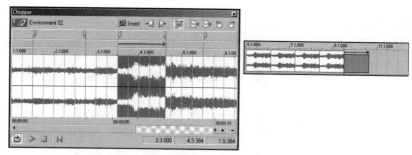

▶ If the arrow is **equal** to the length of the selection area, the events will be inserted back to back, in a looping fashion.

▶ By making the arrow **longer** than the selection area, you can insert events in a periodic fashion with a time interval between them by repeatedly clicking the Insert Selection button.

▶ There isn't really much reason to make the arrow shorter than the selection area. When inserting events this way, the entire selection region is still inserted, but the timeline cursor is advanced only to the arrow's position. The next insert will, therefore, cover up the event portion that extends beyond the arrow. This is identical to simply inserting a shorter selection area with the arrow linked to the area, with the exception that the last event inserted would have been longer. This is also a fast way of creating stutter effects without changing a selection size.

One simple example of how the Chopper can be effectively used is by changing a drum line to create an interesting break:

1. Find and select a beat in the Chopper. In the example, the initial kick is selected.

2. Click the Link Arrow to Selection button so that this feature is turned off.

3. Drag the mouse on the arrow bar to extend the arrow to 1.3 in the Chopper. This is two full beats.

4. Place the timeline cursor on Beat 1 of the measure where you want the break to begin.

5. Click the Insert Selection button. The example uses six repetitions.

6. Click the Link Arrow to Selection button so that this feature is turned on. The arrow is now the same size as the selection. In the example, it equals one beat.

7. Insert the selection to create back-to-back loops. In the example, a kick roll is created that serves as an introduction back into the resumption of the main percussion pattern at 9.1.

Figure 4.15 shows the results of this procedure. Drum breaks and rolls are common in many styles of music. The regular periodic nature of Chopper event inserts makes creating these sorts of patterns easier.

Figure 4.15
The Chopper can be used to break up a beat and create rolls.

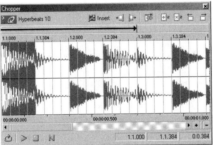

The initial kick is isolated in the Chopper.

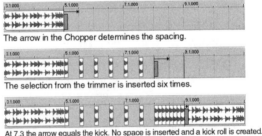

The arrow in the Chopper determines the spacing.

The selection from the trimmer is inserted six times.

At 7.3 the arrow equals the kick. No space is inserted and a kick roll is created.

You can also work backwards from events on the timeline and in the Chopper. Right-click an event on the timeline and, from the context menu, choose Select in the Chopper. The portion of the media file that is being used in the event on the timeline will be used as the selection area in the Chopper.

Project Management

Besides the actual process of finishing up the musical parts of the song, ACID project management becomes more of a concern as a project matures. For example, once you have a song that you really like, you can use the Save As command to create a new version of the song that you can continue to modify, safe in the knowledge that the original is preserved. Since project files are relatively small, there is no reason not to archive projects or even the evolution of a project over time. You'll certainly wish you had when your label wants you to start work on your second album.

Backing Up Projects

Projects can automatically be backed up as you work. This will give you some security in case the original file is deleted or becomes corrupt. These *.acd-bak files can be opened with the File > Open command and saved. Backup files can be automatically created every time you save the project if the Create project file backups on save (.acd-bak) item is selected in the Preferences dialog on the General tab (Options > Preferences). More information on project preferences can be found in the appendix.

Recovering Projects

Normal project files (*.acd) reference the media files on your computer and point to their location. If these files are moved (or their names are changed), ACID will not be able to reference them. For example, if you use the file D:\loops\funk\bass04.wav in the original project and then move it to a new hard disk drive, possibly now named the E:\ drive, the ACID projects that reference this file will be unable to find it in its original location. When you open a project that references files that have been moved, ACID prompts you with a warning message noting that the file(s) cannot be found (see Figure 5.16). The easiest way to recover these broken links is to select the Search for missing file item and click the OK button. In the Search For Missing Files dialog box, it might be faster to narrow ACID's search by specifying the hard drive that the file(s) have been moved to in the Look in list. After ACID has found the file, even if the entire drive has not been searched, click the OK button. If the relative locations of the other files in the project remain the same (meaning that you have moved ALL of your loops to a new drive or location), ACID will automatically find the remainder of the media files. If not, ACID will prompt you again for each file that has been moved to a new location or been renamed.

Figure 4.16
The Search For Missing Files dialog box.

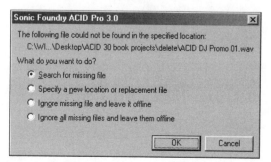

Saving Projects with Embedded Media

Projects can be saved with the media embedded within a single compressed file, allowing you to more easily transfer a project to another computer. While the project file with the media saved within it can be quite large (easily more than 10 MB), it is typically much smaller than the sum of the original project file and its uncompressed media files. To save a project with the media included, from the File menu, select Save As. From the Save As type list, select ACID Project With Embedded Media (*.acd-zip). Enter a name, browse for a location to save the file, and click the Save button.

To reverse this process and extract the original media files from an *.acd-zip file, from the File menu, select Export Loops. Browse for a location to save the files to and click the Save button. It is not a bad idea to create a new folder to store these files in, because there can sometimes be quite a few files in a project. You can select a format for the new media files from the Save as type list (for example, *.wav). Selecting a compressed format such as *.mp3 can save room on your disk, but the quality of the loops may suffer. See Chapter 10 on "Publishing" for more information on file formats, compression, and quality.

Projects with embedded media cannot simply be saved as a new file with a different name using the Save As command. When you attempt to do this, the Copy all media with project item is chosen in the bottom of the Save As dialog. If you uncheck this box and attempt to continue, ACID will prompt you that this cannot be done and the box will be rechecked. When you save the file, all of the media files will also be saved in the folder in the WAV file format.

5

Recording
Vocals and Solos

Perhaps the most challenging, yet rewarding, part of composing an ACID-based song is creating your own unique sounds and loops. One of the best things about loop-based music creation is that all of the instruments and parts you put together are high-quality professional recordings. Fortunately, ACID has all of the tools you need to not only record a lead guitar or vocal track but also to edit and enhance these performances. This chapter covers the basics, such as setting up your hardware, and ends with advanced topics on quality.

Hardware

For the home studio enthusiast, gear is the primary consideration if you want quality. Most of us have at least a decent sound card and stereo system that allow us to produce some pretty amazing output with ACID. Recording and input are, however, another matter. Recording loops into your computer and into ACID definitely requires more hardware than the cheap microphone that came packaged with your sound card. Once again, it is well beyond the scope of this book to give specific recommendations on how to set up a professional studio, although this would obviously be the ideal situation. Instead, the following section on hardware will recommend some things that the interested amateur or enthusiast might find helpful in creating a decent home recording studio without building a booth and covering the walls with acoustic tile.

Noise

The single biggest problem with recording outside a dedicated studio is noise. Beside the basic considerations of keeping the dog quiet and the windows shut to block traffic noises, there are a surprising number of things that can ruin a home recording. Chief among them is the refrigerator, which you may not notice turning on and off until the recording light goes on. And there are even more insidious noise generators that you can't hear with your ears, including the hum of electricity in the wires of your house, not to mention the mess of noise-generating electronics known as a personal computer.

Environmental Noise

Unfortunately, when using ACID, your computer can be a primary source of background noise. There really isn't much you can do about the whir of fans and the click of the hard disks without isolating your computer box from the monitor, mouse, and microphones. You may be able to place the box in another room and run the wires to your semi-isolated environment. Another idea is to isolate your computer in a cabinet beneath your desk, making sure that your computer continues to have adequate air circulation for cooling purposes. If you are really a techno-geek, you could install a whisper-quiet water-cooling system on your PC.

NOTE

Use extreme caution when putting your PC in a cabinet. Keeping your PC cool is critical, and maintaining air circulation is how this is done. If you do insert your PC into an isolating cabinet, overheating is easy to diagnose: Your computer will suddenly start to crash more often and for no apparent reason. While occasional overheating and crashing is rarely fatal to a PC, it is not particularly good for it, either.

There are some filters that come with ACID that can be used to minimize constant background noises (including some of the EQ plug-ins, the Noise Gate plug-in, and the Noise Reduction plug-in), but these are all used after the damage has already been done. Using these tools is less than ideal, but they are extremely useful when you have no other choice. Highly directional microphones can also be useful if you simply cannot isolate your computer.

Electronic Noise

While vocal and acoustic recordings need to be done in the best possible environment, electronic instruments (for example, keyboards, theramins, and other MIDI devices) that feed directly into your hardware will not suffer from a noisy studio or basement. These instruments may be plugged directly into the back of your sound card. This does not mean that you are home free, however—computers are amazingly noisy. Between the power supply, the hard disks, and all of the various components, there is quite a lot of electronic interference flowing around inside your computer. This noise can cause a low-level hum directly on the sound card (especially cheaper ones) or even through the cables that come from your instruments, especially from microphones. Again, plug-ins can be used to eliminate this constant hum after the fact, but this is less than ideal. One solution is to set the noise floor in recording to a level where all of the various hums are not audible (see the following section on recording in ACID); you can always increase the volume of quiet recordings later.

Higher-quality (and, of course, more expensive) sound cards targeted at musicians and recording engineers are much more electronically quiet than the more widely available general-purpose cards. In addition to being internally quieter, these cards are frequently better shielded from external electronic noise sources, including other components within the PC.

Solutions

The first step in detecting unwanted background noise is to watch the meters in ACID's record dialog box. When you are ready to record, if there is a constant flicker of green at the bottom of the meter, even below 57 dB, it means there is some kind of background noise being recorded, either environmental or electronic. The solution to this is to reduce the gain in your audio hardware's mixer on the device from which you are recording until you have eliminated the flicker. Of course, you don't want to turn the gain down so far that you don't record the quietest parts of what you want to record. Not having the meters peak very high may not be a problem, since you can always turn up the volume once the track is recorded in ACID. If some background noise is recorded, turning up the volume on a track will also increase the volume of the background noise. You may have to balance lower recording levels against recording some small amount of background noise. Obviously, you'll want to experiment and get the kinks worked out before you get the musicians into the studio.

There may be times where it is simply impossible to control background noise 100 percent. In these cases, there are a number of very powerful audio effects (FX) plug-ins that can be used to eliminate noise in post-production in ACID. Noise Gate is a straightforward effect that is used to set the lowest level of noise that can be heard in a track. Compression can be used in conjunction with Noise Gate to increase the volume without increasing background noise (see the end of Chapter 8 on "Mixing"). The various equalization (EQ) plug-ins can be used to very good effect to diminish background noise that occurs at a particular frequency. Finally, Sonic Foundry also sells a separate Noise Reduction plug-in, which is tailored to this kind of work. Again, not to beat a dead horse, but these solutions are all last resorts and are not highly recommended.

NOTE

Although these effects are of the highest quality and are used by professionals in almost every project, they should still be considered tools of last resort. There is no substitute for a good recording in the first place.

External Solutions

One solution that should not be overlooked is to record to a dedicated device such as a tape deck (preferably a DAT deck) or an MD player. While this means that you won't be using ACID as your recording studio and you'll lose some convenience, the many noisy complications that are inherent in recording into a computer are completely avoided by going this route. Using even a mediocre microphone and a Walkman-type tape recorder can often produce better recordings than a poor sound card on a noisy computer. There can be issues with tape playback speed and synchronization, however.

Recordable MP3 players and MD players avoid syncing problems by recording digitally, but these formats are compressed, so you'll take a quality hit going this route (although it may still be better than a background hum). Small digital tape machines (DAT) solve both problems by recording CD-quality audio (or better) in a precise digital format. These machines become more affordable and widely available every year. As with MP3 and MD recording, you can also often transfer these recordings directly into your computer through a pure digital connection (if your hardware supports this), such as digital optical, coaxial, SPDIF, or IEEE-1394. Finally, DV camcorders can also be used to create high-quality digital recordings that can be transferred to your computer digitally. While you probably don't want to go out and purchase a camcorder for your audio studio, you can add audio recording to your self-justification list of why you need to buy a camcorder. It cannot be stressed strongly enough that you **must** use an external microphone if you use this method. Camcorder motors and electronics are often internally even noisier than your computer and are easily picked up by onboard mikes, which defeats the whole purpose of using a dedicated recording device. Even moving the camera one meter away will almost certainly completely isolate it from the microphone.

Using one of these solutions eliminates one of the great features of ACID, which is that you can record directly into the timeline of ACID in perfect sync while playing back a project. The rest of this chapter focuses on recording into ACID using your computer's sound card.

Microphones

The quality of your microphone is directly related to the quality of your recording. Professional-level microphones are available starting at just under $100 and are really worth the minor investment. There are many types of microphones available, depending on the intended use. Again, it is not really within the scope of this book to detail microphone dynamics, but here are a few general ideas to get you on the right track. It probably goes without saying that the plastic microphones that come with many sound cards or computers are not particularly well suited to recording quality music. If this is your first serious microphone purchase, I'd highly recommend that you go to your local audio shop and talk to the salespeople there. You can probably save money by ordering on the Internet, but spending an extra $10 to talk to an expert is worth it. The service at local shops is usually quite good as well and can include allowing you to buy a mike, try it out for a week, and bring it back if it isn't exactly what you need. Another huge advantage is that the folks at these shops will often be interested in what you are trying to do and will have a wealth of advice beyond just microphones.

Here are some microphone basics:

> ▶ **Directional mics**—Directional mics come in a number of varieties. Uni-directional mics record in only one direction (forward), are good at isolating the subject, and do not pick up peripheral noises. Shotgun mics are one example of a uni-directional mic and are great general-purpose microphones that can be used from a distance if necessary. However, they typically don't have a response range adequate for music. Bi-directional mics record in a two-lobed pattern and can provide a nice spatial sense to a recording. Omni-directional mics record in a wide pattern and may be suitable for acoustic music in an isolated studio, but they are a poor choice if you need to minimize background noise.

> ▶ **Cardioid mics**—This style of microphone picks up noise from a broader area than a directional mic but is still good at eliminating unwanted environmental noise. This is a common type of pickup pattern and a good choice in a general-purpose microphone.

▶ Close mic techniques—Getting the microphone in close to the subject of the recording is an excellent way to eliminate environmental noise. Minimize explosive consonants (for example, "P") in vocal performances by using a pop filter (baffle), which can easily be created with a coat hanger and a nylon stocking.

If most of your recording is going to be done with a specific instrument, it may be best to buy a microphone specialized to that use. For example, when recording an acoustic guitar, you might want to use a piezoelectric pickup mic, while ribbon microphones are an excellent choice for vocalists and horn players. This is obviously a huge topic, and engineers argue endlessly over the best microphone for a particular application. Suffice it to say that buying a quality mic doesn't need to cost a lot but is well worth the expenditure. A great place to begin your research is **http://arts.ucsc.edu/ems/music/tech_background/TE-20/teces_20.html**.

NOTE

Computer sound cards typically have eighth-inch stereo mini-plug inputs. Most quality microphones are mono, which is not a problem. Microphones do have many different types of connections, however, with XLR being the most popular in professional mics. One-eighth, one-quarter, and RCA connections can also be found. Make sure you can find the proper adapter for your sound card before you buy the microphone: XLR-to-mini-plug adapters can be expensive.

CHAPTER 5

Monitoring

One of the best features of recording directly into ACID through your sound card is that ACID functions as a miniature studio. Once you have a good microphone and have isolated your recording environment as much as possible, the final step is figuring out how to monitor your project in ACID as you record. ACID is a multitrack recording device, after all. Unlike when creating a final mix (as discussed in Chapter 8), there is really only one choice in monitoring ACID while recording: headphones. Headphones can be directly connected to your sound card or even to some computer speakers. Since monitoring in this case simply involves playing back a project for reference while you sing or play along, the quality of the headphones is really unimportant. You do not need to use headphones when using electronic instruments, which are plugged directly into your computer.

Recording into ACID

ACID is a virtual multitrack recording studio, allowing you to record original performances directly into a project. A keyboard player, for example, could use a set of jazz loops to set up a project with a bass line and drums and then record the keyboard part over it. The project could start out structured with a key progression (as discussed in Chapter 3) and have breaks and solo sections built right in. Since the process of recording is no more difficult than pressing the Record button, multiple takes can be recorded and the best one chosen for the final master song. Better still, multiple takes give you the opportunity to select the best parts of each take and combine them into a single flawless performance.

Recording into a Track

The basic metaphor for ACID is a multitrack studio. Each track in ACID contains one media file. When recording into ACID, all new parts are saved to a media file on your computer and inserted into a new track on the timeline. Unlike conventional studios, ACID is basically unlimited in the number of tracks that can be used.

To record into ACID:

1. Move the timeline cursor to the position where you want to start recording.
2. On the Transport bar, click the Record button or press Ctrl + R on your keyboard.
3. In the Record dialog, select Audio in the Record type field.
4. Click the Start button. The project begins playback and the recording starts.
5. Click the Stop button to end the recording.

A media file is saved to your computer and a new track is inserted into the project with an event that contains the recording. The name of the file and the location where the file is saved can be set up in the Record dialog box in the File name and Record folder boxes. It is a pretty good idea to set up a folder dedicated to holding your recordings instead of using the default location where ACID was installed.

Figure 5.1
The Record dialog box.

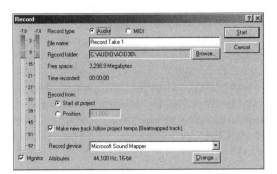

The files are automatically named and numbered according to a default scheme: Record Take 1.wav, Record Take 2.wav, etc. While the file name can be changed in the Record dialog, ACID defaults back to this numbering for every take. As with all tracks, the name of the track is taken from the name of the associated media file (this can also be changed—see Figure 5.2).

Figure 5.2
Tracks 3, 4, and 5
recorded into an ACID
project. Note that
tracks 3 and 4 were
muted while Track 5
was recorded.

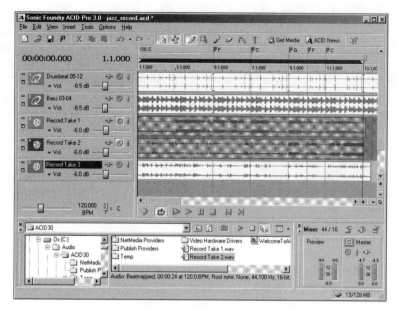

By default, performances are recorded as special ACID Beatmapped files which are then placed
in Beatmapped tracks. This means that the media files contain extra information about the
tempo of the file and where the beat falls within that file. If you use this file in another project,
the media will automatically conform to the tempo and beat of the other project.

TIP

It may be easiest to record short sections of a song at a time, although when
you move on to the next section, more takes will be created. You might want
to work on one section at a time and mix all of those takes down to a single
track before moving on (see the section on "Working with Takes").

Recording can be started at any position by selecting the Position item in the Record from area
of the Record dialog box. Position is entered in measures.beats.seconds (in thousandths of a
second). Since editing and trimming events in ACID is so easy, starting the recording a few
measures before the place where you actually need to begin performing (a pre-roll) is a good
idea. When the Position item is selected, the start of the recording is indicated by—and can be
determined by—the timeline cursor position.

The Make new track follow project tempo (Beatmapped track) item is selected by default. This
adds tempo information to the file when it is saved and does not affect the sound of the file at
all. It does, however, allow ACID to automatically line up events created in the track and make
pitch and tempo changes along with the project. Files that have not been recorded in ACID can
also have tempo information saved to them to take advantage of these ACID features. This is
called Beatmapping and is discussed in Chapter 9.

CHAPTER 5

Since the tempo of the project you are recording into is defined by ACID, it is very straightforward to add this information into the recorded file. A single audio file can have only one tempo in ACID (even if the piece changes tempo on the timeline) and can be set to only one key or root note. Most popular songs do not have tempo changes, so this isn't usually a problem. Loops recorded in ACID will have a tempo dictated by the project tempo. Most songs do have key changes, and these can be a part of an ACID project (as discussed in Chapter 4). Since the key often changes, the root note of a recorded loop is not set in ACID. This means that as the key changes on the timeline, the pitch of any recorded loops will not change. Key changes in the performance are an inherent part of the performance and, of course, will match the project's key changes (if you so desire). If you use the loop in another project, the key may not match the project. You can set the key in the Track Properties window on the Stretch tab. In the Root note list, select the key of the performance. Root note and other Track Properties are discussed in more detail in Chapter 9.

Troubleshooting

Figuring out how to record on your computer is not always easy. The combination of hardware, drivers, and software level interface makes troubleshooting a less than intuitive task. And while it is fairly straightforward to isolate output problems, since you can hear whether your card is working or not, input and recording problems cannot always be fixed by ear. To simplify this procedure and avoid crashes, it is best to close other applications while working through this process.

The first step in verifying proper recording setup is to monitor the recording meters in the Record dialog box in ACID. When everything is set up, any noises will cause the bottom of the meter to bounce up and down. If there is some green that is moving but the levels never get very high, even when taping the microphone, then the input gain is too low but everything is working otherwise. If there is no green visible at all, then something else is wrong.

I don't mean to be patronizing, but you should check to make sure your microphone is hooked up to the sound card correctly. Most consumer-level sound cards have two eighth-inch input jacks, one for a microphone and one for an auxiliary device (such as a Walkman or CD player). On other cards, one input may be balanced and the other unbalanced. Without going into too much detail, this means that one is designed for an unamplified microphone, while the other is designed to work with an amplified signal from an auxiliary device. Some microphones also have an on/off switch that you should check—your card may even have to have batteries.

Once you have verified that your hardware is properly configured, the next step is to find the mixer properties for the sound card. The drivers that come with the card often allow you to select the type of input device(s) used for recording and set the gain. Unfortunately, this can be different for every sound card. The following procedure is fairly generic for a large number of Windows sound cards.

To view the Windows volume control:

1. Click the Windows Start button.

2. From the Start menu, select Settings and then Control Panel.

3. In the Control Panel, double-click Multimedia. This opens the Multimedia Properties dialog box.

4. On the Audio tab, make sure Show volume control on the taskbar is chosen (see Figure 5.3).

Figure 5.3
Check Show volume control on the taskbar to display a speaker icon on the taskbar.

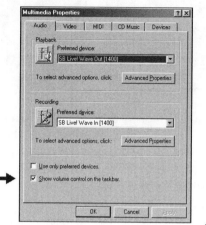

Show volume control on the taskbar ➡

↑
Speaker Icon on taskbar

Keeping the Volume control on the taskbar is not mandatory, but it can be a convenient way to quickly access Windows mixer controls. Some sound cards add their own proprietary controls on top of Windows basic controls (see Figure 5.4). The procedure for adjusting the audio mix in a sound card varies depending on your version of Windows, but it is basically like this:

1. On the taskbar, double-click the volume icon.

2. In the Play Control dialog box, from the Options menu, select Properties.

3. In the Properties dialog box, in the Adjust volume for groupbox, choose the Recording option.

4. In the Show the following volume controls for box, make sure the Microphone option is chosen. This controls which devices are available for mixing, not whether they are turned on or off.

5. Click the OK button.

6. In the Recording Control dialog box (see Figure 5.4), use the sliders to adjust the gain. Close the dialog box when finished.

Again, unfortunately, this is a rather typically convoluted procedure to accomplish the simple goal of turning on the microphone and adjusting its volume. You may have noticed in Step 3 that there may have also been a Microphone option in the Playback Properties dialog—there is no reason you can't use this control instead. The gain can be monitored in real time on the meters in the ACID Recording dialog box. By switching back and forth between the sound card's mixer panel and the Recording dialog box, you can eventually get the gain set properly.

CHAPTER 5

Figure 5.4
The Record Control
dialog box, on the left,
is a standard Windows
feature. The mixer
panel, on the right, is
for an SB Live! sound
card and is really just a
front end to the
Windows controls with
a few extra, proprietary
features.

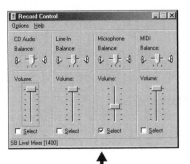

Microphone option selected

Which brings up the question of what the "proper" gain is for the microphone. As with the output mix in ACID, the primary variable is clipping. Make sure that the maximum level on the meters never exceeds the top of the meter. Sound and data are certainly lost at this level, and distortion may occur. Beyond this basic rule, however, there is a pretty broad range of good settings. Some things to consider include the following:

▶ Correction for quiet recordings is rather easy in ACID, so if you are going to err, err on the side of keeping the volume low enough to prevent clipping in all situations. Meters that jump into the red during average recording conditions are probably set too high.

▶ Setting the gain too high can also introduce and enhance unwanted background noise. Due to the environmental and electronic background conditions previously discussed, there is almost always some kind of background noise that becomes more and more apparent with higher gain. By keeping the gain lower, you can avoid recording this noise altogether. Once again, correcting the gain on output and using ACID filters to eliminate background noise is not a difficult thing, but it is an extra step you may be able to avoid by setting the recording gain properly.

▶ Trust the meters to show you what your ears cannot hear. Meters that go all the way to the top are indications of clipping, whether you can hear any distortion or not. (See Chapter 2 for more information on clipping.) Background noise that causes the meters to bounce even in the quietest recording situations reveals problems that may not be apparent to the ear.

NOTE
The meter in ACID's Record dialog box does not peak above 0 dB. This means that there is no clipping indicator as there is with the meters in the Mixer window. You should consider the gain as being set too high if the meter ever reads 0 dB, since it will never read higher. Have your performer play as loud as he/she can given the current setup and set your level accordingly.

Recording Options

A number of recording options can be controlled from within ACID. These options are distinct from the gain/mixing options of your sound card, previously discussed. In fact, you cannot control the gain of the recording in ACID at all. Here is what you can control:

▶ The File name and location can be set in the Record dialog box.

▶ To change the quality of the recording, go to the Audio tab of the Project Properties dialog box and Click the Change button at the bottom. In the Advanced Audio Preferences dialog box (Options > Preferences >Audio tab > Advanced), click the Record latency tab. By default, the Automatically detect and offset for hardware recording latency option is checked. This compensates for the delay that may occur between the time you click the Start button and the time when recording begins. In most cases, you do not need to change this, but if the beginnings of your recordings are being cut off, you may need to adjust this manually.

▶ Also in the Preferences dialog box on the Audio tab, if Microsoft Sound Mapper is selected from the Audio device type field, you cannot select different hardware devices (in cases where you may have two or more sound cards on one computer). Select a device other than Microsoft Sound Mapper (for example, Windows Classic Wave Driver) and then, in the Record dialog box, select the device you want to record from on the Record device list.

Pre-roll

Pre-roll refers to starting the playback before the point where you want the recording to begin. Although ACID does not have a specific tool or procedure to do this, starting the recording process a measure or two early and then editing the take is a good idea. The simple nature of editing takes (trimming, splitting, and so on) makes this quite effortless.

TIP

Since it is difficult to begin recording and come in on Measure 1, Beat 1 of a performance, inserting a measure or two (or whatever your musicians are comfortable with) of silence at the start of a song is a good idea. From the Insert menu, select Time and enter a length of time (in measures.beats.milliseconds).

When the Position item is selected in the Record dialog box, the start of the recording is indicated by and can be determined by the timeline cursor position. If the timeline cursor is at any position in the project other than the very beginning, the Position item is automatically selected.

CHAPTER 5

Working with Takes

Takes are different versions or performances of the same thing. In a typical studio session, many different takes of a song or part of a song may be recorded. In the bad old days, the entire band played live into a microphone or two that was then mixed straight to tape. If the drummer screwed up, the entire performance had to be repeated. With the advent of the multi-track studio, each part was recorded to a separate track on a tape. This way, the rest of the band could go home while the drummer got his act together, recording his takes against the good takes of the band. Or famous pop artists could sing along with a previous take of a song sung by Mr. Sinatra in another studio in another part of the world.

In movies and music recording, takes are different versions of the same section of a project. In movies, a director might film the same scene ten times, getting ten different takes; scene 5 take 1, scene 5 take 2, and so on. In music, the "scene" is usually indicated by the measure; measure 5 take 1, measure 5 take 2, and so on. Takes in ACID are handled in two different ways. The first is simply a naming convention—that is, ACID automatically names the files recorded using a naming and numbering scheme that can help with take organization. The second is to create automatically looping takes. This method allows you to use ACID looping playback to automatically play a region over and over again while continuously recording takes. Although a single file in a single track is created using this method, each take is marked in the file with regions that can be quickly accessed to find the best one.

Each method has its own advantages and disadvantages. For example, recording takes one file and one track at a time requires a lot of starting and stopping and can result in a cluttered workspace, since a new track is created every time. But it is also easier to quickly audition the various takes since they are allocated in separate tracks. In the end, both methods may be useful at different times and in different situations.

Takes by Tracks

Takes in ACID may be recorded into separate tracks. Each time you click the Stop button in the Record dialog box, a media file is saved and a new track is created. When you repeat the recording procedure from the same starting location, a new take, media file, and track are created just below the last. The takes are identified by file name, which then determines the track name. Figure 5.5 shows three takes inserted into three consecutive tracks: Record Take 1, Record Take 2, and Record Take 3. The corresponding media files are, logically enough, Record Take 1.wav, Record Take 2.wav, and Record Take 3.wav. These names are only names and do not actually mean anything in ACID. You can name your tracks and files by any naming scheme you want, this is just the default automatic procedure.

Figure 5.5
Tracks 3, 4, and 5 are
three consecutively
recorded takes in ACID.

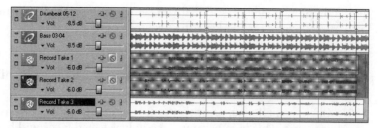

NOTE

Before you record the next take, make sure you click the Mute button on the
last take to silence it (as shown in Fig. 5.5).

By muting and unmuting the various takes (tracks), you can preview them against the main
project to choose the best one.

The whole purpose of recording takes is to get the best possible performances into the song. You
don't need to select the single best media file or track but, instead, can split up the events that
make up the various takes, choose the best parts of each, and create a composite performance of
the best of the best (see Figure 5.6).

Splitting Up the Takes

Events are easily split by positioning the timeline cursor on an event where you want a split to
occur and then pressing the S key on your keyboard. Since you will probably want only one
take at any particular time, you can split all of the takes at the same time and at the same
position by selecting all of the events. Looping the playback one section at a time and then
soloing one take at a time will allow you to audit the best version.

To audit and select portions of takes:

1. Create a Loop Region that encompasses the section of the project that you want
   to work on.

2. Press the L key on your keyboard to turn on Loop Playback.

3. Click the Mute button on all of the takes except the first one.

4. Click the Play button on the Transport bar or press the spacebar on your
   keyboard.

5. Use Markers to identify the locations where you want to split the events: Press
   M on your keyboard during playback.

6. Mute the first take, unmute the second, and verify the split positions or create a
   new one.

7. Repeat with all of the takes.

CHAPTER 5

The purpose of dropping markers is so that you cannot split on the fly during playback. It is best to work in short sections so the markers don't get too complicated.

To split multiple takes:

1. Unmute all of the takes. Since only one portion of a take will likely be playing at any one time, all tracks can be played back.

2. Click the first take, press the Shift key, and then click the last take to select all of the takes. This is important since only selected takes will be split, and you would like to split all of them at the same location.

3. Press the number of the marker along the top of your keyboard (not the number pad) to move the timeline cursor to that marker.

4. Press S to split all of the takes.

5. Delete the split portions of the takes that you don't want—typically, all but one event at any one time.

Figure 5.6

Tracks 3, 4, and 5 are three takes of the same section of music. The best parts of each take have been isolated into individual events, creating a seamless composite take. This is the same set of takes shown in Figure 5.5.

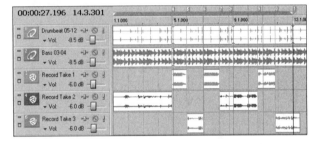

Once you have split and selected all of the events you want to keep, you will likely need to adjust the individual events by dragging their edges and using fade envelopes to get everything just right.

NOTE

Remember that just because you have deleted portions of the event, that doesn't mean you have deleted anything in the original recorded media file. You can always change your mind about which take to use where by dragging the edges of a split-up event to recover the portions that have been deleted from the project.

Mixing Down the Takes to a Single Track

Once you have selected the composite performance that is made up of the best events from the various takes, you can simplify the project by mixing the multiple-take tracks down to a single track (see Figure 5.7). While this will greatly simplify the project, it also more or less locks you into your specific choices and limits your creativity in the final mix. This means that deleted portions cannot be recovered without re-inserting the old takes again, splitting them up, and adding them back in.

To mix down the takes:

1. Mute all of the tracks in the project except the take tracks.
2. From the Tools menu, select Render to New Track or press Ctrl+M on your keyboard.
3. In the Render to New Track dialog box, browse for a location and enter a name for the file to be created from the mixed-down tracks. Click the Save button.
4. After the render process, a new track is inserted into the project. Draw an event in that track that corresponds to the takes.
5. Delete the tracks that were mixed down by selecting them and pressing the Delete key on your keyboard.

Figure 5.7
Track 3 is the mixed-down, composite version of the three take tracks shown in Figure 5.6.

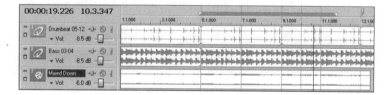

Automatic Looping Takes

Every time you click the Start and Stop button in the Record dialog box, a new track and a new file are created. Takes can also automatically be recorded to a single track as you use looping playback to continuously record takes without interruption.

To automatically create looping takes:

1. Create a loop region above the timeline on the Marker bar. The loop region should probably start a few measures before the actual position where you want to begin recording to give the performers time to get ready for their cue.
2. Click the Loop button on the transport controls.
3. Position the timeline cursor at the beginning of the Loop region.
4. Click the Record button. Make sure the position in the Record from section is correct (at the beginning of the Loop region).
5. Click the Start button to begin recording.
6. Playback will loop, and you can continue to record takes until you are satisfied. Click the Stop button to stop.

When the recording is stopped, the new media file is saved to your hard disk, a new track is created, and an event is inserted into the timeline. This event will extend well beyond the loop region and is as long as the source media file. If you have recorded five takes, the total length will be five times as long as the loop region (see Figure 5.8). Click the track header for the new track to select it and open the Track Properties window (View > Track Properties or Alt+6) to view the media file. In the Track Properties window, the media file is divided up into a number of regions, each representing a single take and named as such (see Figure 5.8).

Figure 5.8
Multiple takes recorded into a single track, a single event, and a single media file. The media file displayed in the Track Properties window is divided into regions.

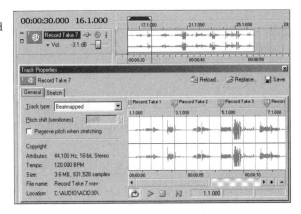

As the timeline stands at the end of recording, the event and its takes are not particularly useful, since additional takes continue after the loop region and into the next part of the song. When you click the Stop button, you are left with a single long event on the timeline that can be two, three, or more times as long as what you need, depending on how many takes you recorded. The media file is broken up into individual regions, however, and these can be accessed from the Chopper window.

The various regions can thus be inserted into the loop region using the Chopper window:

1. Delete the event that was initially placed on the timeline after recording. Remember, this deletes the event and not the media file.

2. Click the timeline in the recorded track at the point where recording began (that is, where you want to insert the take).

3. Open the Chopper window (View > Chopper or Alt+2).

4. Press the number on the top of the keyboard corresponding to the region (take) that you want to use in the project. The region is immediately selected, and the cursor on the timeline cursor changes to indicate the area where the region will be inserted (see Figure 5.9).

5. Click the Insert button to insert the region (take) into the timeline at the loop region.

To use other takes, repeat the above procedure and insert new events directly over the previous takes. There is no reason to delete the existing events, because they will be covered by the newly inserted take. This is a very fast way of trying out the various takes in the recorded media file to find the one that works.

Figure 5.9
The Chopper window can be used to insert regions (takes) into the timeline.

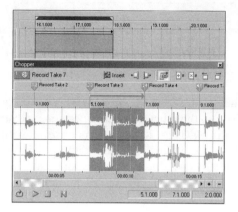

This method does not allow you to audition the takes against the project quite as easily as creating takes one at a time in individual tracks. Another minor disadvantage is that the source media file for the event on the timeline is many times larger than it needs to be, since only a small part is used in the project. This can be solved by mixing the track down to a new file, as previously discussed. The overwhelming advantage to using this method is in the actual recording of the performances. Performers can quickly record a number of takes without the interruption of starting and stopping all of the time.

Recording MIDI

While recording an audio source is a fundamentally different operation from recording MIDI data, the procedure for doing so is very similar. Audio is recorded as sounds, and MIDI is recorded as data that can be used to recreate the performance (for example, what note was played, how hard the key was pressed, and how long the note lasted). MIDI can be recorded into individual tracks or multiple takes can be recorded into a single file by looping the playback. MIDI setup and configuration are dealt with in much more detail in Chapter 10.

MIDI instruments come in many varieties, the most common being a keyboard or synthesizer. Many MIDI instruments have internal circuitry to produce sounds, which are sometimes of a very high quality. If you want to record the actual sound that comes out of a MIDI device instead of recording the MIDI data, use the procedures described above that are used to record any audio signal. The following deals exclusively with recording MIDI data:

1. Move the timeline cursor to the position where you want to start recording.
2. On the Transport bar, click the Record button or press Ctrl+R on your keyboard.

3. In the Record dialog box, select the MIDI option Record type.

4. Click the Start button. The project begins playback and the recording starts.

5. Click the Stop button to end the recording.

Figure 5.10

Track 2 is a MIDI track that was recorded into ACID.

As shown in Figure 5.10, a MIDI track is inserted into the project containing the MIDI data you just played. While you can also use the other procedure previously discussed and record multiple takes as the project loops the playback, MIDI data is not saved with the additional region information that ACID adds to audio files. This makes it impossible to instantly isolate takes by selecting a region and limits the usefulness of this technique. Adding regions in the Track Properties window and clicking the Save button on MIDI tracks does not appear to do anything.

As mentioned previously, the basic process of recording MIDI is similar to recording audio, but the type of data recording and how it is configured is completely different. See Chapter 10 on MIDI for a full explanation.

6

Mastering the Mix

One of the last things that you will do before committing a song to posterity is adjust the final mix. Mixing, a basic and critical part of any song, was introduced in Chapter 2. On the most fundamental level, mixing is used to prevent clipping, which is a common mistake that happens when the volume of a project exceeds the maximum. This section is going to discuss the more subtle and subjective aspects of mixing, which should not be ignored. As a subjective art, however, what constitutes a good mix can be a difficult thing to judge and is always up for debate. It is not an easy art and requires patience and practice—perfectly good songs can be ruined by bad mixing techniques.

Mixing a Master

Mixing and mastering are related but separate concepts. Both involve adjusting the relative volumes of various tracks and so on to produce a song that sounds good. A rough mix may be performed in the studio, but, typically, mixing takes longer than the recording process. Mastering, on the other hand, is done to make sure all songs on an album sound like they belong together spatially and are the same volume, among other things. In ACID, mixing can be thought of as what happens on the timeline and with tracks, while mastering is what occurs in the Mixer window, which is the part of ACID used to modify the output before it goes to your speakers. This is a useful, but informal, definition.

Home computer-based music and Internet distribution bring new elements to the mastering game. In summary, ACID projects should follow a flow from Creation to Mixing > Mastering > Rendering:

▶ Creation is where you create structure, locate media, and draw your song. This will probably consume 90 percent of your time in ACID.

▶ Mixing is done concurrently with creation or shortly after a song has matured. This is where you get a song to sound good, emphasizing sounds and ideas, increasing the spatial environment, and so on. This is mostly done at the track level, and you want to maintain maximum quality (cleanest, widest dynamic range, and so on) and flexibility (in other words, leave room for further mixing).

CHAPTER 6

> Mastering is the last thing done before the final song is rendered. Modern distribution via 24-bit 48 kHz DAT or 8-bit 11 kHz streaming media has complicated this process, so you need to consider the final destination at this stage. Songs destined for the Internet may benefit from dithering and compression, while songs intended for a CD-ROM may suffer from these effects. Using higher-quality settings for mixing (for example, 24-bit 48 kHz) is not a bad idea, but it's not necessary either. You will need to change these in the mastering phase to match the destination requirements.

> Rendering can affect the quality of your song more than any other aspect of mixing. In this chapter, the discussion will focus on 100 percent best quality. Some aspects of mixing can affect how a song sounds when a file is compressed and streamed over the Internet. These aspects and rendering in general are dealt with in Chapter 9 on "Publishing."

The Studio Environment

One extremely important variable in creating a final mix is the studio environment. Equipment, speakers, speaker placement, and the room acoustics all heavily influence the sound of a song. While this book is not going to go into how to build a proper studio, it is important to realize that your song is going to sound different when it is played on different systems. This can be frustrating, on the one hand, but liberating, on the other. Even if you build the Perfect Studio, your song is still going to be played back on both the latest 5.1 surround systems and also out of tiny laptop speakers, so it is impossible to control how the song is going to sound in the end.

NOTE

Lucas THX theater sound is an interesting example of controlling the environment. The exact placement of speakers, volume levels, and so on is precisely dictated in the THX standards. Theaters must meet these requirements in order to receive THX certification. THX mixing studios are likewise standardized. By specifying the mixing and playback environments, mixing engineers can be confident that the mix they are creating will sound pretty much as they intend it to in any THX-certified theater.

Headphones vs. Speakers

Given the above difficulties, creating a final mix can be a very challenging task. For many of us, headphones may be a good choice for monitoring the mix. This is especially true if you would otherwise be using normal computer speakers to monitor ACID. Even some of the higher-end four- and five-speaker systems for computers are not particularly good for music and are really designed for gamers. This often means that the rear speakers are too loud and the bass through the subwoofer is too heavy. Headphones present their own problems, however (see following note).

A good pair of monitors is essential. Many mix masters studiously avoid the use of subwoofers and surround sound. In any case, you don't need giant, expensive speakers, just good ones.

NOTE

One of the technical editors on this book (and one who has a lot of studio experience) writes: "I NEVER mix with headphones because of the Fletcher-Munson curves and the effect of cupping the ears. It is more important to mix at very low volume levels (F-M curves again), but without headphones. Average PC speakers will yield a better mix, if done right, than phones 99 out of 100 times." —A.W.

The Fletcher-Munson curves show the human ear's sensitivity to loudness vs. frequency. What they indicate is that humans hear low and high frequencies better at high volume than at low volume.

Digital Out

A good solution is to get a sound card with digital output and send a pure digital signal to your stereo equipment. While this can also be the perfect professional setup when the digital signal is sent to a studio board and speakers, in a home studio this can add another level of complexity to the mix. The sound coming from ACID is mixed, then sent through the sound card (which often has its own mixing and balancing properties), and finally out to your stereo, which also adjusts the signal. One way to standardize the audio is to play a CD on your stereo's CD player, balance everything properly, then play the same CD on your computer, and try to duplicate the sound. This is not easy, but it is an extremely important and valuable skill. Most engineers still carry five or so reference CDs around for just this purpose. It doesn't really matter which CDs you use, but they should probably be of the same genre as your music. If you have a difficult time determining whether a CD has a good mix (as opposed to just good music), try asking around on the Internet to find out what some real pros use. If you aren't already a recording engineer, I think you will be very surprised at the depth of the discussions that go on. You are sure to learn some amazing things.

There are also some software applications that can help you mix a finished audio file to match the characteristics (for example, equalization) of a given song or audio sample. Keep in mind that this is an after-ACID procedure that does not give you as much control over your mix as ACID does, but it can be an excellent way to polish a finished project.

TIP

Unless you are a professional engineer in a well-designed studio, you are just going to have to wing it. The only real test is to burn a final mix to a CD and listen to it on a couple of different systems to see how it sounds in the real world.

CHAPTER 6

Subwoofers

With more and more home systems coming standard with subwoofers, the controversy over whether you should mix using a subwoofer is only going to heat up more. Many conventional studios do not use subwoofers during mixing, and many engineers are used to mixing without them. The only advice offered here is the same general advice for any mixing environment: Don't count on your listening audience to have the same equipment you do. Subwoofers can distort the bass line, making it seem stronger than it really is, resulting in a loss of your bass line on some systems.

If It Sounds Good…

In the end, the only way to tell if you are mixing properly, beyond going to a professional studio, is to burn a CD of your music and listen to it on your target system. Compare your mix with other CDs that you like. Is the bass all you can hear at reasonable volumes? Can people who don't know the words to your song understand the vocal parts? Pick CDs in the same genre as your music, listen to them, and set up the volume, equalization, and balance the way you like it. Position a chair in the sweet spot. Listen. Pop in your CD. Listen. Ask your friends. Listen.

One word of caution, however: Just as some music is good and some bad, so some mixing on commercial CDs is good and some is bad. Don't compare your mixes to just any CD—carefully pick a few standards that you really like. Finally, to trump everything that comes before or after this sentence in this book, remember what Duke Ellington said (and Peter Schickele oft quotes): "If it sounds good, it is good."

Mixing ACID

Mixing has been briefly discussed a number of times in this book already. It is definitely a basic part of any song and project. ACID allows a huge amount of flexibility in mixing, far beyond most conventional hardware studio environments. In addition to simple yet broadly effective volume and panning controls, the great variety of audio plug-ins and effects available in ACID really enhances your mixing ability.

As you already know, ACID is analogous to a multitrack mixing environment. The entire program can be thought of in terms of a real-world digital mixing console, something like the stylized representation of a mixer shown in Figure 6.1. You can see from the illustration the various parts that correspond to the ACID UI.

Figure 6.1
A stylized mixing
console.

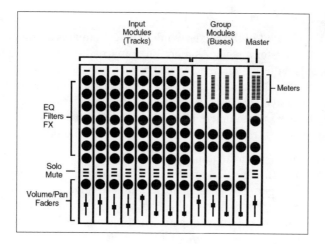

▶ The Input Modules on the mixer are where the various instruments and microphones are plugged in. They correspond to ACID tracks, each of which also has a part of the total mix in the form of a media file or loop. Along the top of each Input Module you may find a piece of masking tape with the name of the input. Of course, ACID tracks can easily be renamed without a magic marker.

▶ As with real-world mixers, each track in ACID has a fader that is used to control the volume and panning. ACID tracks also have an FX button for effects and EQ, Solo, and Mute buttons, just as boards in the real world often do.

▶ The Group Modules (also called *busses*) on the mixer are used to group specified Input Modules to modify and mix them as a unit. This may be done to create more manageable sub-groups in a large mix or, more typically, to apply the same effect or EQ to a group of inputs—for example, reverb (sometimes called the Echo Bus). In ACID, the Busses in the mixer are analogous to the Group Modules and serve the same purpose. You can add FX to a bus and then assign individual tracks to that bus.

▶ The Master output controls the final volume. Final equalization and FX can be added to the mix at this point. The fader on the busses in the Mixer window have two halves, one for each stereo channel, left and right.

▶ The meters in the Mixer window let you visually monitor the volume. Real-world mixers may also have meters on every Input Module.

NOTE
No auxiliary busses are visible in ACID's default configuration. To add a bus to the Mixer window, click the Insert Bus button.

Clipping Redux

In ACID, clipping is indicated in the Mixer window by red squares at the top of the various meters, particularly the Master meters. As mentioned in Chapter 2, clipping occurs when the volume or gain exceeds 0 dB, which in an analog or real-world stereo system means that the system is being overdriven. This can result in distortion or even damage to equipment. Clipping in ACID will not result in damage to your equipment, but it may result in distortion caused by lost signals above the peak (meaning it is clipped off). Unfortunately, the world is not so simple. The peak where clipping occurs is not necessarily 0 dB in the digital realm (but it should be).

Some engineers recommend recording up to 0 dB and not over, especially on systems where clipping does not occur until +1 dB. As previously mentioned, using lower values (perhaps from −13 dB to −9 dB) is perfectly acceptable and, indeed, gives you more room for future mixing. The only down side is a small possibility of a reduction in the total dynamic range of a song; you may want to turn the volume up a bit when playing back your songs when compared with other songs that have been more aggressively mixed.

It must be emphasized that in a digital mix in ACID, clipping occurs at 0 dB and must be avoided. Bringing the levels up to 0 dB should be done only at the very last step and only if you feel it is really necessary. There is no shame in allowing your listeners to adjust the volume of their stereo to the levels they prefer!

TIP

Engineers who create commercials for television and radio sometimes used to cheat when setting the peak volume. Of course, the object is to get your commercial noticed, so getting the maximum playback volume is critical (while still avoiding clipping). Commercial mixes are almost always right up to the top of the meter. The trick mixing engineers used to use was to create a reference signal before the commercial that was artificially low. Then, when the playback engineer at the studio sets up the volume for the commercial using the reference signal, the volume is set up higher than it should be. Modern equipment and automatic gain controls largely make this technique ineffective today.

Clipping means wave amplitudes above a certain point being cut off. Clipping results in distortion and can be seen in the waveform of media files, such as the event pictured in Figure 6.2. You can see that many of the wave peaks go all the way to the top and if you zoom in far enough you can see the actual squaring off of individual waves. Clipping in a media file and thus in an event on the timeline (as pictured) does not result in clipping in ACID. You can always play back a clipped and distorted media file in ACID at a lower volume. This will not fix the clipping problem, which is inherent in the media file and cannot be fixed. Ignoring the clipping warnings in an ACID project will result in rendered media files that are clipped like the file pictured.

Figure 6.2
Clipping can be
visually identified in
the waveform of events
on the timeline. In this
case, clipping is an
inherent part of the
media file.

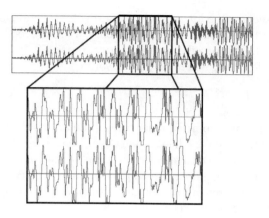

Loudness

Clipping can be monitored by watching the peaks in the mix on the Master meter in the mixer. While increasing the various track volumes and using other mixing techniques to make the peak volume equal to 0 dB is a rough way of maximizing the loudness without clipping, this is not the best way to make the entire mix louder. Peaks in the loudness can be caused by very short bursts of sound—for example, from musical hits or snare drum beats. You can therefore increase the overall loudness of a mix by decreasing the volume of a few of these short bursts and increasing the volume of the rest of the piece overall. One way to do this is to modify the overall dynamics using an effect such as Graphic Dynamics or Multi-Band Dynamics. Even easier, you can use the Track Compressor plug-in on a track that is causing the highest peak. This will decrease the overall dynamics of the track, but the effect will be minimal in the overall mix.

NOTE
The arms race in loudness has resulted in CDs getting louder and louder at the cost of dynamics. Resist the urge to engage in this one-upsmanship and mix wisely, my son. Dynamic range is exciting; loudness is not.

The real battle here is Loudness versus Dynamics. No one wants to sacrifice dynamics in a mix. Most popular music never dips below a certain threshold except at times where there is complete silence. This lowest volume may be −40dB or −50dB, but whatever its value, the total range between the softest and loudest part of a song is considered to be the total dynamic range. Pushing the loudness too high and using compression to do this lessens the total dynamic range. Leaving the peak volume at a lower level is always safe. Unfortunately, there is a very real competition to be heard in the real world, and engineers really try to push the edge to make sure their music is heard. This edge is different and more competitive in different genres of music, with rock-metal-dance music always catching the top of the meters and classical being much less competitive (in addition to having a much greater dynamic range). People may perceive your music as less intense than other music in the same genre simply because the volume is lower. Obviously, this is unfair. Turning up the volume a bit on the playback system solves this problem, but you don't have that luxury.

CHAPTER 6

As a general rule in ACID, keeping the loudness down during the creation and mixing process is a good idea (perhaps from −13 to −9dB) to give you plenty of mixing room. The only time you *may* want to kick it up to 0 dB is during the final mastering, immediately before your song is immortalized to a CD. Don't feel obligated to do this, however.

Volume Envelopes

Envelopes should be thought of as automated fader controls on any track and, therefore, automated mixing controls. Envelopes can be very effectively used to control brief spikes in an event that cause clipping or can be used to temporarily increase the volume of a track for emphasis. While more time consuming than allowing the volume to be controlled exclusively by the volume fader on a track and remain flat throughout a project, envelopes are extremely powerful and very worthwhile when used correctly.

Volume envelopes when used as mixing tools might be considered a manual form of compression in that you can reduce the gain of individual peaks in a track, thus preventing occasional clipping problems. Larger and more frequent clipping may be more easily fixed by using Track Compression, which automatically reduces peaks track wide (this is discussed later in this chapter). Volume envelopes are especially useful in reducing one-time peaks caused by pops or clicks in the audio track that may be the result of any number of things, including dropping the microphone during recording or even by vocal plosives (such as "p").

To use envelopes to eliminate clipping and allow you to turn up the volume of the track overall, you must first identify the places where the clipping occurs. To do this:

1. Solo the track that is the primary culprit.

2. Press the spacebar on your keyboard to play the track.

3. As it is playing back, press the M key on your keyboard when the red Clipping Indicator above the Master meter in the Mixer turns on.

4. You will need to stop playback and then continue playback after the clipped section to reset the Clipping Indicator (or quickly click the indicators to reset them). This process might need to be repeated several times.

Again, since this procedure is being used only to fix a small number of isolated problems, this shouldn't be too much work. If you are finding many places where clipping is occurring, it may indicate that the track is well suited to automatic adjustment with compression.

Once the problem sections have been identified, the clipping can be eliminated with a volume envelope (see Figure 6.3). This is a fairly easy procedure:

1. Press the number key along the top of your keyboard to jump to the first marker that corresponds with a problem section (as marked in the previous procedure). Unless you have psychic powers, the actual clipping will occur somewhere just before the marker.

2. Zoom in on the project and identify the section that is causing the clipping. You will certainly need to zoom in time, allowing you more precise control, but it may also be useful to zoom vertically or to change the track height so the waveform is more clearly seen.

3. Press the V key on your keyboard to insert a Volume envelope (or to make a pre-existing volume envelope visible).

4. Add four nodes (key points) to the envelope: two closely spaced before the clipping and two closely spaced after. The exact position is not critical and can be adjusted later. Three points should be used for peaks of a very short duration.

5. Drag the volume envelope line between the points downward to decrease the volume.

It is very useful at this point to create a loop region above the section you are working on (drag the mouse in the marker bar above any loop regions that already exist), press L to turn looping playback on (and change the loop region color to dark blue), and play back the section while you are making adjustments.

Figure 6.3
A volume envelope can be used to fix momentary clipping problems in isolated sections.

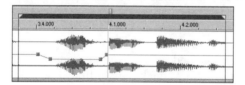

Remember to periodically reset the Clipping Indicators in the Mixer window either by stopping and restarting playback (spacebar) or by clicking the indicators. After you have eliminated the clipping, delete the marker (right-click it and select Delete) and move on to the next section. It is best to leave the envelope between the two outside points at some angle so that the volume decrease and the return to the main volume level is not too abrupt. You can reverse this technique to briefly increase the volume for emphasis or for sections that are too soft.

Grouping and Busses

Tracks can be grouped together and modified as a unit using Busses (see Figure 6.4). One reason for doing this is to more easily control the volume of a group of tracks with a single fader. Applying identical effects to groups of instruments that are supposed to sound like they originated from the same space is another excellent reason to group. To group tracks on a bus, click the Insert Bus button in the Mixer window to create a new bus (for example, Bus A). Then, in the Track Header of the tracks you want to group (one at a time), click the Bus Assignment button and, from the menu, select the new bus .

Figure 6.4
Tracks 1 and 3 are grouped to Bus A, while tracks 2 and 5 are grouped to Bus B. Track 4 is not routed through any bus and, along with Bus A and B, goes through the Master bus.

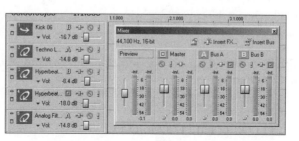

Space and Panning

Space, or the spatial sense of a song, describes the perceived environment the song is being performed in. From a small coffee shop with a folk musician to mystical flute music played in the Taj Mahal, space is a very important part of the mix. How space is perceived in a mix is another topic that could fill a book. In the context of mixing, space is most easily created by panning tracks (meaning instruments and parts) left or right to create the illusion that, for example, the drummer is in the back and center with a trumpet solo up front, while the bass player is hanging off to the right and the piano player is back and to the left. It is easy to overdo panning, so this is something to be careful with. Panning can also solve some volume and clipping problems in ACID: The volume might not be too high, but all of the tracks are bunched up in the center. Panning is not the only way to add perceived space to a mix, however. In particular, see Chapter 8 for more information on reverb and space, where additional ideas are discussed.

Panning to Create Space

Panning individual parts of a song contained in a track is a primary method of creating a feeling of space and realism in a mix. To pan a track, click the Multipurpose fader mode button and select Pan. The fader now controls panning. Listen to music of the genre you are mixing and note which instruments and parts are where. Also listen to different genres and see how these vary as well. Very broadly speaking, pop and rock tend to bunch up in the center, since most parts in these songs are coming out of amplifiers and are not localized with the performers. Jazz, on the other hand, has instruments that are very easy to localize in space on a recording. Drums tend to be in the center. Pianos tend to be off to one side or another. Vocals tend to be in the center. The bass part is a special case—the bass itself is usually off to one side, but because of the way we perceive low-frequency sounds, the bass usually is pretty balanced in the center. In classical music, instrument position is more or less strictly determined, while electronic music is completely unshackled. Panning beyond 30 percent left or right needs to be done with caution, since this can result in an artificial feel to the mix.

Unlike Volume envelopes, Panning envelopes are not particularly useful in natural-sounding mixes. It is a rare recording indeed in which the piano is wheeled about the stage. Instead, panning envelopes are most useful in electronic and dance music. They should be considered an effect tool, not a mixing tool.

Panning to Solve Volume Problems

Sometimes volume problems may be caused by having the entire mix bunched up in the center. By moving instruments and parts to the left or right, you can not only solve loudness and clipping problems but also increase the special characteristics of a mix. Panning can be controlled using the Fader on the various tracks; click the Multipurpose fade mode button to switch the function to a Pan Fader.

FX and Space

There are many other sometimes-surprising ways to create space in a song. Many of these are plug-ins and effects (FX) that you can add to a track or to a final mix. The following list contains a few ideas, with more information on each contained in the relevant section in Chapter 8.

▶ **Reverb**—Reverb is an all-purpose space-generating machine widely used in many mixes. Reverb simulates the bouncing of sound off the walls of a room. Indeed, the presets available in the Reverb FX plug-ins in ACID allow you to select the particular room size and brightness from a list. Reverb can be carefully used at the track level, but it might result in a rather strange mix if the singer is in a small room and the piano player is in cavern. More typically, reverb would be added to the Master bus in the Mixer window as one of the final modifiers in a song.

▶ **Amplitude Modulation**—This varies the volume of a sound or track rapidly and periodically over time and can make a track sound bigger.

▶ **Chorus**—Chorus is used to make a track or instrument sound more full by adding additional voices to it. Each of these additional voices is delayed a bit, which has the side effect of creating an illusion of space.

▶ **Delay**—The delay plug-ins are the most straightforward and easy to understand FX when creating space. Delay can be thought of as a simple, controlled echo effect.

▶ **Equalization**—Increasing the prominence of the higher frequency ranges in a mix can simulate perceived depth or make a song sound as if it were recorded in a larger room.

There are additional creative ways to create space in a song, including the very cool Acoustic Mirror plug-in, which can be purchased from Sonic Foundry.

Track FX

The use of FX has an entire chapter (see Chapter 8) devoted to it, but there are three effects that are particularly important to mixing: Compression, Noise Gate, and Equalization. The discussion of these effects is limited to description in this chapter; actual use is detailed in the following chapter. Track Compression is a very powerful effect that can really bring out a track in a mix, especially in recordings that have sections that are too quiet. Track Noise Gate is a general-purpose tool for eliminating low-level background hums and static, and it can fix problems introduced by the Compression effect. Sonic Foundry Track EQ is automatically inserted into every track by default, although the levels are flat, so no changes are made to a track. Together, these effects move beyond the simple volume faders on the tracks to more advanced mixing.

Track FX are generally simpler versions of some of the other effects available from Sonic Foundry, such as the XFX series of plug-ins. Some types of effects work better on a project level, such as using Reverb to create a room atmosphere for an entire song. Some effects are best used at the track level, such as using a Noise Gate to remove the hum of a camera motor in the soundtrack of a video clip. Track FX are optimized for ease of use on tracks but can be used at the bus and project level as well. Likewise, there is no reason not to use ExpressFX or XFX on the track level either.

Compression

Track compression is another excellent way to emphasize a track in a song, but it differs significantly from equalization. Equalization and Compression can be used in concert to improve the sound of a track. Compression is extremely widely used and is a primary tool in any engineer's toolbox, especially in popular music. Almost all popular music you hear has had some compression applied to it, most commonly at the track level. Many people now feel that compression is overused nowadays. In reality, it is bad compression that is overused. Compression is a powerful and useful tool that should be intelligently used where needed (for example, to cover for musicians who cannot control their own dynamics). Compression is an excellent effect to use early in a chain of plug-ins (see Chapter 8).

NOTE

Be cautious about using compression since it takes away some of the dynamic range. By making the loud parts softer, the total expressive range of the track is more limited. While this can be (and is) used to bring a part out, it can also harm the overall quality of the track. Compression may not be useful on most commercial loops, which are usually high-quality, professionally recorded and mixed files.

Compression is an automated way to variably adjust the volume or consistency of level of a track, raising all valleys or diminishing all peaks. Either way results in a smaller dynamic range for the track overall. Figure 6.5 shows a voiceover narration that was not recorded particularly well, with the narrator perhaps turning away or moving away from the microphone at a number of points. This has resulted in sections of the file being too quiet (notice especially the middle part of the top event). Simply increasing the volume of the track would not work, since this would also raise the volume of the parts that are loud enough, making them too loud and possibly causing clipping. By applying compression to the track, the peaks can be reduced and then the overall volume can be raised without problems.

Figure 6.5

An uneven narration before and after applying compression. By reducing the peaks (and thus reducing the overall dynamic range), the gain can be increased on the track (to bring out softer parts) without causing clipping.

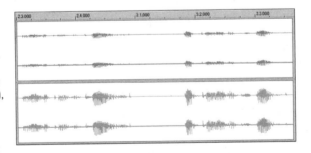

The best place to use compression in ACID is at the track level. The danger of squashing a song into dynamic oblivion increases greatly when compression is used at the bus or project level. Sonic Foundry Track Compression is the simplest of the compression plug-ins. Using it usually results in an increase in the loudness of a track, although this isn't necessarily the case. To apply Track Compression:

1. Click the Solo button on the track to isolate it.

2. Click the Track FX button. This opens the Audio Plug-In dialog.

3. In the Audio Plug-In dialog, click the Edit Chain button. This opens the Plug-In Chooser dialog.

4. In the Audio > FX folder, double-click the Sonic Foundry Track Compressor item (or select it and click the Add button).

5. Click the OK button. This closes the Plug-in Chooser dialog box and puts you back in the Audio Plug-In dialog with the Track Compressor selected (see Figure 6.6).

6. In the Track Compression dialog, adjust the effect (see the following section).

Figure 6.6
The Sonic Foundry
Track Compression
dialog box.

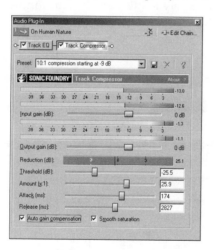

To fix a voiceover narration that is too quiet in some places, you'd want to first reduce (compress) the peaks and then raise the Output gain or the volume of the track as a whole. Solo the track and play it back while adjusting the compression, all the while monitoring the Master meter in the Mixer window.

▶ The Input/Output gain faders and meters control the signal into the effect and out. Usually, you'll want to increase the Output gain to increase the loudness of the track.

▶ The Reduction meter measures how much the peaks are reduced (if they are reduced at all). Right-click the Peak decibel indicator on the right side of the meter to set the range to a more sensitive range: −12 dB to 0 dB.

▶ The Threshold sets the level where the compression begins to take effect (see Figure 6.7). When trying to bring a track out and increase the loudness overall (a

CHAPTER 6

typical use for compression), set the threshold to a lower value but keep it above the level of the parts of the track that are too quiet. You don't want to reduce those sections.

▶ The Amount of compression can be set higher in the voiceover narration example. Too much will result in a very dynamically flat sound, but you don't usually want a large dynamic range in a voiceover narration. Compression is expressed in a ratio—for example, 10:1. This means that for peaks that rise above the Threshold, what was originally (Input) a 10 dB jump in the meter would only result in a 1 dB increase (Output). Because it is a ratio, the louder the peak (the higher above the threshold), the more it is compressed. Setting the Amount to Inf. completely flattens all peaks above the threshold, which can be surprisingly useful at times and is certainly better than clipping, which would simply cut all of this information out.

▶ The Attack and Release parameters set how quickly the plug-in responds to peaks. A quick attack (so the plug-in starts immediately) and a slow release are typical. Too fast of a release can result in very quiet sections (even silence) from having the gain turned up very loud suddenly. This results in background noise becoming audible (referred to a breathing or pumping effect). The Smooth Saturation item can also help with making the compression seem more natural.

▶ The Auto gain compensation is a very important part of this plug-in and is very useful in normalizing a voiceover narration.

Figure 6.7
The Threshold slider sets the level above which compression occurs. Waves that peak below the threshold remain unaffected. The lower waveform shows the results of applying compression.

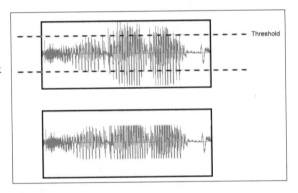

Sonic Foundry also has two more capable and flexible FX that can be used for compression—the Graphics Dynamics and Multi-Band Dynamics plug-ins. See Chapter 8 on FX for more information on these.

Consider taking the time to go through a track and use volume envelopes to adjust individual peaks and valleys to solve small problems. While this may be a lot of work, the results can be worth it. This can be especially worthwhile in improving voiceovers in video narration or the lead vocals in a song, which are always critical aspects of a project.

Compression tends to increase background noise, especially during periods of silence. The Attack and Release controls can help eliminate this, but many times the only solution is to use a Noise Gate plug-in just after the Compression plug-in in the FX chain.

Noise Gate

Noise Gate is a simple method of eliminating background noise from a track by setting the threshold for the minimum level of sound that is audible. The Track Noise Gate and XFX 2 Noise Gate plug-ins are especially useful in reducing the intensity of background hums caused by computer equipment or camera motors in the recording environment, as well as hisses or static. The Noise Gate plug-in is added to a track in the same way a Compression plug-in is added (previously described) and is usually used after Compression in a chain. The basic procedure is to first solo the track so you can concentrate on it, play back the project to listen to the track (looping playback of a short section usually helps), and gradually increase the Threshold (see Figure 6.8) until the background noise is eliminated. It may not be possible to completely eliminate the noise without creating problems in the audio that you want to keep. A short Attack and a longer Release will improve the smoothness of the effect and prevent sharp jumps and drops in gain. See the next chapter for more information about Noise Gating.

Figure 6.8
The Threshold slider sets the level below which the audio is silenced and would be applied to both stereo channels in the above waveform.

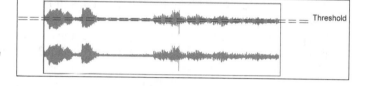

Equalization

Equalization is the next level in mixing after you have eliminated clipping from a song. Remember that clipping is the result of the volume peaking out too high in a song, thus cutting off some parts of the song (see the earlier part of this chapter for more detailed info). Roughly speaking, this means that the volume is too high overall, but clipping can occur at what seems to be lower volumes. Trust the clipping meters in ACID and not your ears. Sometimes a mix can be very bass heavy, causing clipping at lower frequencies. Lowering the volume of higher frequency tracks will not solve these problems. Clipping is, therefore, only an indication of problems and you will need to use equalization to analyze more subtle mixing problems.

Equalization should be used to balance the song overall or on the track level to color/distinguish instruments. Equalization can be done at the track level with individual loops, to groups of tracks assigned to a bus, and as a final step to the project as a whole. There are a number of different equalization plug-ins available from Sonic Foundry. These include:

- ▶ Track EQ
- ▶ ExpressFX Equalization
- ▶ Graphic EQ
- ▶ Paragraphic EQ
- ▶ Parametric EQ

All do basically the same thing, with the difference being in the level of control and how that control is achieved through the effect dialog box. Each of the effects can be applied to any of the levels (track, grouped tracks, project) as discussed below.

CHAPTER 6

Track EQ

Every track has its own default equalization plug-in that can be used to balance the sound of an individual loop. To equalize a track:

1.   Click the Solo button on the track to isolate it.

2.   Click the Track FX button.

3.   In the Audio Plug-In dialog box, click the Track EQ button.

4.   Without closing the Track EQ dialog box, click the timeline to shift the application's focus to the timeline.

5.   Press the spacebar to begin playback (or click the Play button on the Transport bar).

6.   Go back to the Track EQ dialog and adjust the equalization (see following section).

The default Track EQ plug-in is more than adequate for most purposes (see Figure 6.9). It is divided into four frequency bands: Low Shelf, Band 2, Band 3, and High Shelf. The easiest way to adjust the equalization is to drag the various band indicators on the graphic display (see Figure 6.8). Dragging a number up increases the gain, and dragging down decreases the gain. Dragging the number left and right changes the central frequency for Bands 2 and 3, and the width of the band is controlled by adjusting the Bandwidth slider on bands 2 and 3. The Rolloff in bands 1 and 4 sets the steepness for the rolloff curve. The number on the graphic display for these bands marks the beginning of the rolloff. While the Track EQ plug-in is the default, any of Sonic Foundry's EQ FX can be used at the track level. It would be redundant, and of questionable value, to use two or more EQ FX in the same FX chain.

Figure 6.9
Basic Track EQ plug-in.

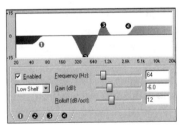

Track EQ might be best implemented across a number of different tracks individually. In other words, instead of only boosting the frequencies between 1,000 Hz and 4,000 Hz on a vocal line to bring it out more, you might also want to decrease that same range in a few other tracks that might interfere. This is more subtle and effective than simply adjusting the volume of the two competing tracks, although it is more difficult to perform.

Group Track EQ (Bus EQ)

Tracks can be grouped to apply equalization to them together as a unit. This is done by assigning individual tracks to a bus and then applying an Assignable FX to the bus. Assignable FX can be any audio plug-in, including the Track EQ plug-in.

To equalize a group of tracks:

1. Click the Insert Bus button in the Mixer window.

2. In the new Bus "X" monitor (where "X" is the letter of the Bus), click the Assignable FX button.

3. In the Plug-In Chooser dialog, locate and double-click the Track EQ plug-in. If an FX has already been added, click the Edit Chain button to open the Plug-In Chooser dialog.

4. Click the OK button. The Audio Plug-In dialog opens with the Track EQ controls (and the Plug-In Chooser dialog closes).

5. In the Track Header, click the Bus Assignment button on the tracks you want to equalize as a group (one at a time) and, from the menu, select the Bus that has the equalization assigned to it.

6. Click the Solo button on the bus to isolate it.

7. Without closing the Track EQ dialog, click the timeline to shift the application's focus to the timeline. Press the spacebar to begin playback (or click the Play button on the Transport bar).

8. Go back to the Track EQ dialog and adjust the equalization (as previously detailed).

Applying FX to a bus is a very effective way to quickly apply unified effects and is dealt with in more detail in Chapter 8.

Project EQ

Project-level equalization as a last step is a very useful and highly recommended procedure. To some extent, the equalization has been controlled all along by adjusting the volumes of the various tracks to get a proper balance, but the ease with which you can modify the whole sound of a song with one effect is powerfully simple.

Once again, there are a number of different equalization plug-ins that can be used. In this example, the Track EQ is used again because of its simplicity. To equalize a project:

1. Click the Master FX button on the Master bus in the Mixer window.

2. In the Plug-In Chooser dialog, locate and double-click the Track EQ plug-in. If an FX has already been added, click the Edit Chain button to open the Plug-In Chooser dialog.

3. Click the OK button. The Audio Plug-In dialog opens with the Track EQ controls (and the Plug-In Chooser dialog closes).

CHAPTER 6

4. Without closing the Track EQ dialog, click the timeline to shift the application's focus to the timeline. Press the Spacebar to begin playback (or click the Play button on the Transport bar).

5. Go back to the Track EQ dialog and adjust the equalization (as previously detailed).

NOTE

The effect of the equalization plug-in (or any plug-in) can be toggled on and off by clearing and checking the small box on the plug-in's button in the Audio Plug-In dialog. After tweaking for a while, you can easily forget what the original track sounded like and may find that you were better off before you started messing around with all the toys. Toggle, listen, toggle.

Equalization can also be used to influence many other subtle aspects of a song. For example, the higher frequency ranges can be altered to simulate perceived depth or make a song sound as if it were recorded in a larger room. While adding reverb would be a more direct way to do this, you shouldn't underestimate the power of using an EQ plug-in at the project level at the end of a project.

FX Chains

More than one effect can be used at a time on a single track, bus, or project. FX are applied in a particular order in an FX Chain. The order of plug-ins can be important in the final sound. Some FX belong very late in the chain (such as EQ and Reverb) and some earlier (Compression). Others should be used in a particular order. Track FX plug-ins are usually applied in this order: Compression, Noise Gate, and, finally, EQ. This is not a hard and fast rule, and there may be creative reasons why you'd want to alter this sequence. FX chains and ordering are discussed in more detail in the next chapter.

Figure 6.10
Three effects applied in a chain to a track in the Audio Plug-In dialog.

7

FX

As we saw in Chapter 6, FX are special audio processes that change and modify a basic sound. FX can be used to clean up an audio file that has problems or liven up a flawless but flat sound. They can be completely unnoticed by the listener or can warp a song in unmistakably unnatural ways. FX are ubiquitous in music: Every CD you listen to has been modified with some kind of FX. Even the equalization on your home stereo can be considered an effect, since it modifies the original sound. In ACID, FX are powerful and often fun tools for turning a good basic mix into a truly professional auditory treat for the ears. One word of caution, however: Though effects are readily available, they are typically most effective when used sparingly or with a specific purpose in mind. Nothing ruins a project or muddies a mix quicker than a wash of effects.

NOTE

Audio effects are called FX throughout the ACID UI. The actual FX, however, may also be referred to as plug-ins. Plug-ins are small but sophisticated computer programs that are designed to work within another larger program. FX become available in ACID when audio effects plug-ins are installed. Sonic Foundry and a few other companies sell DirectX audio plug-ins for use with any compatible program—ACID, for example.

Types of ACID FX

FX in ACID could be sorted a few different ways. In a very broad way, the FX can be divided into effects that repair or fix problems with audio files and FX that are used in more special and creative ways. There is quite a lot of overlap between these two categories, but it is still a useful distinction nonetheless. Table 7.1 gives you an idea of how FX can be categorized:

Table 7.1

A classification scheme to group FX plug-ins.

Repair	Creative
Compression	Amplitude Modulation
Dither	Chorus
Dynamics	Delay
Equalization	Distortion
Graphic Dynamics	XPressFX Stutter
Graphic EQ	Flange
Multi-Band Dynamics	Gapper/Snipper
Noise Gate	Multi-Tap Delay
Smooth/Enhance	Phaser (Flange/Wah-wah)
Paragraphic EQ	Reverb
Parametric EQ	Simple Delay
Pitch Shift	Vibrato
Time Stretch	Wah-wah

Again, just because an effect is in the Repair column doesn't mean it can't be used in interesting and creative ways. For example, the Time Stretch plug-in is usually used to change the duration of an audio file without noticeably distorting it otherwise. Beyond a certain point, however, stretching or compressing a file is going to do funky things to it, but that may be exactly what you're looking for. And just because I've chosen to put an effect in the Repair or Creative column (as in Table 7.1), that doesn't mean it can't be used in very subtle and natural sounding ways. The Reverb plug-in is a great example: It is widely used in music to improve the spatial aspects of a recording and doesn't usually sound like an artificial effect; instead, it imitates a natural environment or room. Table 7.2 shows some other ways ACID FX might be categorized. Notice that many plug-ins end up being included in more than one category.

Table 7.2

FX plug-ins grouped by effect type.

Category	Effect
Delay/Chorus	Chorus, Flange, Phaser, Wah-wah, Delay, Multi-Tap Delay, Simple Delay, Reverb
Modulated	Amplitude Modulation, Phaser, Wah-wah, Flange, Vibrato, Gapper/Snipper, XPressFX Stutter
Dynamic	Noise Gate, Compression, Distortion, Dynamics, Graphic Dynamics, Multi-Band Dynamics
Equalization	Smooth/Enhance, Equalization, Graphic EQ, Paragraphic EQ, Parametric EQ
Pitch	Vibrato, Pitch Shift, Chorus, Flange, Phaser, Wah-wah
Special	Dither, Time Stretch

NOTE

While ACID Pro comes with all of the plug-ins discussed in this chapter, not all versions of ACID do. See the Sonic Foundry Web site for more information about your version and the availability of upgrades and additional plug-in packages.

FX in Action

FX can be added to a project anywhere you see a green FX button, as indicated in Figure 7.1 (see the next section on "Where should FX Go?"). To view the FX installed on your computer, click the FX button. This opens the Plug-In Chooser dialog box (see Figure 7.2). At the top of the dialog box is a folder selector that allows you to move around the various plug-in folders if you happen to have a complex array of FX. By default, the FX subfolder in the Audio folder is opened. This is where ACID puts all of the DirectX compatible audio plug-ins it scanned for and detected when ACID was installed. Every time you run it, ACID detects newly installed plug-ins and makes them available in the Plug-In Chooser.

Figure 7.1
Various places you can add FX in ACID.

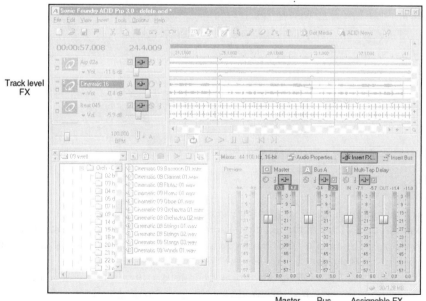

▶ To add an effect, click the FX button to open the Plug-In Chooser dialog box. Then select the plug-in you want to use from the list and click the Add button. This places a button with the effect's name on it at the top of the dialog box. Multiple plug-ins can be used at a time and they are lined up in a chain across this top area. When you are finished, click the OK button. The Plug-In Chooser dialog box closes and the Audio Plug-In dialog box opens with the last plug-in inserted active, meaning that the button in the chain at the top of the dialog box is depressed and the controls for the plug-in are visible.

▶ The check box on a plug-in button means that it is being used to modify the audio signal passing through the chain. De-selecting, or unchecking, the box prevents the effect from modifying the signal without removing it from the chain. This is commonly known as bypassing the effect.

▶ To remove a plug-in from the chain, right-click the effect's button at the top of the Audio Plug-In window and, from the context menu, choose Remove.

Click the X in the top-right corner of the dialog box to close the Audio Plug-In window. This window can also remain on the workspace or docked in the Windows Docking Area at the bottom of the program. Subsequent FX button presses anywhere in ACID will open the Audio Plug-In window or display an existing chain in the window if it is already open.

Figure 7.2
The Plug-in Chooser dialog box is accessed the first time you press an FX button or by pressing the Edit Chain button in the Audio Plug-in window.

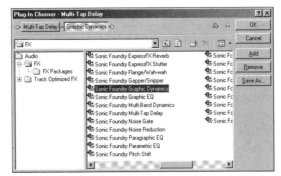

Experimenting

Every effect has its own array of controls that are used to modify the parameters of the plug-in. These are discussed in detail later in the chapter. There are some general procedures that will allow you to effectively audition and modify effects. Effects can be modified as the project is playing back, which means that you can change the effects variables in real-time while you listen to the results. With the Audio Plug-In window open to the plug-in that you want to work on, click on the timeline (or press Alt + 0 [zero]) to set the focus to the timeline and press Play. It is often useful to use a looped playback of a shorter section of a project to hear the results of an effect. While playback continues, go back to the Audio Plug-In window and modify the effect. Of course, in the end, the entire project will be mixed together—events, tracks, busses, and effects. At this stage, it would be very difficult to subtly tweak an effect within the complexity of an entire project, so it is necessary to isolate the output of the project so you can hear what you are doing.

▶ Isolate the target of the FX, either a track or a bus, by clicking the Solo button.

▶ Isolate the specific effect in a chain of effects by unchecking all of the other effects in the chain.

▶ Reduce the gain of the Dry out slider while working with an effect to hear the processed signal more clearly.

The ultimate goal is to get an effect to mesh perfectly with a project. As you experiment, gradually reverse each of the above and fine tune the effect. Start by increasing the gain on the Dry signal and mix the effect itself with the unprocessed signal. Then add the other effects in the chain back in. Finally, un-solo the track or bus and adjust the effect in relation to the final mix.

Saving your project is especially important when working with effects. It is extremely easy to get carried away and forget what the original sounded like or even the goal that you were working towards. And in the course of a few minutes, it is possible to make so many changes that it is difficult to get back to the original sound. One simple idea is to do a Save As and save the project to a new name. This guarantees you can always get back to the original.

Where should FX go?

There are two places that FX can be added in ACID: into a track or into the Mixer window. Within the Mixer window, there are three places where FX might go: into an Assignable FX, into a pre-existing bus, or into the Master bus (see Figure 7.1).

Track-Level FX

Track FX apply only to a single track and, thus, only to a single audio file or loop. Click the Track FX button to add an effect at this level. While all effects can be used at any location, some effects work better at some levels. FX that work well on the track level would be ones that are used to fix problems in a media file. For example, a Noise Gate would be perfect at the track level for a media file that has a background hum. Using it at the project level would be overkill and would harm a project. For example, you should use caution when using a Reverb effect at the track level. Since this is used to place the music in a spatial environment, it might seem strange to have your sax solo track in a cavernous hall and your piano track in a virtual bathroom.

Bus-Level FX (Multiple Tracks)

There are two distinct purposes for busses: to group tracks and to route tracks to hardware devices. Within the context of tracks, bus FX would most commonly be used to group tracks and apply the same effect to all of them with identical settings. Perhaps one example would be to apply equalization to a group of tracks to bring them out of the mix as a unit. This is also a more appropriate location for a Reverb effect, where the grouping of the tracks ensures the instruments sound like they are in the same virtual space.

To use effects at a bus level, you must first insert a bus into the project by clicking the Insert bus button in the Mixer window. Then assign specific tracks to the bus by clicking the Bus button (initially concentric squares and assigned to Microsoft Sound Mapper) in each track and assigning it to the bus (for example, Bus A). Finally, click the FX button on the bus in the Mixer window and select a plug-in.

One great advantage to using busses this way is that you can use envelopes on the track to animate the level of the effect over time in the project, much like you use Volume or Pan envelopes. Assignable FX also share this advantage as well.

Assignable FX

Assignable FX are added to the Mixer window and are the most powerful and effective way to add effects for many reasons. Individual tracks can be routed through an Assignable FX and into the final mix. Multiple tracks can be sent through an Assignable FX bus, making this a convenient way to efficiently reuse an effect and group tracks. One powerful advantage to using effects this way is that they can be modified by envelopes on the timeline, much like Volume or Pan envelopes. This lets you fade effects in and out and otherwise animate the level of the effect over time. Assignable FX busses in the Mixer have two sets of faders that control the input gain of the effect and the final output.

NOTE

You must right-click the Multipurpose Fader Mode button and select Pre Volume to use the Volume and FX fader to adjust the Dry/Wet mix.

To use Assignable FX, click the Insert Assignable FX button in the Mixer window. Then select an effect from the Plug-In window that automatically opens. Paradoxically, you do not need to assign tracks to the Assignable FX bus the way you would a hardware or group bus. Instead, the Assignable FX is available to all tracks and you only need to click the Multipurpose fader mode button and select the FX from the list to adjust the volume of the effect in a particular track.

The main track Volume fader and the FX fader can operate as another set of Dry/Wet faders to control the mix of the effect. By default, Assignable FX are applied after the track volume is set (Post Volume), which means that if the track volume is set to −Inf., nothing leaves the track to be processed by the Assignable FX. Right-click the Multipurpose Fader and change when the Assignable FX is processed by selecting Pre Volume.

NOTE

You must right-click the Multipurpose Fader Mode button and select Pre Volume to use the Volume and FX fader to adjust the Dry/Wet mix. Yes, this is the same as the previous Note, but it is easy to forget, and the FX fader and FX envelopes won't work if you don't do this.

To use envelopes to animate the mix of the effect over time, right-click the blank area of the timeline in the track you want to use envelopes in and select the Assignable FX from the list (for example, FX1). Double-click the envelope to add a node and then drag the node up or down to adjust the gain. The plug-in effect is mixed with whatever the Volume is set to, so use a Volume envelope to further adjust the total mix.

Project-Level FX (Master bus)

You can also add effects to the Master bus in the Mixer window. These effects will then modify the entire audio signal as it is passed out of ACID and to your sound card. Some plug-ins are better than others for use at this stage, and you should carefully consider which FX you use here since you can quickly degrade an entire project with one simple effect. A good example of this is compression, which reduces the dynamic range of an audio signal with the eventual goal of increasing the loudness. Applying compression at the project level risks squashing a song and reducing its liveliness. A much better idea is the more intelligent and selective use of compression on individual tracks that need to be brought out in a mix. On the other hand, the Master bus is the perfect place to apply ambience to a mix with the Reverb effect.

Some FX are better used at the track level and some are better used in the Mixer window, but all options are possible for maximum flexibility. Specific recommendations are given after a brief discussion of FX chains in the next section and in the descriptions of the actual plug-ins.

FX Chains

More than one effect can be added to a track or the Mixer window. The specific order is important to the final sound, and some arrangements are recommended over others (as will be discussed shortly). To create an FX chain, simply add multiple plug-ins in the Plug-In Chooser dialog box or click the Edit Chain button in the Audio Plug-In window. Once effects have been added, they appear as buttons in a row at the top of the Audio Plug-In window. To change the order of the effects, drag the buttons to a new location in the chain. To temporarily bypass or disable a plug-in in the chain, uncheck the box on that plug-in's button (see Figure 7.3).

Figure 7.3
A plug-in chain in the
Audio Plug-In window.

In addition to the order of FX being important to the final sound, the way tracks are mixed is important. For example, you could apply a Flange to Track 1 and the same Flange to Track 2. The Flange in each will be applied and then the two tracks will be mixed. Another way to do this is to use Flange as an Assignable FX and then assign the two tracks to the Assignable FX in the Mixer window. In this case, the two tracks will be mixed first and then the Flange will be applied. Sometimes this can make a difference in the final sound. One thing to consider is that if you use an Assignable FX, you only have one effect to modify. If you went with two Track FX, on the other hand, you'd have more control and could isolate the tracks individually as you adjust the effect. The Flange is a good example. Since this effect varies periodically over time, if you used it in two different tracks, they could easily get out of sync. This may be what you want to do, but it would be easier to work with only one effect.

Recommendations on FX Placement

The order of effects in a chain is important to the final sound. The following sections detail where in a chain you might typically find an effect. Keeping in mind that the total effects package in ACID runs through a chain on a track, and then through another chain on the bus and project level, you must also consider that the first effect on the Master bus will also be the first effect after the last track effect. In other words, an early Master bus effect might actually be late in the overall effects chain. The following recommendations are made assuming you are trying to achieve a more traditional or natural sound to your mix. Electronic genres (techno, dub, and so on) and many other types of music may benefit from radical effects ordering, but the explanations that follow will help you understand why the effects are placed in this order and why you might want to ignore that order anyhow.

Since effects can be used in three different places in ACID, deciding where to use an effect is not always a simple matter. You must also consider the order of the effects in the chain as well as the entire signal flow (see ACID's online Help for a great illustration of signal flow), since FX added at the Master bus level will be the final effects in a long overall chain. The following are some recommendations as to where FX are best used: early, middle, or late in a sequence. The total sequence of plug-ins must be added together. For example, a single chain on a track with FX A-B-C would be the same as having FX A on a track routed through an Assignable FX B which was then routed through a bus with FX C. Depending on the purpose, some plug-ins are useful in multiple places. For example, you might use a Noise Gate to eliminate background noise on a track and then use it again at the project level after applying compression to an entire project. These recommendations are not writ large and in stone, however, and should only serve as guidelines to understanding how FX work in ACID.

NOTE
It would be impossible to arrange all of the Sonic Foundry plug-ins in a strict hierarchical list from one to thirty, and this really wouldn't make much sense. Instead, the following is a just a rough guide, with similar plug-ins grouped into paragraphs.

Early

The first FX in a chain are typically the ones used to correct tracks with problems (such as background noise) or to clean up a sound to prepare it for later effects. The **Compression** plug-in is frequently the first effect in a chain and is then quickly followed by a **Noise Gate** to remove any artifacts caused by compression. These both modify the level and dynamics of a sound, so the other related FX would also be used at this stage, **Graphic Dynamics** and **Multi-Band Dynamics**.

The next class of FX that might follow the dynamics FX are the equalization (EQ) filters. These include the XPressFX **Equalization**, **Graphic EQ**, **Paragraphic EQ**, **Parametric EQ**, and **Track EQ**, as well as the **Smooth/Enhance** plug-in. Many mixes end up being too busy and sound muddy from having too many sounds and instruments. Cleaning up individual tracks with equalization early in the mix allows you to emphasize parts by removing unwanted frequencies and generally create a cleaner and brighter mix. Track EQ is a default plug-in on every track. Equalization may also be a nice thing to add at the project level, very late in the total chain, as a final touch up.

Pitch Shift and, especially, **Time Stretch** are special plug-ins that are not usually found in a traditional studio effects chain. These definitely should be the first effect in a chain.

Middle

After the signal is cleaned up with dynamics and equalization, many of the more special effects are added. **Distortion** on a guitar part would come immediately after these effects. This might be followed by the various pitch effects, such as **Vibrato**, the **Gapper/Snipper** effect, and the XPressFX **Stutter** plug-in.

Next in line would be the modulation-type effects, such as the **Amplitude Modulation** FX and the **Flanger/Wah-wah/Phaser** FX. This would also be the time to add delay effects like **Chorus**, **Delay**, **Multi-Tap Delay**, and **Simple Delay**.

Late

The last effects in a chain are best used at the project level as Master bus FX. A **Reverb** effect is often the last effect used in a chain. Reverb is also a delay-type effect and adds space to a mix, simulating various room types and environments. Use caution when applying reverb at the track level, so that various tracks don't sound like they were recorded in different rooms (although reverb is commonly used on drums and vocals to bring these parts out of a mix). EQ filters can also be used at the project level to polish a mix in the final stages, although it is better to take the time and use EQ more precisely at the track level to highlight individual parts and instruments.

The **Dither** effect is another special plug-in that is particular to computer music and digital processing. It is used to fix problems that are caused by rendering a project at a lower bit-depth from the source media. For example, when using media from a DAT at 24 bit and creating a final song for the Internet at 8 bit, Dithering as the last step can eliminate some problems that might be caused. Some projects contain a mix of different types of media, perhaps using commercial loops at a 16-bit depth with recorded tracks at 24 bit. In these cases, the Dither plug-in is most efficiently used as the last effect only in the tracks that have a higher bit depth than the project's bit depth. Avoid using Dithering twice, at both the track and the project level.

Summary of Sonic Foundry FX

Sonic Foundry has developed a wide range of effects for use with its flagship Sound Forge editing tool. These effects have been created to comply with DirectX standards and will work with any application that supports DirectX audio plug-ins, including ACID, of course. ACID Pro 3.0 ships with the full compliment of basic FX from Sonic Foundry for sale separately as XFX1, XFX2, and XFX3. Other versions of ACID 3.0 may come with other plug-in sets, such as XPressFX. There are a couple of other more advanced plug-ins made by Sonic Foundry that are not included (notably Noise Reduction and Acoustic Mirror), but the effects that are included are formidable, varied, and capable.

NOTE

There are a number of different versions of ACID available from Sonic
Foundry, from free promotional versions to inexpensive Style versions to the
Pro version (see the Introduction). Not all versions have all of the FX,
although the Pro version comes with the works.

Track FX

All Track FX are included in all but the XPress (promotional) version of ACID. These basic
effects are some of the most important and fundamental filters that you need when sweetening
and cleaning up a mix. Although they are optimized for the track level, there is no reason these
FX cannot be used at the bus or project level. All three Track FX plug-ins have XFX counterparts.
Track FX are specifically discussed at the end of the previous chapter.

Track FX are not the same as Track Optimized FX, which are a subset of plug-ins that are
recommended for use at the track level by Sonic Foundry and are contained in a separate folder
in the Plug-In Chooser dialog box. These are a subset of all of the FX available from Sonic
Foundry. You can use any FX at the track level, not just the Track Optimized FX.

XPressFX

XPressFX are all simplified versions of the professional XFX plug-ins from Sonic Foundry and
are not included with ACID Pro. These FX are certainly capable and more than adequate for
many operations. If you have purchased a version of ACID that does not include the full set of
XFX plug-ins, XPressFX are an economical alternative to purchasing more expensive plug-ins.
XPressFX are listed following the corresponding XFX in the pages that follow.

NOTE

It is important to note that while the control and flexibility of the XPressFX
plug-ins are more limited when compared to the XFX, the quality is not.

XFX

The Sonic Foundry XFX series of plug-ins is a professional series of DirectX effects available for
use in compatible programs, like ACID. ACID Pro comes with the full set of XFX plug-ins:
XFX1, XFX2, and XFX3. Other versions may not have all of these plug-ins, which are available
for purchase from Sonic Foundry.

DirectX Audio Plug-ins

The XFX and XPressFX audio plug-ins from Sonic Foundry are all DirectX compliant. Any
DirectX audio plug-ins from other companies will work in ACID. DirectX compatibility means
that the plug-ins follow a strict set of programming guidelines from Microsoft that result in a

standardized plug-in architecture. This allows other companies (such as Twelve Tone Systems) to create effects for ACID and likewise allows Sonic Foundry to create effects for use in other programs (such as Cakewalk/SONAR).

General FX Concepts

Many effects share a core set of controls that are the same for every plug-in. The following section details many of these controls and how they are used. Each plug-in also has its own set of controls that are particular to that plug-in. These controls are detailed in the description of the specific plug-in later in the chapter.

Presets

At the top of every plug-in dialog box is a preset drop-down list. This unassuming little feature might not jump out at you as the first thing that you'd want to play, but it really should. The first reason is that it contains a list of settings that were created by the audio professionals at Sonic Foundry and are specifically designed to show off the effect in a wide variety of situations. These presets can also serve as great jumping off points for creating your own customized effects. One of the best things about the presets is that they auto-position the effect's controls, allowing you to see what settings were required to produce a specific effect. This is the first step to learning how to create interesting effect settings.

Which brings us to the second reason this list is vital: You can save your own custom presets to the list. Here's how:

▶ To save your own presets, first type a name for your preset and then click the Save button to the right of the list.

▶ To modify one of your own presets, select it from the list, modify the parameters in the dialog box, and then click the Save button.

▶ To delete one of your own presets, select it from the list and click the Delete button to the right of the Save button.

The presets from Sonic Foundry are protected and cannot be saved with modifications or deleted, but you can start with a Foundry preset and save it to a new name.

Dry/Wet

Dry is a term used to describe a signal that is unmodified by an effect. Wet, therefore, refers to the signal after it has been modified. The strength or prominence of the effect can be subtly controlled by adjusting the wet and dry mix. Many of the effects have Dry and Wet sliders that can be used to control this mix, although sometimes the Wet slider is named after the plug-in— for example, the Chorus effect slider that controls the Wet signal is called Chorus Out. XpressFX typically control the Wet/Dry mix with a single slider labeled with the name of the effect (Wet) on one end and Original (Dry) at the other, with the center of the slider being a 50/50 mix. FX that are added as Assignable FX can also be controlled by using the Multi-purpose Fader to set the dry/wet mix of the FX. Make sure to right-click the Multipurpose Fader and select Pre Volume to use the fader in this way. Figure 7.4 displays many of the different ways you can adjust the dry/wet mix.

Figure 7.4
The various forms that
the basic Dry/Wet mix
faders can take.

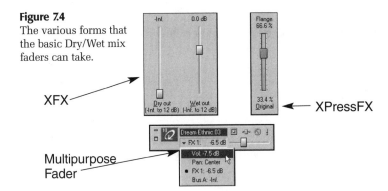

XFX

XPressFX

Multipurpose
Fader

Assignable FX also let you use FX Envelopes, which automate the gain over time of the FX in exactly the same way that the Multi-purpose Fade allows you to set the gain. Using both Volume and FX envelopes, you can animate the Dry/Wet mix over time.

The In and Out faders in the Mixer window of an Assignable FX bus are not the same as the Wet/Dry controls within the FX. The Volume control on the track and the In slider in the Assignable FX in the Mixer window both control the Input gain as it is fed into the plug-in, much like a pre-amp. Setting the gain on the Dry mix to 0 percent or − Inf. results in a signal that is 100 percent modified by the effect with none of the original in the mix. Setting the gain to − Inf. on the In slider of an Assignable FX results in no sound being fed into the plug-in. Setting the gain to − Inf. on Volume control of a track results in no sound coming from the track to go to the Assignable FX when the Multipurpose Fader is set to Post Volume (right-click the Multipurpose Fader to change this). Some FX, especially in the XFX series, also have Input sliders that control the level of the signal coming into the plug-in.

NOTE

Turning up the gain on the Wet/Out slider allows you to more clearly hear the results of changes made in the Audio Plug-In dialog box. After you get a sound you like, mix the dry signal back in for a more subtle, realistic, or natural sound.

Rate and Hertz (Hz)

Many effects are modulated and can periodically vary over time. The period of this variation is measured in cycles per second, or Hertz (Hz), the measurement used in ACID for the Rate controls on the plug-ins. For example, 1 Hz is one cycle per second, 10 Hz is ten cycles per second, and 0.1 Hz is one cycle every ten seconds. This is a very logical and easy way to talk about periodic variation, and it is very easy to instantly see that 2 Hz is twice per second and 7 Hz is seven times per second. However, it is less intuitive once the period drops below once per second. In this case, the smaller the fraction, the slower the period. You can quickly calculate the proper Rate to set by dividing one by the period you want. So, to get a period of once every seven seconds, you'd divide one by seven (1/7) and get a Rate of 0.143 Hz. The Rate range in ACID is from twenty times a second (20 Hz) to once every 1,000 seconds (almost seventeen minutes: 0.001 Hz).

Table 7.3

Measuring the periodicity of an effect in Hertz.

Period in Seconds	Hertz (Hz)
1	1.000
2	0.500
3	0.333
4	0.250
5	0.200
6	0.167
7	0.143
8	0.125
9	0.111
10	0.100
20	0.050

Calculating Rates

Many of the effects that modulate or cycle over time (for example, Delay, Flange/Wah-wah, and Stutter) can easily and effectively be synchronized to the beat of a song. The Rate for these effects is measured in cycles per second and project tempo is set to beats per minute (bpm), so divide 60 seconds in a minute by the number of beats per minute to get the delay in seconds. By default, ACID projects are 120 bpm, so:

> 60 seconds / 120bpm = 0.500 seconds between beats

Next, you need to convert this into cycles per second:

> 1 second / 0.500 seconds for one beat = 2.000Hz

So, if you wanted a "wah" on every beat, you'd need a Rate of 2.000 Hz, or two cycles per second. For a 140 bpm project, we get 2.331 Hz, and for 100 bpm, a rate of 1.667 Hz. Flanges often have much longer cycles that you might want to synchronize in terms of measures. Since tempo is typically annotated in terms of a quarter note = one beat and, by default, ACID has four beats in a measure, you only have to multiply the number of seconds by four and convert to Hertz (Hz).

> 60 seconds / 155 bpm = 0.387 seconds for one beat* 4 beats a measure = 0.774 seconds for one measure

Converting this to cycles per second:

> 1 cycle / 0.774 seconds = 1.292 Hz

For multiple-measure flanges, multiply the seconds per measure by the number of measures that you want the flange to occur over (often 4, 8, 12, or 16 measures):

$$1 \text{ cycle} / (0.774 \text{ sec.} * 16 \text{ measure flange}) = 0.161 \text{ Hz}$$

See Chapter 3 on tempo and time signature for more information on measures and phrasing.

Frequency (Pitch)

All of the equalization effects operate on the frequency of the sound. Frequency is a strict definition of the pitch or key in terms of the number of waves of sound per second, measured from peak to peak in a pure tone. Cycles per second are measured in Hertz (Hz).

The note A is used as the foundation of the Western scale and is defined as 440 waves per second, or 440 Hz, at somewhere around the middle of a piano. Obviously, music and instruments had existed long before oscilloscopes and Hertz, and people had been tuning instruments by ear for millennium. In 1939, the International Standards Association (ISA), along with scientists and musicians, decided that 440Hz was A, and this has been the standard ever since. It wasn't completely arbitrary, though; before 1939, A was closer to 435 Hz, but it was very close to a nice even number and standardization is a very important idea. This standardization is not entirely unlike sensibly setting the freezing point of water to 0°C and the boiling point to 100°C.

An octave in the Western scale is, by definition, either one-half the frequency or double the frequency of whatever note you start from. So one octave up from the middle A (440 Hz) is 880 Hz. This relationship is very simply related in the frequency graphs on the EQ plug-ins or on the equalizer on your stereo. Figure 7.5 has a line much like the scale on the graphs in the EQ plug-ins. Notice that the frequencies don't increase in a linear fashion. If they did, the scale numbers would read 20, 40, 60, 80, 100, etc. Instead, the scale doubles at every point. This means that the equalizers are not linear but instead mark octaves. Each horizontal hash mark on an EQ graph or fader is twice as much as the previous one, indicated by a doubling in the frequency, and equal to one octave. The keyboard below the scale in the illustration is a standard 88-key piano keyboard; the lines represent the standard tuning of a six-string guitar. This should give you some idea of what the various frequencies sound like in the real world.

Figure 7.5
The scale from an EQ frequency graph compared to an 88-key keyboard and a six-string guitar. All frequencies are in Hertz (Hz).

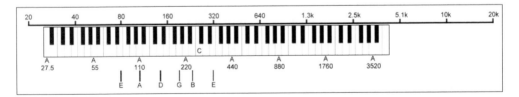

8

FX Dictionary

The previous chapter detailed the use of FX and plug-ins generally. This chapter is devoted to a thorough explanation of the various effects that come with ACID Pro. Not all of these effects are included in all versions of ACID, and many other effects are available from Sonic Foundry and other vendors. These explanations are meant to be concise and helpful, but the only way to really understand what is going on is to use your ears and experiment with these yourself in ACID.

Amplitude Modulation (XFX 3)

Amplitude adjusts the gain (volume or amplitude) of a sound at specific user-selected frequencies in a periodic manner (that is, it is modulated). This can be used to change the spatial characteristics of a sound and has traditionally been used to create a tremolo sound in guitar (for example, the cool surf/spy guitar or the spacey guitar parts in grand Sixties instrumentals) or organ parts. Tremolo is, by definition, a modulation of the volume, which is not to be confused with vibrato (although it often is), which is a modulation of the pitch. Amplitude refers to the peaks of the waves in a sound. These peaks can be seen in the waveform of events on the timeline—the larger the peak, the greater the amplitude and the louder the sound (see Figure 8.1). Here's how it works:

▶ The **Amplitude** slider sets the level of the minimum gain in the effect. In other words, setting the Amplitude slider to the lowest level (−Inf.) will result in the largest variation in amplitude and the greatest effect. Setting the slider to the highest level (0 dB) means that the lowest point will not be low at all and the plug-in will have very little effect.

▶ The **Graph** must be used to set the shape of the modulation curve. Set the overall frequency of the modulation—for example, 1 Hz or once a second—and then use the graph to shape how the modulation actually occurs within that single cycle of one second. Click the line on the graph to add a square node and drag the node to a new position. Try a few of the presets to see a few of the graphs set up by audio professionals. The **Blend graph edges** check box can be used to smooth the transition from the end of the graph back to the beginning of the next cycle.

▶ The **Mod. freq.** is the rate, or period, of the modulation in cycles per second (Hz). This controls the speed of the tremolo.

▶ The **Stereo pan** controls whether the modulation also pans back and forth across the two stereo channels of a file. This can be used to roughly simulate a rotating speaker effect used in some classic real-world organs (such as the Hammond B3) and speakers (Leslies, for example). Try a Mod. Freq. of at least 2 Hz, set the Amplitude very low, and set the Stereo pan to a higher percentage to simulate this effect.

▶ Use a **Low-pass start freq.** filter to tone down the higher frequencies, which can sometimes seem to be emphasized by an Amplitude effect.

Figure 8.1
The top waveform is the original loop file and the bottom is the same waveform modified by the Amplitude Modulation plug-in, using the Wacky preset.

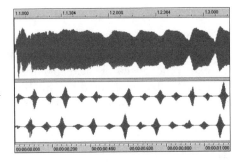

Calculating Rates

It is very useful to synchronize the Amplitude Modulation effect with the tempo and beat of a project. Amplitude Modulation is a faster-period effect that may occur on the beat or often multiple times each beat. See the previous discussion on calculating rates in the "General FX Controls" section of this chapter for information about how to calculate and synchronize this effect with a project.

ExpressFX Amplitude Modulation (ExpressFX 2)

The ExpressFX Amplitude Modulation plug-in has only a Rate, Depth, and Wet/Dry mix slider and lacks the other controls of the XFX version of this plug-in.

ExpressFX Stutter (ExpressFX 1)

The ExpressFX Stutter plug-in is most closely related to the Amplitude Modulation plug-in and works by periodically muting (lowering the gain of) an event to produce anything from a strobing effect to creating stranger pitch artifacts. Unlike the Gapper/Snipper plug-in, this effect does not alter the original length of the event. Unusual pitch overtone and undertones can be made with very short (less than 10 ms) Silence and Sound settings. Hold the Ctrl key while dragging the slider to move the two sliders in smaller increments. Move the Stutter slider all the way to the top to hear the results of the effect more clearly.

▶ **Silence** sets the duration of the muted section. Longer Silence durations (up to 200 ms) with shorter Sound settings produce popping-type stutters.

▶ **Sound** sets the duration of the non-muted section. Longer Sound durations with shorter Silence settings produce effects more like the Amplitude Modulation plug-in.

▶ **Add space** adds a spatial sense (not at time gap) to the effect by panning the sound between the left and right stereo channels.

The Stutter plug-in seems to react slowly to changes, and the preview on the timeline might take a second or two to update if you are continuously looping playback while you work.

TIP

One of the earliest amplitude modulation effects (from earlier in the last century) was created by mechanically spinning or rotating a speaker, commonly in an electric organ and most famously in Hammond organs and Leslie speakers. The volume decreased as the speaker pointed away from the listener and increased as it pointed towards the listener (amplitude modulation). The physical movement of the speaker could also produce tonal changes (vibrato) as a result of a Doppler shift, increasing the pitch slightly as the speaker spun towards you and decreasing the pitch as it spun away.

Chorus (XFX 1)

A chorus is, by definition, composed of more than one member. The Chorus effect can make a single instrument or voice sound like multiple instruments or voices. No matter how much skill or practice a group of performers has, the members will not play or sing in perfect unison. If the Chorus effect simply added more voices with perfect computer precision in unison, it would result only in a louder output. Therefore, the Chorus effect allows you to control how much out of sync the various parts are (delay) and how much it varies (modulation).

Interestingly, the Chorus effect is the foundation of a number of other effects. Since a chorus can be two voices (in the broader definition of voice, meaning any single instrument), with the original first and then the chorused voice, if you add a large enough delay, you have a Delay effect. Add another voice and you get a Multi-Tap Delay. Change the Modulation rate and depth and add a little feedback, and you get a Phaser, a Flange, or a Wah-wah. The Chorus is a very powerful and flexible effect with possibilities far beyond simple presentation of multiple voices.

Table 8.1 details some of the differences, although the flexibility of ACID means that most of these parameters have much greater variability.

CHAPTER 8

Table 8.1

Delay-related effects and how they differ.

Effect	Typical Delay	Notes
Chorus	More than 20ms but less than 50ms	While the delay itself is not noticeable as a separate delay, the effect of it is heard as another voice.
Delay	Greater than 50ms (often much more)	Simple Chorus effect with a longer and clearly noticeable delay or echo effect. Delay effects are not modulated.
Flange/ Wah-wah/Phaser	Between 0.1 and 20ms	Delay is not heard as a delay or echo. Also has the addition of distortion or feedback and a noticeable sweeping modulation that varies from a few times a second to once every dozen seconds or so. These FX usually use only one additional voice.

Although the Chorus effect is the foundation of many other effects, it is not always easy to derive these other specialized effects from the Chorus plug-in, and the additional controls that are specific to the Phaser give you more flexibility when dealing with that effect. For flanges, on the other hand, the Chorus plug-in has additional controls that allow you to set the delay and control the all-important feedback, which sometimes makes the Chorus a more powerful flanger than the Flange FX. Some of the presets in the Chorus do produce very nice flanges, phasers, and wah-wahs, so don't underestimate this plug-in as a simple tool only for adding additional voices and richness to a track.

▶ Select the **Invert the chorus phase** item to set the phase of the wave peaks to be 180 degrees out of phase with the original. The Dry out slider, which mixes the original signal with the processed signal, must be set higher for the phase to be heard. **Invert the feedback phase** does the same thing, but only to the feedback, so the Feedback slider must be set at a higher level for this to be noticeable.

▶ The **Chorus size** determines the number of additional voices added, from one to three.

▶ **Feedback** is an important element in the Flange-type effects. It can also be a way to increase the number of apparent voices by adding subtle echoes to the signal.

▶ The **Chorus out delay** is simply the delay of the voices.

▶ **Modulation rate** and **depth** control the variation of the delay. Set the depth to higher levels to vary further from the delay setting as a percent of the total delay. The modulation rate can be heard more clearly when the depth is greater. Flange-type effects use larger depth settings.

▶ Check **Attenuate high frequencies above** to mute or soften the higher frequencies that can come to dominate some applications of the Chorus plug-in. This is called a Low-pass filter in some other plug-ins, since it allows everything below the selected frequency to pass through.

ExpressFX Chorus (ExpressFX 2)

The ExpressFX Chorus does not allow you to specify the delay time, add feedback, or attenuate high frequencies with a low-pass filter.

Compressor (Track)

Compression is an automated way to variably adjust the volume of a track, ultimately raising all valleys and diminishing all peaks. By doing so, the overall loudness of a track can be increased without causing clipping in places where the volume is already high. This is a very widely used effect in popular music production and results in a loss of dynamic range in a song. This may be fine in full-speed-ahead pop music, but you should use caution when using compression in genres where dynamics are important. That being said, compression can be a lifesaver when you are working with a track that must be made louder to stand out in a mix or when you are fixing a recording with uneven levels. As the name suggests, the Track Compressor is best used intelligently at the track level, although there is no technical reason why you couldn't use it at the project level as well. See the discussion in the Graphic Dynamics plug-in entry later in this chapter or the section on mixing in the previous chapter for a much more detailed explanation on how to use compression properly in a mix.

Compression is not all work and no play, however. More creative uses of compression can cause very interesting and effective distortions, especially in guitar parts, creating awesome chunky guitars.

Distortion (XFX 3)

Distortion is caused by turning up the volume too much, which can cause distortion or clipping in the amplifier or the speakers. Clipping in an ACID project is a related concept, and it results in distortion, usually unwanted. An intentional distortion effect has been used effectively, especially in noisy or dirty electric rock guitar parts, causing a fuzzy or raspy sound. Originally, distortion was caused by the amplifiers, speakers, and tubes used for electric guitars. Modern distortion boxes and plug-ins can simulate these to some extent, and some of the presets in the Distortion plug-in refer to transistors and tubes. Of course, this has many other applications beyond guitar parts. Perhaps surprisingly, the Distortion FX plug-in can be used to create space or even to remove noise below a certain threshold, much like a noise gate filter. Since distortion is applied to the signal above a certain level, it is sometimes useful to apply compression just before distortion in an effects chain to boost some of the quieter parts of the signal. Here is how the Distortion FX works:

▶ The **Graph** controls the level of the effect in terms of Input versus Output. Click the line on the graph to add nodes and drag them up or down. Try some of the presets to get an idea of what some typical distortion settings look like on the graph. A diagonal line from bottom left to top right means that the input and the output are equal and no distortion occurs.

CHAPTER 8

▶ The **Graph polarity edit mode** sets the behavior of the effect: Individual only affects the graphs as seen; Synchronize matches the X/Y values to the graph and tends to yield a raspy sound; and the Mirror X, Y, and X/Y sets these values to the opposite, or mirror, of the graph. The **Positive/Negative** button determines which of the two graphs (lines) is being edited, with the line displayed on the button being the one that is black with the opposite graph displayed in a lighter gray in the background. Positive is the part of the wave in a waveform that is above the −Inf. center line and Negative is the part of the wave that is below that line.

▶ The **Slew rate** in the real world is a measure of an amplifier's ability to follow the input signal. Higher numbers are better, with 100 resulting in no change. This means that lowering the slew rate simulates the distortion plug-in not keeping up with changes in amplitude in the signal. The result is a characteristic type of noise in the output signal.

▶ Check the **Low-pass start freq.** to attenuate or soften the higher frequencies. As the name implies, this filter allows everything below the selected frequency to pass and filters everything above it.

ExpressFX Distortion (XFX1)

The ExpressFX version of Distortion does not have a graph to customize the effect or a Low pass start freq. filter.

Dither

Dithering is the process of smoothing rough edges in digital media. An analog signal is a continuous signal, but when a sound is recorded on a computer, it must be recorded in a digital format. This digital format is necessarily composed of individual discrete parts called *quanta*. The more pieces (quanta) the sound is broken up into, the greater the fidelity and quality of the digitization. The number of pieces is expressed in terms of the sample rate, or number of samples every second. Each piece, in turn, can be measured by the amount of computer bits that are used to describe it, with more being better. This can be expressed in terms of the resolution or depth (bit depth) of the recording.

Sometimes the process of moving from a higher bit depth recording to a lower one can result in the addition of noisy artifacts in the signal. For example, when converting down from a 24-bit DAT source to 16 bit for an audio CD, some information is necessarily lost. In this case, the information lost is likely to be minor, but the situation becomes more serious if you are converting down all the way to 8-bit for a small file destined for the Internet. Down converting can sometimes be heard as a tinny echo in spoken word recordings, a static crackle after percussion beats, or a distortion in low-level (volume) signals.

The Dither plug-in smooths the sharp noise that sometimes results from such a conversion by adding a random hiss to the down conversion artifacts and then changing the frequency of this noise so that it can no longer be heard—or is at least less noticeable to human perception. This comes at a minor price of adding a background hiss, but it allows more of the original low-level signal to be maintained in the down-converted sound. The effect of the dither plug-in can be very difficult to hear, since it is not designed to change a sound or song; it is instead used to try to preserve the original sound as much as possible through the conversion process to a lower bit depth. While you can set the audio characteristics when you render the final song, you will not be able to preview the effects of the Dither plug-in on your project unless you set the Project Properties to the target audio format. Simple drum and percussion parts with silence between the beats can reveal the Dither most clearly—individual beats are strongly affected by decreasing the bit depth and can be surrounded by static-like clicks and distortion which can be easily masked by the random hiss added by the Dither plug-in. In the end, as with all plug-ins and effects, if it sounds better with a Dither, you should use it.

This is definitely one plug-in that you want to try out whenever you are having problems getting a high-quality yet highly compressed (file size) file for streaming over the Internet. Keep in mind, though, that Dithering does nothing for problems caused by lowering the sample rate (44.1 kHz to 22.1 kHz), and do not confuse "bit depth" with the Internet/streaming/data transfer specific term "bitrate" (expressed in Kbits per second), which also is unaffected by Dithering.

▶ Select the bit-depth that you are converting to with the **Quantization depth** control. For example, if you are converting an audio track from 24 bit to 16 bit for an audio CD, you'd set the Quantization depth to 16 bit (default). Dithering is more important when down converting to 8 bit.

▶ The **Dither depth** sets resolution of the dithering, so half-bit results in a smoother dither.

▶ **Noise shape type** sets the type of noise reduction that is used in combination with the dithering to remove the hiss that is added as a part of the dithering process. The ACID Help file cautions against using noise shaping with files with lower sample rates such as 22 kHz, because it ends up pushing the noise into frequencies that are very noticeable.

Dithering should be done on individual tracks if only some tracks will be down converted, but it is more typically used on the entire project as the very last plug-in, especially when down converting for the Internet. You should definitely avoid using Dither twice, both at the track and the project level.

Track Dither

This plug-in is referenced in the Help file but did not install with Build 189 of ACID 3.0. From the screen shot in the Help, it appears that the Track Dither plug-in is identical to the Sonic Foundry Dither plug-in.

ExpressFX

ExpressFX are listed as sub-entries beneath the name of the effect. For example, ExpressFX Dither is listed under the Dither plug-in. ExpressFX Stutter is listed under Stutter.

CHAPTER 8

Flange/Wah-wah (Phaser–XFX 3)

This is really three related plug-ins in one: Flange, Wah-wah, and Phaser. You can select the specific plug-in by choosing the radio button that corresponds to the effect that you want to use. Wah-wah and Phaser are united by their common effect of periodically shifting or modulating the frequencies that are dominant in the output. Flanging is also a periodic effect, but it works by modulating the delay of a chorus of parts. This is probably one of the most fun plug-ins of the bunch, and you should definitely click through the three radio buttons to hear the difference between these three effects for yourself.

Flange is more difficult to describe but is an instantly recognizable sweeping sound where different frequencies in a sound are smoothly enhanced in a periodic fashion. This is actually a special case of the phaser, and you'll notice that the Flange effect doesn't use the Center Frequency or Resonance Control. It sounds a bit like singing a long "ooh" sound and gradually transitioning to a long "eee" and back. Flanging is widely used in techno and other electronic music. Surprisingly, flanging is also similar to a chorus effect except that the effect is varied periodically over time and the delay used is usually less than 10 ms—too short for humans to perceive (see the Chorus plug-in section for important details). Since it is varied by shortening and lengthening the delayed signal, this creates a periodic shift in pitch (shortening the delayed signal causes an increased pitch).

▶ The **Rate** is the number of cycles per second (Hz) of the effect. Flanges tend to have slower rates and produce a pronounced sweeping effect.

▶ The **Depth** determines the range in the amount of the delay. The delay itself cannot be controlled with this plug-in (see the Chorus effect).

Wah-wah is the onomatopoetic term for an effect often used in electric funk guitar. It creates an almost vocal effect on guitar (and other instrument) parts, almost as if one were singing, "Wah." Although this is not a hard-and-fast rule by any means, flanging usually takes place over a longer period, measured in seconds and tens of seconds, while wah-wah and phasing take place over a shorter period of time. In ACID, this is completely irrelevant since any period can be chosen for either effect.

Phaser effects refer not to Star Trek but to the waves in a sound. Sound waves, as with waves of water, have peaks and troughs. The distance between two troughs is the frequency of the sound, which defines the tone or pitch of the sound. By chorusing the original sound, you can have two instances of the same sound playing together. When the waves are moving together, they are in phase; waves that peak while others are in a trough are said to be out of phase. The Phaser plug-in periodically reinforces some parts of a sound and weakens others by moving them in and out of phasing. Selecting either the Wah-wah or Phaser effects reveals two more controls in the Audio Plug-In window:

▶ The **Center frequency** is the tonal center of the sweeping effect. Slide this around to achieve a more intense or more subtle effect.

► **Resonance** is when two sounds work together to reinforce each other, making the total louder or more intense than the sum of the parts. The slider in this plug-in controls the phase of the multiple voices in this effect, with higher percentages meaning that the sounds are more in phase, resulting in more reinforcement and a more intense sound.

Calculating Rates

Phaser and Wah-wah effects can easily and effectively be synchronized to the beat of a song. See the previous discussion on Calculating Rates in the General FX Controls section of this chapter for information about how to calculate and synchronize this effect with a project.

ExpressFX Flange/Wah-wah

The ExpressFX Flange/Wah-wah does not have a Phaser effect option. It also does not have the Wah-wah Center Frequency control, which is centered around 1,000 Hz and cannot be changed, nor does it have a Resonance slider, which is set at roughly 70 percent and also cannot be changed.

Gapper/Snipper (XFX 3)

This plug-in works by inserting silence (Gapper) or by cutting material out (Snipper) periodically. At higher rates, a tremolo-like effect is achieved by modulation of volume. In practice, given the same settings in the Audio Plug-in window, the Gapper produces a slightly harsher and more clearly delineated stutter (since there are clear areas of silence), while the Snipper produces a softer, more continuous one. Figure 8.2 graphically displays the effects of the Gapper/Snipper on a waveform. The media file is a spoken word file that helps to visualize the results of this plug-in and is not meant as an example of a typical use. You can see that the Gapper event has silence inserted, but no material from the original is lost; it is pushed down the timeline, making the event longer. The Snipper, on the other hand, removes material, moves it left to be flush with the start of the cut (butt-splice), leaves no sections of silence, and results in a shorter event. These are the Gapper/Snipper controls:

► **Freq. to gap/snip events** sets the period of the stuttering in Hz (cycles per second). "Event" here refers to a gap inserted or a snip removed and not ACID events on the timeline.

► **Length of one event** sets the duration of the gap inserted or the section removed.

► **Fade edges of each event** prevents the slight clicking or popping sound that can occur from sharp edges created by the effect. It is measured as a percentage of the length of the gap/snip.

► **Percent of original** shows how the (Freq. * Length) combine to affect the original event. The Gapper expresses this in terms of +100 percent since it is inserting material (silence), making the event longer. The Snipper uses percentages of less than 100 since the resulting event is shorter than the original.

Figure 8.2
The effects of the Gapper/Snipper on a spoken-word media file.

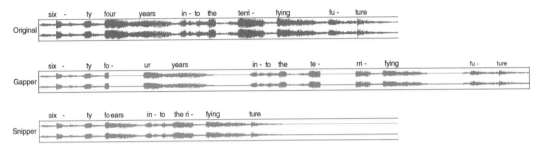

Calculating Rates

It is very useful to synchronize the Gapper/Snipper effect with the tempo and beat of a project. The Gapper/Snipper effect is a faster-period effect that may occur on the beat or often multiple times each beat. See the previous discussion on "Calculating Rates" in the General FX Controls section of this chapter for information about how to calculate and synchronize this effect with a project.

ExpressFX Stutter

The ExpressFX Stutter plug-in shares a similar name and may, at first, seem like a simple, derivative version of the Gapper/Snipper FX. It is not. As a unique plug-in that is much more closely related to the Amplitude Modulation plug-in than anything else, it is included in this dictionary in its own main entry (see Stutter) and not a sub-entry. The rest of the ExpressFX are defined as sub-entries beneath the main XFX plug-in's entry.

Graphic Dynamics (XFX 2)

This is the first of a number of dynamics plug-ins that can be used to precisely control the compression, limiting, and expansion of a sound in ACID. By and large, the specific tool you use to adjust the dynamics is a matter of personal preference, although some plug-ins are tailored to particular uses (such as Compression and Noise Gate). The Graphic Dynamics plug-in is particularly well suited to perform detailed compression across all frequencies in a track and is similar to, but more flexible than, the Track Compressor. Compression is the process of lowering peaks in a signal and raising valleys with the ultimate goal of increasing the loudness of a track overall. Expansion is the opposite and adds dynamic range to a track; low-level (volume) signals are lower and high-level signals are made higher. Limiting is hard/absolute compression and is a way to make sure the peaks in a waveform never go above a certain level. It is another way you can increase the overall loudness of the track without causing clipping. See "Mixing" in Chapter 7 for more information on effective use of compression.

The Graphics Dynamics and Multi-Band Dynamics plug-ins are probably the two most difficult plug-ins to understand due to the large number of controls and the subtle but important ways they affect an audio signal. One suggestion is to try out the various presets on a track to listen to and see the various types of graphs that have been designed by the engineers at Sonic Foundry. One difficulty with exploring this and other correction plug-ins in ACID is that media files and loops from commercial vendors are recorded and engineered by professionals who have already (hopefully) optimized the dynamics and equalization.

Here is what you will find:

▶ The **Output gain** sets the volume of the processed signal. The usual goal of applying compression is to increase the overall loudness and you can do that with this fader.

▶ The **Auto gain compensation** is a very important part of this plug-in and is very useful in normalizing a signal. This will automatically raise the gain on the quiet parts, resulting in a smoother compression overall. More than likely, you'll also want to manually increase the Output gain slightly whether this is checked or not.

▶ The **Sync stereo gain** means that the compression/limiting is applied to both stereo channels equally. If you have a situation where one channel is peaking out and the other is fine, make sure this option is not selected. Compression will then be applied to both channels independently.

▶ The **Graph** is the heart of this effect. When you first start, the line on the graph runs from bottom left to top right. This is known as the zero line and means that you are not changing the dynamics of the signal, because the vertical Out is equal to the horizontal In. To add a point or node on the line, click on the line and drag it to a new position. To delete a node, double-click it. You'll notice that the line already has one node on it at the -24, -24 dB position. This is a standard place where you might want to slowly ease into the compression and is the Threshold in this plug-in. If you look at a few of the presets, you'll see that while this node moves up and down in volume (gain), it is always at the X = Y position. The compression presets start on the zero line at an angle to the right and below the line. This is what compression looks like. Noise gating is the process of eliminating unwanted low-level background noise. In this case, you want to start by adding a node at a low gain and then drag the line down and away, again decreasing the output gain. See Figure 7.9 and the following example.

The graph allows you to do both at the same time. A good example of where you might want to use compression and noise gating is when working with a spoken-word recording using the microphone on a camcorder. It's not a good idea to do this, but sometimes you have no choice. Since the subject is talking into the camera from a distance and the microphone usually isn't of the highest quality, you might get some very uneven recording levels—especially if the camera operator is also talking, creating sections that are much louder. In order to increase the gain for the quieter parts, you need to first reduce the gain of the really loud parts and then increase the whole thing together. The final result will have much less dynamic range (difference between the quiet and loud parts).

Camcorders also usually introduce annoying background motor noise. This can become especially prominent when the gain is turned up. So at the same time you are working with some compression on the graph, you might also want to use a noise gate. Figure 8.3 shows what the graph might look like to solve this problem. In the figure, the relatively steep slope of the noise gate starting at −60 dB means the noise is cut out fairly quickly and sharply. The compression slope is more gradual and results in an easing in of the compression at −24 dB as the gain increases. By the time the gain in the input hits 0 dB, it is being compressed by −12 dB. This is typical since low-level sounds are, of course, harder to hear. Noise gating is frequently a vertical line at a particular gain (a hard gate). If you wanted to do a hard limit (compression), you would create a horizontal line at some upper limit. Expansion would involve dragging the graph line above the zero line, but this is rarely done.

Figure 8.3

Compression and Noise Gating in the Graphic Dynamics plug-in.

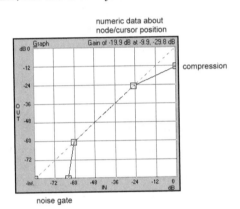

▶ The **Attack** and **Release** parameters set how quickly the plug-in responds to peaks. A quick attack (so the plug-in starts immediately) and a slow release are typical. Too fast of a release can result in very quiet sections (even silence), while having the gain turned up very loud suddenly results in background noise becoming audible. This is referred to as a breathing, or pumping, effect

▶ The **Threshold** sets the level where the compression begins to take effect. This slider moves the default threshold node on the graph line up and down while maintaining the relative X:Y ratio.

▶ The **Ratio** slider sets the slope of the compression line, raising and lowering the final node on the graph. The zero line is at a ratio of 1:1, resulting in no compression. A 2:0 ratio above 124 dB means that for every 2 dB increase in gain above 124 dB, the gain will be reduced 1 dB. So 122 dB signals will be lowered to 123 dB, 112 dB In to 118 dB Out and 0 dB In to −12 dB Out.

Graphic EQ (XFX 2)

This is the first of a number of equalization plug-ins that can be used to adjust the overall tonal qualities of a sound or song. The specific type of equalization you use is largely a matter of personal preference, although you may find some EQ plug-ins easier to use than others for specific uses (some suggestions are given within the plug-in definitions).

NOTE

It is not highly recommended that you use multiple EQ plug-ins in a chain. At a maximum, you may want to use EQ at the track level to fix a few problems and maybe then on the Master bus in the Mixer to polish off a project. You should think very carefully about what you are doing and whether there is a better way to more efficiently do the same thing. This is actually good advice for all plug-ins!

The Graphic EQ actually is a very nice blend of simplicity and power. All three tabs in the plug-in window control the same parameters, and when you move a slider on one, the sliders and envelope nodes on the other move with it. This gives you a great way to very quickly set up a rough EQ curve on the **10 Band** tab, then move to the **20 Band** tab and make a few more minor adjustments, and finally move to the **Envelope** tab, which offers the greatest level of control. Figure 8.4 shows an exploded view of all three tabs with the same settings in the plug-in. Each **slider** on the 10 Band corresponds to a pair of sliders on the 20 Band. Initially the number of nodes on the envelope line corresponds to the complexity and variation in the sliders (for example, a flat line needs only two nodes), but additional nodes can be added by clicking and dragging the envelope line. You can delete nodes that you have added by double-clicking or right-clicking them. Dragging nodes or sliders up and down (vertically) controls the gain at any specific frequencies. Nodes can also be dragged left and right (horizontally) to fine-tune the exact frequency of the node. The overall volume of the signal leaving the plug-in can be controlled with the **Output gain** fader.

The **Accuracy** list simply adjusts the quality of the plug-in. Higher quality means that your computer needs to work harder. If you have a slower machine (say a 500 MHz CPU) or if your project is particularly complex (using a lot of tracks and/or effects), you might want to use the Medium or Low settings. As you'll notice from the list, higher bands are easier to process, so you can get away with using the lower Accuracy items when applying EQ only to the upper frequencies. This really affects only timeline playback of the project in real time. You should definitely use High whenever you render, as the computer will take as much time as it needs to create the final output.

Equalization can be used to bring a track or part out of a mix. You can do this at the track level to clean up the sound of a track. This is especially useful if you are using a loop or media file that has a number of different instruments and you want to focus on one in particular. The trick is to figure out which frequencies to boost. To give you a rough idea of the range of frequencies, a typical 88-key piano keyboard ranges from about 27 Hz to 4,200 Hz, with middle C at about

CHAPTER 8

262 Hz, which can serve as an arbitrary divider between high and low frequencies. It would be impossible to make a recommendation about which frequencies to boost for the human voice, since it covers such a large range. By playing back a section of a project (with a loop region) with a track soloed and adjusting the sliders on the 10 Band tab one by one, you can hear which ones emphasize the part you want to bring out. Then you can move on to the other tabs for greater accuracy (see Figure 8.4).

Equalization can also be very effectively used at the project and bus level. In these cases, you wouldn't want to solo the track while trying to bring a part out of the overall mix, but the procedure would be the same. EQ can also be used to bring brightness back to a mix or track that has been compressed or otherwise modified. Surprisingly, a gentle boosting of the high frequency band can also add a greater spatial sense to a mix. As you might know, sub-woofers produce the lowest frequencies and home stereos usually only have one. This is because the very low frequencies are non-directional (in smaller spaces). The higher the frequency, the easier it is to identify the location of the sound. The higher frequencies are, therefore, more important to the perceived spatial aspects of a mix. Finally, EQ can be used to minimize constant-frequency background noises, whether low-frequency hums or high-frequency hisses. The Notch frequencies around 450 Hz are an example of a preset that might be used for such a purpose. EQ can also be used to reduce pops and crackles as well, just as long as the frequency of these artifacts remains constant.

Figure 8.4

The Graphic EQ plug-in tabs from the top: 10 Band (most Coarse), 20 Band, and Envelope (finest control).

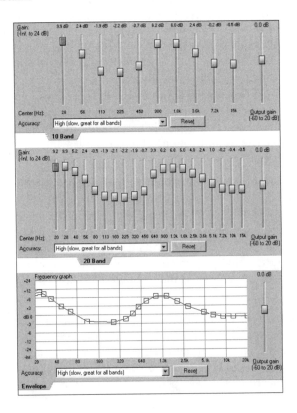

ExpressFX Equalization

ExpressFX Equalization is limited to only three bands of frequencies to adjust: Bass, Mid, and Treble.

Track Equalization

This is a simple equalization plug-in that is automatically added to every track, although the controls are flat, meaning that they do not alter the audio signal in the default configuration. Track EQ is designed to be simple and easy to use. There are much more complex and flexible equalization plug-ins that you can use (Paragraphic EQ, for example), but this FX should be adequate in many situations. There is no reason that you cannot use this plug-in at the bus or project level, despite its name. Track Equalization was dealt with in more detail in the previous chapter on mixing.

Multi-Band Dynamics (XFX 2)

The Multi-Bands Dynamics plug-in takes compression one step further by allowing you to apply compression at specific frequencies instead of broadly across the entire spectrum (see the explanations of compression in the Graphic Dynamics entry and in Chapter 7 on mixing). This kind of custom tailoring can allow you to target your compression more precisely, potentially avoiding some of the pitfalls of compression. This is not necessarily easy, but there are some cases where this is very important. Any time you can identify clear peaks or spikes in a signal, either by ear or by looking for very sharp and narrow spikes in the waveform, you should consider this plug-in instead of squashing the entire track with one of the broader effects. This is especially true with pops or clicks or when a vocalist spits a "p" into the microphone. In all of these cases, the sound probably occupies a fairly narrow frequency range that is different from the material you want to keep, which often occupies a much broader frequency. The tricky part is figuring out the frequency of the noise you want to compress. You cannot perform noise gating with this plug-in.

First off, you can apply compression (or limiting where the Amount slider is set to 50:1) to four individual bands: two on the first page of the plug-in and two on the other. You can use one or all four, but you'll definitely want to work one band at a time by selecting the **Solo** option on the band you are modifying. Bands are activated by un-checking the **Band # bypass** option at the bottom of the dialog box.

Identify the section of the event that has a typical example of something that you want to compress, say a "p" in the microphone. On the timeline, create a loop region around one section that is causing problems, turn looping playback on, and click the Play button. As with all plug-ins, you'll want to preview the soloed track while you make adjustments. Click the **Preset** list and select Reduce loud plosives. This is a great place to start. This sets the **Threshold** to -15 dB: This is the point above which the compression begins. For this preset, the compression is fairly sharp with an **Amount** of 32.0:1. If we used the Graphic Dynamics plug-in, it would look like Figure 8.5.

Figure 8.5
Compression applied
to all signals of all
frequencies above
− 15 dB at a 32:1 ratio
in the Graphic
Dynamics plug-in.

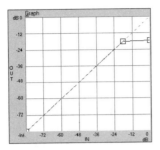

In the Multi-Band Dynamics case, however, the compression is going to apply only to a limited range of frequencies. The Type of band in this case is a Low-shelf, which means that all frequencies below the frequency specified by the frequency slider will be compressed—in this example, 500 Hz. In summary, all sounds between the lowest sound possible (20 Hz) and 500 Hz will be compressed (almost limited at 32:1) when they rise above − 15 dB. Hopefully, this will catch the plosives.

A trickier example would be harsh "s" sounds, which can also cause problems when blown into a microphone, but at a completely different frequency from the plosives. From the Preset list, select the Reduce loud sibilants item. Unfortunately, the presets seem to affect only Band 1, so it is not possible to use the presets on two separate bands, one for sibilants and one for plosives. This time the Type is **Band-notch** and the **Center** of the frequency that is going to be compressed is at 5,000 Hz with a **Width** of 1.0 octave. The threshold is set very low at − 30 dB with a 25:1 compression. Figure 8.6 shows what the Low-shelf and the Band-notch might look like in the Track EQ plug-in, with the low-shelf being identified on the left with a 1 and the one octave band-notch at 5,000 Hz identified by the 2.

Figure 8.6
Top: The settings used
in Band 1 to eliminate
plosives and in Band 2
to eliminate sibilants.
Bottom: What these two
frequencies might look
like in the Track EQ
plug-in.

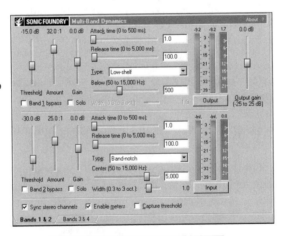

Starting with a preset is a great idea, but these are usually just that—starting points. Make sure the Enable meters item at the bottom of the window is checked and the button below the meters on the band you are working on is set to Output. Then, while the loop region is playing back on the timeline, move the Center slider back and forth to try and zero in on the exact frequency of the "s" or whatever noise you want to compress. The Width slider should also be adjusted to try and minimize the range of frequencies that is being compressed. There is no magic way to do this; it takes time, practice, and a good ear to get it right. You can probably eliminate a few scattered "s" sounds, but eliminating wind in the microphone will be tough to do.

As with the Graphic Dynamics plug-in, the **Attack** and **Release** operate the same way, usually with a fast attack and a slower release. The **Sync stereo channels** item at the bottom of the window is the same as well. Unselect this default option if you are having problems only in one channel.

The final item is one of the most important. The **Capture threshold** box should be selected when you want to automatically find the highest peak(s) that you want to compress. To do this, select the Capture threshold option and then play back the section of the track that has the problem. The Threshold slider becomes disabled and the labels around it turn red. Now, when peaks occur, the Threshold slider automatically adjusts to that level. Now you can drag the Threshold slider down slightly to make sure you compress these peaks. To the left of the main meters is a third red meter. This is the compression meter, which operates from the top down, allowing you to see when compression is occurring and by how much. If the meter is not moving, you are not hitting your target. If it is constantly bouncing all the way to the bottom, you are probably squashing the track too much (or you have really poor source audio that cannot be fixed).

Multi-Tap Delay (XFX 1)

Multi-Tap Delay is a more complicated version of the Simple Delay effect. Both essentially create echoes from a signal, simulating audio waves bouncing off a surface. This can be used to create perceived space in a song, but it is more commonly used as an interesting special effect (Reverb is a more natural way to create space with delays). Instead of a single echo (as created in the Simple Delay FX), the Multi-Tap Delay creates multiple echoes. This can be used to simulate canyon walls at different distances or more complex spaces where echoes return at different times. There are also quite a few other controls that can be used to subtly modify the delayed signal. As with the Simple Delay plug-in, this FX is most effective with solo voice or instrument parts that can clearly show the effect of the delay. The delay can continue well after the event on the timeline ends.

Here is what to do:

▶ The **Input gain** sets the level of the signal coming into the effect. It is set to 0.0 dB by default and this represents no change in gain. Anything less will diminish the volume.

▶ The **Dry out** and **Wet out** faders are usually used to mix the original signal with the processed signal, but it is a slightly different situation in this effect. With some FX (dynamics, equalization, and so on), you might want to turn the Dry fader all the way down to −Inf. for maximum effect. With this effect, you need to hear the Dry out (original) signal or the echo won't make any sense. Hearing only the echo and not the sound that caused it would be odd indeed. Usually, the Wet out fader gain will be the same as or lower than the Dry out gain. These controls set the gain for the entire effect; the gain of individual taps can be set below.

▶ The **Number of taps** sets the number of delayed signals that will be returned as echoes. As you move the slider to add more taps, the numbers on the **Current tap** list become active one by one. All of the controls below this list apply to whichever Current tap is selected; to modify the third tap, make sure at least three taps are available and then select the radio button before the 3. Taps appear on the graph as lines, with the active Tap being red.

▶ The **Tap gain** sets the initial volume of the processed signal for each tap. One reasonable way to determine the gain for each tap is to make taps with greater delay times also have lower volumes. The gain of each tap is visually represented on the graph. The tap gain can be set to +/− 100 percent with negative values being 180 degrees out of phase, meaning that the peaks of negative and positive waves occur at different times. This can be important in any delay effect (such as Chorus) since waves that occur in sync can reinforce each other and sound like a unison signal. In other words, an earlier and louder delay can mask a later delay if the two are completely in phase. Altering the Tap gain +/− can solve this problem and add space to the effect when this occurs.

▶ The **Graph** visually represents the gain and the delay (see Figure 8.7). You cannot change anything on the graph directly. The **Graph Resolution** allows you to view more or less detail on the graph. The number selected in milliseconds determines the total length of the graph, from 500 ms to 5000 ms.

Figure 8.7
The graph displays the information about Tap 4 in the effect (which is represented by a red line). The other taps are displayed on both sides of the Gain line in gray.

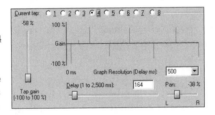

▶ The **Delay** sets the time of the echo return in milliseconds (ms). Hold the Ctrl key down while dragging the slider to more accurately position the delay. The line on the graph above will move in response to the movement of this slider. Each tap can be at any delay setting, but it might be more convenient if the shortest delay is Tap 1, the next one is Tap 2, and so on.

▶ The **Pan** control allows you to set the stereo panning of the delays. This is important since this effect is used to simulate multiple echoes coming from walls at different distances, and also different directions, from the listener. It might help you to think about a room or location and the position of the listener in the room as you adjust the plug-in. Each tap can be thought of as modifying the echo from a single wall.

▶ The **Mod. rate** sets the modulation in the pitch of the individual delays. This creates a more realistic effect instead of a relentlessly perfect computer delay. Subtle manipulation will allow the delayed signals to be more easily differentiated from the Dry out signal. The **Mod. depth** determines the strength of the modulation.

▶ The **Feedback** can also set up additional delay-type effects by running the delays through the filter again.

▶ The **Low-pass start freq.** allows you to add a filter that filters out some of the higher frequencies (letting lower frequencies pass through). The frequency set here determines where the filter starts, with frequencies above this level being filtered. High-frequency sounds are important in our perception of depth; filtering out these frequencies can create a warmer and less harsh effect.

Calculating Rates

It is very useful to synchronize the Multi-Tap Delay effect with the tempo and beat of a project. See the previous discussion on calculating rates in the "General FX Controls" section of this chapter for information about how to calculate and synchronize this effect with a project.

Noise Gate (XFX2)

Noise Gate is primarily used to eliminate low-level background noise from a sound and is a special case of applying a dynamics plug-in. See Figure 8.8 for a comparison of what the settings in the Noise gate plug-in might look like in the Graphic Dynamics plug-in. You can see in the example that the Threshold is set to −32 dB. Sounds below this threshold are silence to −Inf. The line in the graph is vertical, meaning that everything is cut off with no roll-off. Noise gates are especially useful in eliminating constant low-level noises from electronic hums to video camera motor noises. Figure 7.8 in the previous chapter and the Noise Gate Help file show two events with waveforms that display a low-level hum that could be eliminated with a noise gate.

CHAPTER 8

Figure 8.8
What the Noise Gate plug-in might look like as expressed on the graph in the Graphic Dynamics plug-in.

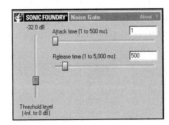
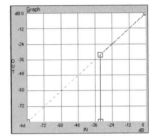

To use the Noise Gate:

▶ The **Threshold** sets the minimum level a sound must reach to pass through the filter. All sounds below the threshold are silenced.

▶ The **Attack** and **Release** parameters set how quickly the plug-in responds to peaks. A quick attack (so the plug-in starts immediately) and a slow release are typical. Too fast of a release can result in very quiet sections (even silence); having the gain turned up very loud suddenly results in background noise becoming audible. Too slow of an attack can mean that some background noise will still be apparent before the plug-in kicks in.

Track Noise Gate

I cannot see any difference at all between the Track Noise Gate and the XFX Noise Gate, and it is likely that they are identical.

Paragraphic EQ

Paragraphic EQ is another visual or graphic equalization plug-in that allows you to see the various frequencies and how they are being modified. It is actually very similar to the Track EQ plug-in (they even share many of the same presets) except that it has two additional bands. Figure 8.9 shows some of the similarities. The plug-in automatically calculates smooth curves between the various adjustments, resulting in smoother transitions, which is something that the graph on the Graphic EQ does not do.

Figure 8.9
The same settings in both the Track EQ and Paragraphic EQ plug-in.

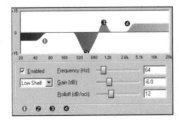
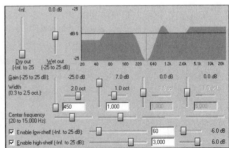

Like the Track EQ, the Paragraphic EQ has bands that you can customize and adjust individually, although this EQ has a total of six: four distinct main areas plus a low- and a high-shelf (see Figure 8.10). In the Track EQ plug-in, the various controls are found on four tabs. In the Paragraphic EQ, all of the controls are on a single page, which can make the plug-in look intimidating. There are four bands just below the graph, while the low- and high-shelf bands are at the bottom of the window (these are called shelves because of the flat ends to the equalization curves).

▶ The only additional control that the Paragraphic EQ has is **Dry/Wet** mix faders, which control the mix of the original signal with the processed signal.

▶ The four bands below the graph are gray until you touch the **Gain** fader for a band.

▶ The bands default to a **Center frequency** of 100 Hz, 300 Hz, 1000 Hz, and 5000 Hz. After adjusting the gain to make the band active, drag the slider to change the center frequency. Although they default from lowest to highest, left to right, there is no reason to leave them that way. The left-most band could just as easily center at 9,000 Hz if you desire. As with most sliders in ACID, hold the Ctrl key while dragging a slider to make it more sensitive and move in smaller increments. You can use the slider to conveniently sweep up and down the frequency range while playing the track back to quickly target what you need.

▶ The **Width** is set by the middle slider (see Figure 8.10) and is measured in terms of octaves.

Figure 8.10
The band controls on the Paragraphic EQ plug-in.

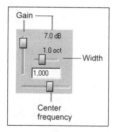

▶ Select the **Enable low-shelf** or **Enable high-shelf** options to use these bands as well. The first slider controls the **frequency** that the shelf roll-off begins at and the last smaller slider controls the **gain**.

As with many other effects, the best way to work with this plug-in is to solo the track you are using it on, create a loop region on the timeline, and play the project back while you modify the various parameters. For example, imagine you have an annoying hum that you want to get rid of—this plug-in is well suited to this use. There are two ways to figure out the frequency of the hum. In both cases, to isolate the noise you'd pick a section of the event that has no content and that is as silent as possible. Then, while that is repeatedly looping, you could increase the gain on one of the bands. Then you could either slide the Center frequency slider back and forth until you made the sound as loud as possible or you could reduce the gain to −Inf. and see if you can make the sound disappear. After finding the frequency as closely as possible, adjusting the width of the band and lowering the gain, go back to the track and preview the EQ settings on a section of the track with content. More than likely, the plug-in is going to have a negative impact on the sound you want to keep as well. You will need to play a balancing game to get rid of as much of the problem as possible without damaging the rest of the track.

Parametric EQ (XFX 2)

The Parametric EQ is another reconfiguration of the same controls that are found in the Graphic, Paragraphic, and Track EQ plug-ins. It has a slightly higher range (up to 22,050 Hz) and an in-line Output gain control, but other than that, it has almost identical Low-shelf, Band 1, Band 2, and High-shelf options like the Track EQ. The difference is that this plug-in is specialized to discretely apply only one specific filter to a track, either to boost a specific band or attenuate it. There are a number of examples in the presets that you might look at to get a feel for the plug-in. The basic controls are similar to the other EQ plug-ins:

- ▶ The **Output gain** controls the volume of the processed signal as it leaves the plug-in.

- ▶ The **Amount** fade is the same as the gain sliders in the other EQs and sets the level at which the selected frequencies are attenuated/boosted.

- ▶ The **Filter style** list is unique to this effect. There are four types of curves that can be selected. The **Low-** and **High frequency shelf** items are like the shelves in the other two plug-ins and create a flat adjustment to the signal below/above the selected **Cutoff frequency** (with a small roll-off). This roll-off is set with the Width slider, which is specifically called the **Transition width** slider in these two cases. The **Band-pass** filter boosts everything outside the selected **Center frequency** of the **Band width** selected and is used to isolate a sound and remove it. This filter will, by default, produce a louder output since most of the frequencies are boosted. The **Band-notch/boost** filter works by isolating a specific frequency and then boosts the gain on that frequency alone, leaving the rest of the frequencies alone.

- ▶ The graph is simply a picture that represents the Filter style and does not reflect any of the control settings.

- ▶ The **Accuracy** list simply adjusts the quality of the plug-in. Higher quality means that your computer needs to work harder. Faster machines (+700 MHz CPU) should use the High setting unless you have a particularly complex project with a lot of effects. This really affects only timeline playback of the project in real time. You should definitely use High whenever you render, because the computer will take as much time as it needs to create the final output.

Pitch Shift

Pitch Shifting is handled very easily, automatically, and effectively by ACID (see Chapter 4). The advantages to using this plug-in over the native pitch shift that ACID does is that the plug-in gives you explicit control over how the shifting takes place. Here is what you will find:

▶ **Semitones to shift pitch by** sets how much the pitch is shifted up or down. By default, the shifting will also change the duration of the media file, although this will not be reflected in events on the timeline or in the waveform. Pitch can be shifted by +/− 50 semitones (half-steps) when the duration is not preserved (see below). Smaller changes can be made with the **Cents to shift pitch by** slider. Logically enough, there are 100 cents in a semitone, which defines the range of this control.

▶ The **Accuracy** list simply adjusts the quality of the plug-in. Higher quality means that your computer needs to work harder. This really affects only timeline playback of the project in real time. You should definitely use High whenever you render, because the computer will take as much time as it needs to create the final output. If you are experiencing problems with playback, you might want to use the High setting and render to a new track (from the Options menu) and create a new media file with the pitch shift settings.

▶ Select the **Apply an anti-alias filter during pitch shift** option to smooth out the effects of this filter when pitch shifting up, especially if the Preserve duration option is being used. This requires more processing power and may deaden the sound a bit, but it can be important in removing some annoying artifacts.

▶ Select the **Preserve duration** option to keep the length of the media file the same as the original. This requires quite a bit more computational power to do well and is not effective beyond +/−12 semitones (one octave): The Semitones slider label changes to reflect this limit. The **Mode** list allows you to select how the plug-in functions and what additional filters are applied. The only way to choose the correct mode is to first guess which one matches your requirements most closely and then listen and experiment.

▶ The bottom of the window has two labels that display information about the shift. The **Musical equivalent** shows the name of the musical interval (for example, 12 semitones = one octave—see Chapter 4) in relation to the shift in semitones, while the **Transposition ratio** shows the ratio the actual frequency is changed (2.0000 is 2:1, or twice the original frequency).

▶ The **Initial time** is always 00:01:00.000 because of some problem with determining the duration of a media file from Windows. Because of this problem, you need to enter the length of the file (which can be found by right-clicking the file in Windows Explorer and selecting Properties from the context menu and then clicking the Details tab) in the Initial time box. Once you have done this, the Final time label will accurately display the change in duration of the file as it is used in ACID. The Preserve duration option must not be checked to use and view these features.

CHAPTER 8

Reverb

One of the most useful and widely used effects, Reverb is a common control on everything from guitar amplifiers to mixing boards. The main goal of Reverb is to subtly add a sense of space or depth to a recording. This is especially useful on recording done with close-miking techniques, which produce extremely clean recordings that are devoid of any background sounds or room reflections. Close-miking works on the assumption that it is easier to start with a clean recording than to have to go in and clean it up later. Almost all of the commercially available loops are extremely clean (with the notable exception of many of the ambient loops and drones). Reverb, therefore, becomes particularly effective in making ACID-created songs sound more alive, with a more realistic sense of space.

Reverb is a delay-type effect and is similar in many ways to the Simple Delay and Multi-Tap Delay FX. You can immediately see from the plug-in window that Reverb has many more controls to subtly adjust the delay and potentially make it sound more natural. On the track level, Reverb can be used to bring a part out of the mix, although it should be used cautiously and with restraint. Here is how Reverb works:

▶ The **Reverberation mode** list is another set of presets that alter many background characteristics of the effect. None of the parameters that are modified by the selections on this list is available for manual adjustment in the plug-in window. The Preset list at the top of the window is a good place to start exploring this and many of the other settings in this complex and important effect.

▶ The **Dry out/Reverb out** fader controls the mix of the original signal with the processed signal. Reverb out is the main part of the effect and is heard as a delay or echo.

▶ The **Early out** fader sets the gain for the first and fastest reflection or echo in the effect. It can be most clearly heard if you turn the Dry out fader all the way down to −Inf.

▶ The **Early reflection style** list has ten modes that allow you to set the bright and very quick reflection that occurs before the main reverb. Again, this can most clearly be heard by turning down the Dry out and Reverb out sliders.

▶ **Decay time** is how quickly the reverb fades out. It affects only the reverb and not the Early reflection and can produce a sort of sustain effect on notes that simulates the characteristics of the room.

▶ The **Pre-delay** determines the main reverb delay or echo and provides the first clue about the size of the virtual space. This slider also affects only the reverb and not the Early reflection.

▶ Select the **Attenuate bass freqs. below** option to set a filter that diminishes everything below the frequency set with the slider. This is similar to a low-shelf filter in the EQ plug-ins.

▶ Likewise, select the **Attenuate high freqs. above** option to set a filter for all frequencies above the one selected with the slider. This is like a high-shelf filter in some of the EQ plug-ins. You should be careful when filtering the higher frequencies since these are the exact frequencies that are most important to the spatial sense of a sound.

While you probably want to use reverb on the Master bus at the end of a project to keep all of the tracks in the same space, you may want to solo one of the primary tracks and adjust the reverb while listening to it alone. Reverb is more clearly heard in solo instrument and voice parts. Of course, before you settle on a final effect setting, you will need to fine tune the reverb for the whole project.

ExpressFX Reverb

This effect has fewer controls than the XFX Reverb plug-in but still produces a very high-quality and satisfying reverb. The different controls with their less technical names make this plug-in easier to use in many cases.

▶ The **Preset list** and **Room type** lists work together to set the overall operation of the effect. Select a Preset first and then a Room type to modify it. As with the XFX Reverb plug-in, the Room type sets internal parameters that cannot be adjusted by the user.

▶ The **Room size** slider essentially adjusts the delay time and has a similar effect as the Pre-delay slider in the XFX Reverb effect.

▶ The **Liveliness** slider controls how quickly the reverb fades out and is the same as the Decay time slider in the XFX Reverb effect.

▶ The **Reverb/Original** fader controls the mix of the original signal with the processed signal.

Simple Delay

This is a variation of the Multi-Tap Delay and has exactly the same effect, except that you are limited to only one delay or echo. The plug-in simulates the reflection of sound off a surface and what it sounds like as it returns. The further away the surface, the longer the delay in the return of the echo. By creating a delayed signal in this effect, the illusion of perceived depth or large room size can be simulated. This is not a particularly subtle effect and simulates very large spaces. The Reverb effect is better suited to simulating smaller spaces more realistically. Even so, the Simple Delay FX can add some very interesting ambience to a track or project. Adding this to a single, clear track is probably the best way to focus on the effects of this plug-in. Media files that contain solo instruments and voices with even brief areas of silence are good candidates. Keep in mind that adding a delay to a sax solo track in a song may sound very nice and can bring that part out of the mix more, but it is not very realistic to have one instrument playing in a large hall and the rest in a small studio. Try out a few of the presets to get you started with this (and any) plug-in.

▶ The **Dry out** and **Delay out** faders are usually used to mix the original signal with the processed signal, but it is a slightly different situation in this effect. With some FX (such as dynamics, equalization, and the like), you might want to turn the Dry fader all the way down to −Inf. for maximum effect. With this effect, you need to hear the Dry out (original) signal or the echo won't make any sense. Hearing only the echo and not the sound that caused it would be odd. Usually, the Delay out fader gain will be lower than the Dry out gain.

CHAPTER 8

▶ The **Delay time** is set in seconds. The greater the delay the larger the room size or further away the sound-reflecting circuit.

▶ The **Multiple delays (Feedback)** check box sets up the echoes to repeatedly bounce around the simulated space. This can produce some very interesting, if artificial and strange, effects. The delay can continue well after the event on the timeline ends. The feedback of this FX is very different from what the Multi-Tap Delay FX does.

▶ When the Multiple delay box is selected, the **Decay time** slider becomes available. This controls how quickly the echoes fade. Long decays make the simulated space sound more alive and bright, while shorter decays simulate a space where the walls absorb the sound more quickly (although the original echo is still strong).

Calculating Rates

It is very useful to synchronize the Simple Delay effect with the tempo and beat of a project. See the previous discussion on "Calculating Rates" in the "General FX Controls" section of this chapter for information about how to calculate and synchronize this effect with a project.

Smooth/Enhance (XFX 3)

The Smooth/Enhance plug-in is a very special case of an equalization plug-in. It is carefully tuned to eliminate (smooth) some of the artifacts caused by other processes and effects or by problems with the source audio.

The other use is to quickly brighten up a track (enhance), especially one that has been softened with any number of other effects. One example might be a track that has been compressed to make it a bit louder in a mix. This can sometimes result in a flatter, less lively sound. Another notable example is when down sampling. Down sampling is the process of changing the sample rate from, say, an audio CD at 44,100 Hz to 11,025 Hz for distribution over the Internet. The Smooth Enhance plug-in has one simple **Operation** slider that is used to control the effect.

Time Stretch (XFX 1)

Time Stretch is a sophisticated plug-in with many excellent presets that allows you to make a media file shorter or longer without pitch shifting it. Of course, there are limits to this; the less you alter the time, the better results you will get, although you'll be amazed at what you can do. Some types of audio—for example, vocal tracks (especially of yourself)—do not stand up to the rigors of time stretching as well as others. Here is how Time Stretching works:

▶ The **Mode** drop-down list is a sort of preset list that targets specific applications of the plug-in. There are a number of artifacts and problems that can crop up when you alter the duration of a file, so you should first match the type of file you are stretching with some close approximation from the list. Then preview the results and select a different item from the list that looks like it may address the problem.

▶ The **slider** graphically displays the stretching or shrinking. Unfortunately, it does not bear any relation to the actual length of the file in the real world. As you move the slider, a gray bar appears on the slider. The size of the gray bar represents the percentage of change.

▶ The amount of stretching can be measured as a **Percentage** of the original, by default.

▶ You can also specify a desired length of time for the final file by selecting **Time (hr.mn.sc.xxx)** from the Input format list. Then you need to enter the length of the file (which can be found by right-clicking the file in Windows Explorer and selecting Properties from the context menu and then clicking the Details tab) in the **Initial time** box and then type a time into the **Final Time** box or adjust it with the slider.

▶ Finally, you can change the tempo of the file as it might be detected by ACID by selecting **Tempo (bpm)**. Like the Time option, you'll need to enter both the **Initial tempo** (the default initial tempo is always 120 bpm) and the **Final tempo**. This option is ideal when you need to match the tempo of a project with a file that doesn't have beat information or when a file just isn't sounding right in a project. In most cases, ACID automatically takes care of these adjustments very well, but you might need to try some of Mode options with this plug-in if you are having problems.

The waveform of events on tracks that have been time stretched will no longer match up with the output from the track. You can mix the track down to a new track to see the effects (and free up processor cycles by not having to use the plug-in any more). You can also lengthen and shorten loops very quickly and easily using the Track Properties dialog box to modify the beats and change the length of an event, although the Time Stretch FX gives you more flexibility. See "Loops" in Chapter 10 for more information.

Track Compressor

See Compressor (Track).

Vibrato (XFX 3)

Vibrato is technique used by musicians and singers to modulate or oscillate the pitch of a note between the original note and a slightly lower tone. It is used to embellish and make a note more expressive. Incidentally, tremolo is a modulation based on a change in loudness (amplitude) while vibrato is a modulation of pitch. This is a nice, clean distinction between the two that is not widely made in the real world, but it should be. Vibrato is probably best used on individual tracks and not at the project level.

▶ The **Output gain** sets the volume of the processed effect.

▶ The **Semitones** fader sets the range or resolution of the graph which sets the possible range of the effect. It does not determine the actual range of the vibrato, however. As you drag the fader up and down, watch the labels at the top and bottom of the graph. After an envelope has been drawn on the graph, it does not change shape in relation to the graph, but its range changes as the Semitone fader is adjusted.

▶ The **Graph** is where you draw the curve of the vibrato over the period of time set with the Modulation freq. slider. Initially, the envelope line runs from 0 to 0 across the center and is hard to see. Click and drag the center line to add a node and reposition it. Nodes can be deleted by double-clicking them or by right-clicking them. Explore a few of the presets to get an idea of what the Graph is used for. Nodes dragged above the center line increase the pitch, and nodes dragged below the line decrease the pitch.

▶ The **Blend graph edges** option can be used if the start and end nodes on the graph do not line up.

▶ The **Modulation freq.** sets the rate or speed of the vibrato in cycles per second, or Hertz (Hz). See the discussion of rate and Hertz earlier in this chapter for a more detailed explanation.

Although it can be fairly time consuming to perform, you can add vibrato to individual notes in an event by using Vibrato as an Assignable FX, assign a track to the FX bus, and then use envelopes to isolate and apply vibrator to the note. Vibrato in the real world is often used to emphasize notes instead of being used constantly.

Calculating Rates

It is very useful to synchronize the Vibrato effect with the tempo and beat of a project. Vibrato is a faster-period effect that may occur on the beat or often multiple times on each beat. See the previous discussion on "Calculating Rates" in the "General FX Controls" section of this chapter for information about how to calculate and synchronize this effect with a project.

9
Loops

Up until this point, the word "loop" has been used in a very general way, referring to any audio file on your computer that is used in ACID. Loop originally meant a physical loop of audiotape that had the two ends spliced together to create an infinitely repeating audio clip. In much the same way, the archetypical loop file on a computer is a short file that will play back seamlessly end to end—and perhaps most commercial loop files are designed to work that way. But the definition has definitely expanded to include material that will not endlessly and seamlessly loop, and there are a large number of "loops" that don't actually loop.

Within the context of ACID, loops are more than they might seem at first glance. As you've probably noticed by now, an amazingly large variety of loops from many different genres sound pretty good together when mixed in ACID, straight out of the box. This isn't because the audio files were carefully recorded to match one another but instead is a result of background beatmatching and pitch adjustments. This chapter is going to reveal all of the many facets of loops, whether they come from Sonic Foundry, from other commercial loop libraries, or from your own creative talents.

Media Files

There are three broad types of media files that can be used in ACID: audio files, MIDI files, and video files. While all three might have an audio component to them, only audio files can truly be considered proper loops. MIDI files are not composed of actual audio data but instead contain instructions to tell your computer how to create notes. Video files may contain an audio track, and, while you can use only the video portion of one video track in a project at a time, the audio part of a movie file can be used just like any other audio file.

Track Types

Audio files themselves can be divided into three categories, according to the type of track they are inserted into in ACID. The different categories become apparent when media files are inserted into the timeline. Video media files are inserted into a single video track, MIDI files into MIDI tracks, and the more traditional audio media files are inserted into audio tracks. These audio tracks are further divided into Loop, One-Shot, and Beatmapped tracks. Each of these five types of tracks can be recognized with a glance at the track header, which contains an icon identifying the track type, as shown in Figure 9.1.

Figure 9.1
The five various types of tracks in ACID. Notice that the One-Shot track has the same name as the Video track—it is the audio track from the video file.

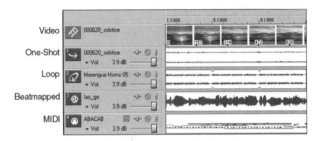

Audio Loops

MIDI and video files are obviously not proper loops and, therefore, will not be referred to as such in this book. As important media components of ACID, each has a chapter devoted to it later, but they will be ignored for now. Instead, the rest of this chapter is going to discuss audio files, which might all be called loops, whether they loop or not. The most popular format for audio files used as loops is the Windows *.wav file format. To Windows or another audio application, the *.wav files that go into an ACID project all look the same. That is to say, although ACID has three different types of audio tracks and thus three different kinds of audio loops, Windows sees these as all the same. The information that ACID uses to separate these types is proprietary to ACID.

ACID Loops

So what makes an ACID loop an ACID Loop? ACID loops are simply audio files available from Sonic Foundry that have had beat, pitch, and tempo information added to them. As mentioned previously, this information is useful only to ACID (and perhaps some other Sonic Foundry projects in the future). At this time, only loops from Sonic Foundry have this additional information, but this is not some carefully guarded secret. Anyone can create ACIDized loops. Information about a media file as it pertains to ACID can be found in the Explorer window and in the Track Properties window for files that have already been inserted into ACID, as shown in Figure 9.2. See the section later in this chapter about ACIDizing your own loops.

Do not construe this to mean that you cannot use other companies' loop files and libraries in ACID. Just about any audio file in any of a large number of popular formats can be used in ACID. These files will not have the beat, pitch, or tempo inherent in an ACID loop, so they will not automatically be adjusted by ACID to match the project—but they will certainly work as well as any other audio file. ACID will take its best guess about tempo and beat information and will very frequently get it right, but pitch information will not be detected. All of this information can be added by the user, as detailed later in this chapter.

Figure 9.2

ACID-related information about a media file (type, duration, tempo, sample rate, bit depth, channels, and compression) can be found in the Explorer window and in the Track Properties window for files that have already been inserted into ACID.

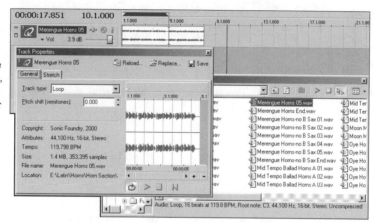

The type of track into which an audio file is inserted can be changed in the Track Properties window. To view the Track Properties window, from the View menu, select Track Properties or press Alt + 6 on your keyboard. To see a specific track's properties, click that track; the Track Properties window will immediately display that track's properties. The General tab in the Track Properties window has the Track type list, which displays and lets you change the type of track for that media file.

Loops

Now we get to the most specific and proper definition of a loop in ACID. Not only are loops audio files, they are audio files that are automatically inserted into a Loop track in ACID. Most, but not all, loops are fairly short, with durations measured in seconds and, much more rarely, tens of seconds. Loop tracks are identified by a loop icon in the track header and are designed to repeat, often seamlessly.

Loop tracks and the media files that they contain that come from Sonic Foundry have beat, pitch, tempo, and type information saved with the file. Any audio files below about thirty seconds in length will be inserted as loops into loop tracks, with ACID's best guess about the beats and tempo. Pitch information will not be included, although pitch is an important aspect of Loop tracks. This is because Loop tracks can be pitch shifted automatically or manually. The Stretch tab in the Track Properties dialog is used to control this information. While most loop files contain pitch information, this is not really necessary for loops that are not primarily tonal in nature, such as drum and percussion parts. Most percussion loops are inserted as loops into Loop tracks and can have pitch information added, but they do not have a root note selected on the Stretch tab.

CHAPTER 9

One of the most obvious aspects of a loop is the fact that it can loop over and over. This looping is displayed on the timeline with notches in the events that mark each repetition. When the Track type of a track is changed from Loop to something else, ACID no longer automatically repeats the media file in the event in a looping manner with notched events (see Figure 9.2).

For commercial loops from Sonic Foundry, a small bit of information is saved with the media file that tells ACID what type of loop the file is and, therefore, the Track type that should be used. For media files that do not have this information, ACID follows a few default rules:

▶ Files with a duration of less than 0.5 seconds will be inserted as One-Shots.

▶ Files with a duration of greater than 0.5 seconds but less than 30 seconds will be inserted as Loops.

▶ Files with a duration greater than 30 seconds will be inserted as Beatmapped.

To change this behavior, select Preferences from the Options menu and, on the Audio tab, change the Open files as loops if between (seconds) item.

One-Shots

One-Shots are non-looping files that are not intended to be looped repeatedly. A One-Shot might be a spoken word vocal performance, an instrumental solo, or a single snare drum beat, among other things. As you can see from the Track Properties window, One-Shots do not have a Stretch tab and are not adjusted to match the key of a project. This can be especially important with vocal performances that may sound bizarre if pitch shifted too much and for the audio part of a video file which may need the audio and video to be synchronized. One-Shot tracks do not change pitch or key as the project changes key. When you record a solo part into an ACID project that changes key with Key markers, you will obviously perform your part responding to the key changes. The performance is inserted into ACID as a One-Shot, so your original performance will change key as you played it, not according to the Key markers in the project.

Again, the type of track that the file is inserted into is not an inherent part of the Windows *.wav file format but is a part of ACID loop files. One-Shot tracks can be changed to Loop tracks by selecting Loop from the Track type list. This changes how the original media file is treated by ACID in the current project, but it does not alter the file on your hard disk. By changing the Track type to Loop, you can add pitch information to the track (by selecting a root note on the Stretch tab) so that a One-Shot can respond to changes in key in a project.

Finally, events in One-Shot tracks do not loop. To repeat a One-Shot over and over, you need to create multiple individual events, since each event in a One-Shot track contains only one occurrence of a media file. Changing the Track type between Loop and One-Shot does more than just change how events occur in a track—it will also alter whether tempo information is used. As you can see in Figure 9.1, when a One-Shot is inserted into a project, the tempo information is ignored and the media file plays back at the rate inherent in the media file. When the Track type is changed to Loop, the tempo information is used and the duration of the media file in the project is changed. In Figure 9.3, the top track is a Loop track and the file repeats three times in one event. The bottom track is the same file in a One-Shot track. The event, of the same duration, does not repeat and the portion after the media file ends is blank. You can also see that the single occurrence of the media file in the One-Shot track is considerably longer than a single repetition in the Loop track, meaning that the file is played back much more quickly. This can result in the file being distorted, although ACID will do its best to prevent this.

Figure 9.3
The same media file as inserted into a Loop track (top) and as inserted into a One-Shot track.

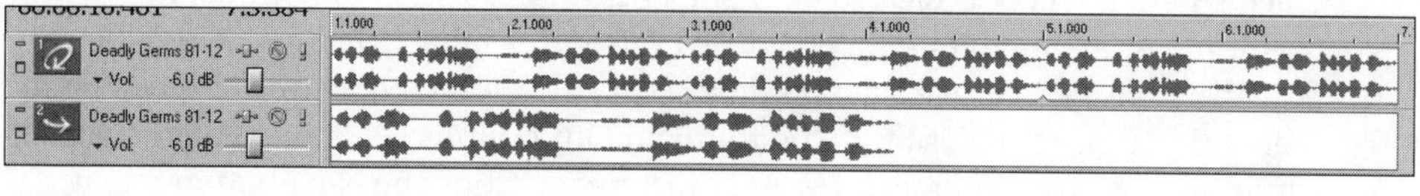

Beatmapped

Beatmapped tracks are designed to be used with much longer media files, perhaps tens of seconds or even minutes long. These files might be entire songs with beat and tempo characteristics. The word "Beatmapping" comes from the technique DJs use when mixing songs seamlessly together. To truly mix two songs together, they need to both be playing at the same tempo. Obviously, songs are recorded at many different tempos, so special turntables (and now CD players and software) are used that can have the playback speed adjusted on them. The DJ then monitors the mix through the headphones (the audience cannot hear this) and beatmatches the new song with the currently playing tune. Once this is done, a perfect transition can be performed by gradually fading one song out while fading the other in. Beatmatching during a live mix is not nearly as easy as it sounds and takes quite a bit of practice.

Beatmatching in ACID serves a similar purpose, but it is much easier. Entire songs inserted into ACID can be easily synchronized to a project's tempo and beat if they are Beatmapped. Most song-length media files are probably either *.mp3 files on your computer or perhaps media files that you have recorded for yourself, so you will have to do almost all Beatmapping when the media file is used in a project. When you insert a longer file into ACID, the Beatmapper dialog box opens to guide you through the process of Beatmapping the media file as it occurs in the project. To start the Beatmapper Wizard, insert a longer media file into an ACID project. By default, the Beatmapper Wizard starts automatically.

You can prevent this behavior by deselecting the Automatically start the Beatmapper Wizard for long files option in the first page of the Wizard's dialog. By default, files that are less than 30 seconds long are opened as loops. To change this behavior, from the Options menu, select Preferences and, on the Audio tab, change the Open files as loops if between (seconds) item. This is used to set a range, with files longer than the range being opened as Beatmapped and files shorter than the range (0.5 seconds) being opened as One-Shots (typically a single drum beat). Manually start the Beatmapper Wizard by clicking the Beatmapper Wizard button on the Stretch tab in the Track Properties window for Beatmap-type tracks. If a longer file is initially inserted into a One-Shot track, you will need to change it to a Beatmapped track to use the Beatmapper Wizard.

1. Begin by determining the first downbeat. A downbeat can be the "One" as you count through a song: One, two, three, four. ACID takes its best guess based on short, sharp peaks in the waveform, which usually indicate percussion parts. The first downbeat is labeled with a timeline cursor in the dialog tagged

CHAPTER 9

"Downbeat." Use the Play button to verify that this is the first downbeat and drag the Downbeat marker to change the position if it is not. The marker and cursor position should be aligned with the very beginning of the first beat. If the song fades in or has some type of introduction that makes it difficult to find the first downbeat, move the Downbeat marker further in on the song to the earliest place where the beat is clear. The first downbeat is used to determine the beginning of the media file in events, so this will trim all material before the first downbeat. You can move the first downbeat back to the beginning of the song in Step 3 if you need to. Use the Zoom In and Out buttons (+ and −) on the scroll bar to increase the accuracy of your adjustments. Click the Next button when finished. The first downbeat can also be adjusted in the Stretch tab of the Track Properties window.

2. Now set the tempo by guessing the length of a single measure. The loop region at the top of the dialog is ACID's estimate of one measure. Click the Play button to listen to the measure. The Metronome is very useful, and you should listen to see if it counts out the 1, 2, 3, 4 of the song. You can also use the waveform and metronome beat lines to see if the measure is lined up correctly. Dragging the left edge of the loop region moves the initial downbeat's location and lengthens the measure. Dragging the right edge of the loop region only lengthens the measure. As the measure is shortened or lengthened, the beats, which evenly divide the measure, also move. Click the Next button.

3. Now you can manually make any final adjustments, because the single measure in Step 2 is extrapolated to Beatmap the entire song. Initially, the single measure isolated in Step 2 is highlighted in the dialog box and continues to serve as a loop region. Use the Measure slider to move to and inspect other measures in the song. The beginning of each measure is marked with an orange marker, which can be dragged to correct errors. Dragging one marker repositions ALL markers in the song and cannot be used to compensate for variation in individual measures caused by tempo variations or beaks. The first downbeat in a measure is audibly indicated by a higher metronome beat. It is not practical or useful to check every single measure—use the slider to examine a few along the entire duration of the file. Click the Next button to move to the Finished step. Changing the position of the measure markers can also be done in the Stretch tab of the Track Properties window.

4. In the last page of the Wizard, you are presented with three options. Click the Finish button after you have selected the options you want to use.

    ▶ Changing the project tempo to match the Beatmapped track will automatically adjust the project's tempo after you click the Next button. This is a good idea if the Beatmapped media file is a major or important part of your project and prevents the file from being distorted by being stretched.

    ▶ The Preserve pitch of Beatmapped track when tempo changes is related to the previous item. When the project's tempo is different from the tempo of the Beatmapped file, or when the tempo changes, this item prevents the pitch of the file from changing.

▶   Select the Save Beatmapper information with file to add a small amount of data to the file and allow it to be used in other ACID projects. If this option is not selected, the media file will be Beatmapped only in the current project. The Save button in the Track Properties window does the same thing.

Outside the Beatmapper Wizard, the Beatmapping of a media file as it is inserted into a track can be adjusted in the Track Properties window on the Stretch tab (see Figure 9.4). The first downbeat and measure adjustments can be adjusted while the main project is being played back to align the media in the Beatmapped track with the project. Use a simple drumbeat to compare the project tempo and beat with the Beatmapped track since there is no metronome associated with this window.

Figure 9.4
The properties set up in the Beatmapper Wizard can be modified manually in the Track Properties window.

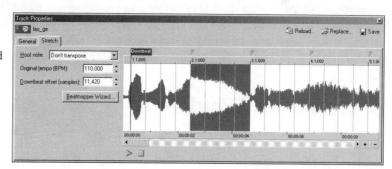

Using much longer media files in a project is a special use of ACID that must be carefully thought out. Perhaps the most obvious use for this is to create your own mix sets, using ACID to Beatmap and then mix together songs to form a continuous mix set. This is not what ACID is primarily designed to do, however. As an original, loop-based composition tool, the use of longer copyrighted material presents a problem;—if not a legal one, then at least an ethical one. When you buy a commercial loop library, you are also buying a license to use these loops in your own projects. When you sample your own loops from other artists' songs, you do not have the legal right to use this material in commercial productions. Sampling a beat or riff of short duration is usually not a problem, especially if you cite the original source, but the longer the sample, the bigger the problem. There is no set number (for example, "ten seconds is OK, but eleven seconds is too long"), and the determination of fair use may also be based on distinctiveness of the sound. Pragmatically speaking, no one is going to care whether you use copyrighted material until and unless you start to make money from it.

Another potential use for longer media files inserted into Beatmapped tracks is to use the file as a template for your own project. This is not a bad idea, especially when you are getting used to ideas of song structure and composition. Take a song you like, insert it into ACID, then mark out the structure of the song using markers (Intro, Verse 1, Refrain, Break, etc.), and use that as an outline for your own piece. There is nothing wrong with—and no shame in—copying the structure from a songwriter you respect.

CHAPTER 9

NOTE

Loop tracks (and media files) are loaded into your computer's active memory (random access memory, or RAM) from your hard disk drive when inserted into a project. One-shot and Beatmapped tracks are not. If you change a large (long) One-shot or Beatmapped track into a Loop track, it may take up significant amounts of RAM and can affect performance.

Finally, you may want to use Beatmapping when inserting longer original media files that you have recorded in your studio. Of course, this avoids all legal and ethical issues you might otherwise face, but it can also be less of an issue in ACID as well. If you want to use media that you have recorded in the distant past, long before you purchased ACID 3.0, you can Beatmap the file as previously outlined. Otherwise, all tracks that are recorded into ACID are automatically Beatmapped and saved with tempo information. These files are not saved with pitch information and, as with all Beatmapped tracks, will not change key as the project does.

Track Properties Window

As mentioned in the previous section, loop files from Sonic Foundry (or any audio files that have been ACIDized) have some information about pitch, beat, and tempo saved with the file that instruct ACID how to deal with it. This information becomes relevant when the loop is inserted into a track in an ACID project. This means that a loop's default properties are identical to those of the track into which it is inserted. While both the loop's properties and its associated track's properties can be changed independently, changes to a loop's properties are permanent and saved to the media file on your hard disk. Changes to a track's properties are saved only to the current project. Many of a loop's properties are displayed in the Explorer window in the Summary View area (click the View button to view/hide this feature) when a media file is selected (see Figure 9.1).

Modifying Existing Loops

The properties of a loop as it occurs in ACID are modified through the Track Properties window. To view a loop's properties once it has been inserted into a project (track), from the View menu, select Track Properties. Click on a track to change the focus of the program to that track and view its properties in the Track Properties window. While a track's properties are initially determined by the information saved with the media file, the track properties are still independent and can be changed. The track properties always supercede the loop's properties. The specific properties that are available depend on the track type, as previously discussed. MIDI and video files can also be inserted into tracks, but not into audio tracks. MIDI and video tracks are dealt with in their own chapters.

TIP

The Save button at the top of the Track Properties window saves any changes in a loop's properties to the media file on your computer. These properties are only informational in nature and do not change the characteristics of the media file. It is analogous to a caption on a picture. Press the Ctrl key on your keyboard while clicking the Save button to open the Save As dialog and create a new media file.

The top of the Track Properties window has three buttons. The Reload button copies the media file back into the project from your hard disk and allows you to discard any changes you have made to the loop's properties. You can think of this as a type of reset button. The second button is the Replace button. This is useful if you have created a track that has been carefully adjusted with audio FX and envelopes, but you'd like to change the particular media file that is being used. Click the Replace button and then browse for the new file that you want to use. This can be especially useful when you want to duplicate a key change sequence (pitch shifting events) with a different instrument. First, duplicate the track and then replace the media file associated with it. The last button is the Save button, which is used to save the loop's properties to the media file on your hard disk. This information does not alter any of the characteristics of the media file and is only information that can be read by ACID and is proprietary to Sonic Foundry. Information that can be saved to a file or be changed includes everything that can be altered in the Track Properties window. This information is saved in the header portion of a media file and not in any of the areas that contain actual audio data. See the section that follows on ACIDizing media files.

General Tab

The General tab in the Track Properties window serves a number of basic purposes: It sets the Track type, displays the loop's properties, and allows you to add media file level markers and regions (see Figure 9.5).

Figure 9.5
The General tab determines the Track type and has a timeline similar to the main timeline in ACID.

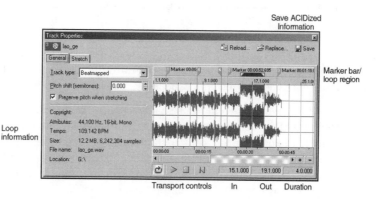

▶ **Track type**—This sets the type of the track for audio files: Loop, One-shot, or Beatmapped. Video tracks and MIDI tracks cannot be changed.

▶ **Pitch shift**—This sets the change in key or pitch of the entire track. You can adjust this parameter by pressing the + and − keys on the numeric keypad on your keyboard after first clicking on the track header of a track.

▶ **Preserve pitch when stretching** (Beatmapped only)—This tells ACID to make sure the pitch of a longer Beatmapped media file does not change when the project's tempo is different from the media file's tempo, which causes stretching. You must select this option in order to access the Pitch shift control in a Beatmapped track.

▶ **Summary of properties**—This displays some of the properties of the media file.

▶ **Transport controls**—These control the playback of the media file. The Loop button repeats the loop region over and over.

▶ **Mark In** (or cursor position), **Mark Out**, and **Duration** of selection area (loop region)—These are displayed below the timeline.

▶ **Timeline**—This is very similar to the timeline in the main program workspace. You can add markers and regions to a media file that will be saved with the file when you click the Save button at the top of the Track Properties window. See Chapter 3 for more information on using markers and regions in ACID.

Stretch Tab

This tab is used to control stretching or compressing in time to accommodate a project's tempo. One-Shot tracks and files are primarily used for media that should never be altered in duration; thus, the Track Properties window in this situation does not have this tab. There is a lot of information on this tab for Loop and Beatmapped tracks, however.

Root Note

The Root Note is the key of a loop. This property of a track can be changed on the Stretch tab in the Track Properties window of Loop and Beatmapped type tracks. The Root Note allows a track to be automatically pitch shifted to match a project or the key changes that occur in a project as a result of Key Change markers. Setting the Root Note to Don't Transpose prevents this from happening. Any time you want a loop to be protected from key changes, you should select Don't Transpose. You'll notice that most percussion and drum loops have Don't Transpose as a Root Note, as well as some vocal loops and, especially, spoken word loops.

Another place where you may want to use a Root Note of Don't Transpose is for your own recorded material, which is automatically inserted into a Beatmapped track. When you record parts into a song with key changes, your performance will musically change key to match the song. If this performance were then further modified by Key Change markers in ACID, this would result in the file not matching the original recording. This is why tracks that you record in ACID do not have key or pitch information saved with them.

Loop Properties–Stretch tab

The Stretch tab for loop-type tracks and files sets how ACID adjusts the loop when it is inserted into a project. It controls the tempo and where the beats fall. For loop files, ACID stretches and compresses smaller subdivisions in the file to force the beat to match the project. This means that the playback of a loop file may vary over time. Here is what you will find on this tab:

▶ **Number of beats**—This is based on how many beats are in the media file, which in turn is based the number of beats in a measure multiplied by the number of measures in the file. Most commercial loops are based on four beats in a measure, so most loops have 4, 8, 12, or 16 beats. This property is critical in determining how the loop matches the tempo of a project. Try changing the tempo on a melodic commercial loop that already has a Number of beats property. If the original Number of beats is 8 and you change it to 16, the loop will play back at half its normal speed in a project. Changing the Number of beats to 4 doubles its speed. While you usually want to leave the number of beats at its default value, there may be times where you can get a loop recorded in a different time signature (for example, 6/8) to fit in an ACID project that is in 4/4 (see Chapter 3 on Time Signature for more information). Doubling the speed by halving the Number of beats is also a great way of creating rolls back into a song after a break.

▶ **Stretching method**—This determines how the media file is stretched to fit the beat and tempo of a project. There are three different methods that can be used, and each is suited to a different purpose. When a track is distorted because of too much stretching or compression, experimentation by trying all three methods is a good way to solve the problem. The default method is **Looping segments** and is a good general purpose choice for most types of loops. **Nonlooping segments** is better for longer and smoother audio files such as pads and ambient background loops. **Pitch shift segments** allows the audio to be pitch shifted as it is stretched. This can prevent artificial sounding artifacts, echoes, and flanging-type noises associated with stretching, but the event may fall out of tune with the rest of the project.

▶ **Force divisions at**—The orange markers in the main timeline mark the beats in the media file. By setting divisions to various different values, you can fine tune how the beats in the file will be matched to the project. For example, set the divisions to Quarter notes and move the beat markers on the timeline to every beat in a 4/4 loop. By default, the beat markers are spaced equidistant. Of course, the beat in a project is evenly divided, so by changing the beat markers on a loop, you cause ACID to automatically stretch the segment of the loop between the two beats to match the project. Sixty-fourth notes give you the greatest degree of control.

▶ **Additional transient detection**—A transient is simply any peak in a waveform—in other words, a sound. ACID can detect these peaks to set the beat markers in a file. The number of beat markers set, and thus the number of transients detected, is determined by the Force divisions at item option. The higher the percent in this item, the greater the accuracy of ACID's beat detection.

CHAPTER 9

▶ **Transport controls**—These control playback and looping just as other ACID transport controls do.

▶ **Cursor position**, **Mark In**, and **Duration** of selection area (loop region)—These are displayed below the timeline.

▶ **Timeline**—The orange markers represent the beats or divisions as determined by the Force divisions at list option. Individual beat markers can be dragged to reposition them. Beat markers that have been repositioned are a lighter color. Right-click the marker bar and select Reset All to undo all of your changes.

The orange beat markers are very important in fine-tuning stretching in ACID (see Figure 9.6). ACID does not simply stretch a media file uniformly, but instead uses these beat markers as reference points and attempts to line these up with the beat of a project. Dark orange markers are the ones that have been detected and positioned by ACID; these have a broken vertical line on the timeline. Light orange markers are beat markers that have been manually added, either by the manufacturer or by the user; these have a solid vertical line on the timeline. Double-click the marker bar above the timeline in the Track Properties window Stretch tab to add another beat marker. You can also increase the number of beat markers added by ACID by increasing the Additional transient detection percentage. Existing markers can be disabled by double-clicking them. All of these changes can be saved by clicking the Save button at the top of the Track Properties window.

Figure 9.6
The Stretch tab of the Track Properties window for a loop file. Zoom in to get a better look at the orange beat (transient) markers.

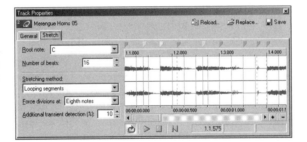

Beatmapped Properties – Stretch tab

The Stretch tab for Beatmapped tracks and files is basically a way to manually modify the characteristics that can be set using the Beatmapper Wizard (see Figure 9.4).

▶ **Original tempo**—This is the tempo of the loop as it was recorded or as you set it in the Beatmapper Wizard. Increasing this value will speed up the media file and decreasing this value will slow down the loop as it is used in a project. Notice that changing the tempo value also has the effect of changing the relative spacing of all of the measure markers on the timeline.

▶ **Downbeat offset**—This is a numerical representation of the position of the first Downbeat marker. The Downbeat marker can be dragged to reposition it or a number can be entered in this box.

▶ **Beatmapper Wizard** button—This starts the Beatmapper Wizard, as previously detailed.

► **Transport controls**—These control playback of the media file.

► **Timeline**—The orange markers divide measures in the loop. Dragging any of the measure markers will resize all of the measure divisions in the media file. This can have the effect of changing the speed of the file in a project, just as changing the Original tempo will. In fact, the tempo will change as you drag these markers, and vice versa. The Downbeat marker sets the first downbeat that is used to set where in a media file an event will start. Downbeat can be changed just like Step 3 of Beatmapper Wizard.

Creating Your Own Loops

There are literally hundreds of gigabytes of loops available in professional loop libraries from Sonic Foundry and other companies. The quality of these loops is typically very high and the variety is immense. Still, there is nothing better than creating your own loops. The source for these loops could be your own vocal or instrumental recordings (see Chapter 6), or you could use audio samples from just about any source. Some excellent sources are audio CDs, movies, television shows, or politicians from the nightly news. Beats, main instrumental refrains, and even solos can make for interesting source material. The samples can be radically split and mixed into completely new forms or distorted beyond recognition with audio effects plug-ins. Rap, hip-hop, and electronica have been major users of sampled material, and these are good places to start looking at the effective use of samples. Perhaps the most interesting result of using popular music for samples is that the new song has a very familiar feel to it, yet is completely different. This is often most surprising and interesting when the samples come from one genre (jazz or classical) and are then used in another (trip-hop or D&B). Remember the television game show, "Name That Tune?" You'd be surprised how short a sample you can use to create an instantly recognizable sample. Perhaps the most recognizable sample ever is a single "ha" from Mr. James Brown.

Legal and Ethical Issues

This book is not a legal tome and doesn't pretend to offer any advice on whether sampling loops from your CDs is legal or not. It is the author's opinion that sampled material of a short duration, say less than ten seconds, is probably OK to use without getting explicit permission from the artist. There is something called "fair use" that is pretty well defined for printed material, but it is less clear for audio. Fair use is used to describe how much material you can quote in printed material (with a citation, of course). For news stories and research, this is an important concept, but does fair use apply to fiction? Poetry? Is your work a parody? Parodies are completely legal, but you'll have to prove it is a parody first. You can see that the issue gets more complex when you talk about art. In music, fair use depends on a number of gray areas: uniqueness of the sample, originality of your piece, citation of work sampled, where your work will be used, fame of the sampled artist, and genre.

Is the sample uniquely a signature of the artist? You would be wise not to try to sell a commercial song using Intel's ubiquitous four tones, even though they last only a second. This is a branded and explicitly copyrighted sound and you'll have a cease-and-desist e-mail before your AMD CPU gets to its next clock cycle. Likewise, many products (for example, Dolby) and artists (Michael Jackson) have very distinctive trademarks (registered or not) that will invite trouble if used in your music. The concept of originality is another gray area. A song that is 50 percent a single sample is clearly not original, yet legislating a percentage, much less measuring and enforcing that percentage, is not feasible.

As with publishing an article, citation is important and is certainly ethical. Make sure you credit where your samples came from: artist, song, composer, and album. Credits and attributions can be in the liner notes of a CD, posted with the song on ACIDplanet, or saved in the header data area of the song in a few formats, such as *.mp3, *.rm, and *.wma. All three formats allow you to save extended information about a song with the file. In ACID, from the File menu, select Render As and choose one of these formats. Then, in the Render As dialog, click the Custom button. Click the Summary tab (*.rm and *.wma) or the ID3 tab (*.mp3) and enter in the Copyright or Comments tab any information you need to properly credit any samples used. Again, this is not a legal issue, but an ethical one. Simply crediting your sources will not protect you from any legal actions and is not the same as getting copyright permission.

Where your creation is used is also important. If you are producing music for a commercial use, the restrictions are certainly much, much higher—so high, in fact, that you probably cannot use sampled material at all in an advertisement. Of course, you can probably get away with this in a small market (and you have probably seen numerous violations of this on local TV), but that doesn't make it any more legal. If you are pressing a commercial CD, the standards are higher than if you are distributing on ACIDplanet (although the denizens of ACIDplanet take a dim view of unoriginal material). I might recommend that you attempt to contact the record company or artist and ask for permission. Most record companies can be reached via e-mail, and it might be a good idea to send them an e-mail. Unfortunately, while I suspect that most fellow musicians would be flattered that you are sampling a bit of their work and would appreciate you asking, record companies and whoever answers the artist's mail will probably automatically say no. There are a number of copyright clearance houses that can be easily found by performing a search on the Web, including **www.ascap.com** and **www.bmi.com**.

NOTE
While we'd all like to do the right thing, getting single-use copyright permission for popular songs is likely to run $500 at a minimum and double that in most situations.

Which brings us full-circle to how recognizable a sample is. The Material Girl is going to be much more tense about you using her material than a relatively unknown band in your area. How the sample is used is important, as well, since using a sample as a tribute to your favorite artist is going to be received quite differently from a parody or satire.

Genre is very important in this discussion as well. Some genres of music are more inclined to tolerate sampling (for example, hip hop) than others. Some types of music out-and-out rely on sampling, such as techno and most electronica forms. Interestingly, we cross into another gray area here between sampling and re-mixing. When are you sampling to create an original piece and when are you remixing a song? Again, there isn't much legal precedent here, but dropping a percussion loop on a Cincinnati Pops Orchestra performance and calling it your own is probably going to raise the ire of Erich Kunzel and the dozens of musicians who have spent a lifetime not getting rich on their art. Remixing as a performance is fine, just as covering a song in your band is fine. Remixing and selling a song definitely requires the original artist's permission, no question about it.

If you do receive a cease-and-desist order, you probably should. And if you work for Acme MegaCorp and your ad just appeared during the Super Bowl, you'd better call your lawyer. The heading for this section is "Legal and Ethical Issues": Just because you think you can get away with it without anyone noticing or suing you doesn't make it right. Finally, turnabout is fair play. When using samples from other artists, imagine that you have worked for years nurturing your talent and suffering for your art when, suddenly, the latest Top 40 tune selling millions of copies prominently features a riff from one of your songs. If that would make you angry, you'd better not use samples at all. While this whole discussion is very gray in legal terms, ethically and artistically, it is not. More information on you and your rights is covered in the chapter on publishing.

TIP

One excellent place to explore this issue more fully is on ACIDplanet (**www.acidplanet.com**) in the Community section. One warning: The use of sampled material from CDs is vehemently opposed by most ACIDplaneteers on ethical and, more importantly, artistic grounds. Don your asbestos suit and prepare for a flamin' if you disagree!

Recording and Editing Loops

Technically speaking, recording your own loops is not difficult and falls into three basic steps: acquiring the source material, editing the source into a loop, and ACIDizing the loop. Again, loop with a lowercase "L" is a general term used to describe audio files used in ACID to create songs. The material you sample may ultimately be used as One-Shots, Loops, or Beatmapped files. No matter how you acquire loop material, you will ultimately want to use ACID to edit them.

Acquiring Source Material

Source material can come from anything that can make a noise or produce an audio signal. Analog instruments or voices that you use a microphone to record can be saved to audio files on your computer using the techniques discussed in Chapter 6. A variation on this is any auxiliary analog source, such as a Walkman or VCR. Using the appropriate connector cables, you can output the audio from these sources into your sound card or I/O interface. Very likely, this will involve an eighth-inch to eighth-inch (male to male) connector for a Walkman or a stereo RCA Y cable from a VCR to one-eighth-inch jack to the sound card. In any case, analog into a sound card is the same as hooking up a microphone. Setting the gain on the input and getting a good quiet signal without any electronic hum is everything. You can record samples straight into a track in the project you are working on. Precise timing is not important, since you can edit later. See "Recording" in Chapter 6 for more information.

Acquiring material from a digital source is easier, since the levels are automatically adjusted. Digital sources might be IEEE-1394 sources such as DV camcorders, coaxial and optical digital connections, and, most commonly, CD-ROM drives in your computer. When sampling from a digital source, you may need to use special software that interfaces with your device, and that will not be dealt with here. Getting audio data from an audio CD also requires special software. Fortunately, the name of that software in this case is ACID:

1.   Insert an audio CD into your CD-ROM drive.

2.   From the Tools menu, select Extract Audio from CD.

3.   In the Extract Audio from CD dialog, select the CD-ROM drive that has the audio CD in it from the list (if you have multiple CD-ROM drives).

4.   Click on the CD track that you want to extract.

5.   Click the OK button.

Figure 9.7
Select multiple tracks to extract by holding the Ctrl key while clicking on CD tracks.

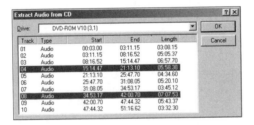

This will extract, or rip, the entire song from the CD to your hard disk drive in an uncompressed form and takes roughly ten to twenty seconds for every minute of audio, depending on the speed of your CD-ROM drive. The final file size will be about 10 MB per minute of audio. The file will be automatically named and saved to the ACID program's root directory. An additional file called a peak file (*.sfk) will also be saved in the same directory as the file. This is a small file that basically contains a picture of the waveform of the file to help ACID display the file more quickly on the timeline. You can delete this file if you want, but ACID will spend some small amount of time recreating it every time you use the media file in a project.

The new media file will be inserted automatically into a track in your project, and the Beatmapper Wizard will start (by default) to begin the process of ACIDizing the media file (see the section on Beatmapping earlier in this chapter). Obviously, fair use precludes using the entire media file in your project, but you can trim events using ACID to get what you want. Events can be trimmed directly on the timeline or by using the Chopper. The Chopper is probably more useful in this case, since you can create multiple regions, providing multiple separate samples from the same media file. Remember that ACID is a non-destructive editor and is not designed to edit source media files. You will not be able to save changes to any media files that are being used in the project. See the next section for more on editing media files using ACID.

Editing Sampled Material

Once you have recorded or extracted the raw source material, you will need to trim the file into a shorter sample and then ACIDize it. This can be done in any audio editing application (such as Sound Forge), but unless you have very special needs or just love working with your sound editor, it is recommended that you use ACID to create new loop files. The reason for this is that you can edit, ACIDize, and render new loop files all at once with ACID.

The basic techniques of using ACID to isolate short samples from a much longer piece are discussed in Chapter 2. Specifically, see the sections on editing and trimming, as well as the section on the Chopper window. Chapter 5 has more information on the Chopper window and how to use regions to isolate sections of a media file. Remember that you can easily copy, paste, and duplicate events on the timeline to use a loop repeatedly. All of this is completely non-destructive and does not alter the original media file. The downside to this is that the larger media file continues to take up space on your hard drive. The other problem is that edits made to events in a project will not be available to other projects, unless you render out. On the upside, you can isolate different loops from different parts of the file. But then again, on the downside, since these are not saved as separate media files, you cannot make the various adjustments to the looped sections or ACIDize them as detailed in the rest of this chapter.

If you have an external sound editing application, you can use it to edit the media file and thus save disk space on your computer (you can also use ACID—see the following paragraph). Right-click either the track that the media file is in, the Track Properties window, or the media file itself in the Explorer window and select Edit in ###, where ### is the name of your preferred sound editor. To specify a sound editor to appear on this menu (you can select up to three), from the Options menu, select Preferences and click the Editing tab. Then, Browse for the applications you want to use under the Editing application boxes. Once you have edited a file and saved it to a new name, the new media file will need to be inserted into the project to be used. Any changes to a loop file will automatically be updated into the project. This can result in some events not matching the media file or the project if the duration of the original media file was changed. Press F5 on your keyboard in ACID's Explorer window if you cannot see the new file. Even if you use an external editor to trim and adjust your loop files, in the end you need to use ACID to ACIDize your files with tempo and key information.

Using ACID as a Loop Editor

ACID is not technically designed as a media file trimmer or editing program, but it is an extremely capable and flexible media file editing environment nonetheless. In fact, you can even add ACID to your list of audio editors in the Preferences dialog. When you right-click a media file and select Edit in acid.exe, another copy of ACID is opened with the selected media file inserted into a track (the only reason to do this is to isolate the loop from a larger project, but this is usually more easily accomplished with the track Solo button). By creating an event, splitting it, trimming it, modifying it with effects, and then Rendering it, you can very effectively change the loop in a myriad of ways. Without opening another copy of ACID, you can also render out a single track by soloing it. Create a selection area (loop region) around the section that you want to use as a new loop file and render. You cannot, however, render a file with the same name. Remember, ACID is a non-destructive editor and you cannot create a file of the same name in the same location as any file used in your project. You must delete, rename, or overwrite the file manually in Windows Explorer. If you are editing a media file that is already in a mature project, with carefully placed events, finely tuned effects, and delicately curved envelopes, you can always replace the source media file for the track with the newly edited media file with a different name. Click the Reload button in the Track Properties window.

Loop Editing Techniques

Editing and trimming media files is basically not a difficult or complex task. It simply requires practice. Creating media files that loop seamlessly and naturally is more involved, and in this discussion "loop" means a formal loop that is intended to repeat over and over. One of the best ways to learn how to do this is to examine some simple drum tracks, where the waveform is clearly visible, and see how the media file is constructed. As you can see in Figure 9.8, you should start with first things first: Beat 1 should fall immediately at the beginning of the media file. Be careful not to cut anything off from Beat 1, but make sure it falls at the beginning. The end of the media file is not just after Beat 4 but is just before (but not including) Beat 1 of the next measure. When starting with longer source material, the initial track type is likely to be a One-Shot or Beatmapped track. In many ways, a One-Shot is simpler and less error prone, but a Beatmapped track gives you more control.

Figure 9.8
An event that reveals a few measures from a larger media file. This event will be used as the basis of the loop to be created.

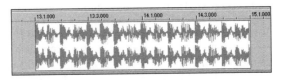

There really isn't much magic to doing this, with trial and error being the only real way to get it right. There are a few bits of advice that might help:

▶ Try out a number of slightly different trimmed files with different names to see which ones work best.

▶ Play with the tempo (see the next section) when ACIDizing a media file to get it to fit.

▶ Use ACID to edit an event based on the media file and then duplicate the event to see how it works as a loop. Then render a single occurrence of the event as a new loop.

▶ Watch out for pops and clicks that can sometimes occur at the edges of sharply edited media files. You can use your audio editor to smooth these out at the fraction of a second level. Again, using ACID and Quick fade audio event edges in the Preference dialog will allow you to prevent these sorts of problems if you render the new loop file with ACID.

Using ACID as your primary loop audio editor has significant advantages. While it isn't formally an audio editing environment, there is no reason why you shouldn't use ACID to trim loops. Trimming ACID events is a very simple process, and you can listen to the media file and future loop against the destination project. ACID can also be used to determine the all-important tempo of a loop. See the next section for the specific procedure.

ACIDizing Sampled Material

ACIDizing means adding that small bit of information to the header of an audio file that tells ACID the type of file (One-Shot, Loop, or Beatmapped) and the pitch, the tempo, and the beat of the file. There is also some other information that may be added—such as markers, regions, and copyright information—but these properties are all secondary to the main goal of creating effective loops. The information that is saved is displayed in the Explorer window and in the Track Properties window. Many characteristics of a loop can be changed in the Track Properties window (for example, root note) and saved to the media file by clicking the Save button at the top of the window.

TIP

By far the best and easiest way to create new loops and automatically ACIDize them is to solo a track and render a loop region (blue or gray bar at the top of the timeline) straight out of ACID to a new media file. Make sure the Render loop region only checkbox is selected in the Render As dialog.

ACIDizing with Beatmapping

No matter whether you want to create a Loop or a Beatmapped final media file, the Beatmapper Wizard is a good tool to use to determine tempo:

1. Insert it into a project and change the Track type to Beatmapped on the General tab in the Track Properties window.

2. Click the Beatmapper Wizard button on the Stretch tab in the Track Properties window.

3. Determine the Downbeat. This doesn't need to be the first downbeat in the media file, since you are creating a shorter loop file and not an entire Beatmapped file. It may even be easier to start the Downbeat at the beginning of the section that contains the loop you want. Then, when you draw an event on the timeline, the event will begin at the downbeat. Click Next.

4. Use the metronome to set the tempo as closely as possible to the media file's natural tempo. Drag the Downbeat marker to move the metronome beats more in line with the media file and adjust the length of a measure to adjust the tempo. The duration of the measure not only sets the tempo, but it is also probably going to be the basis of the loop. Click the Next button.

5. It is important to make sure the beats line up through the whole file. Since you need to determine the tempo for only a short loop section, this step is not as important here, however. Just make sure that the section you want to use as a loop is perfect. Click Next.

6. Select Change project tempo to match Beatmapped track or, from the main timeline, right-click the Track Header and select Use original tempo to set the project tempo to the tempo of the loop. This ensures that the new media loop rendered from the project will not be significantly distorted and will be of a higher quality. You don't need to save the Beatmapped information with the file, since the final goal is to create a new loop file.

7.   Create an event that spans the duration of the loop you want to create.

8.   Test the looping of the event by duplicating it (Ctrl + drag) and repeating it on the timeline. Listen to it and see if it works. Insert a simple drum part and see how it matches the beat. Go back to the Track Properties window and adjust the Downbeat and measure size.

9.   Solo the track, create a loop region around the area that you want to create a loop from, and render the new loop file. In the Render As dialog, make sure the Render loop region only is selected.

10. The new loop file will be saved to your hard disk with the name you have selected. Remember to press F5 in ACID's Explorer window to refresh the window and see any new files. The newly rendered loop will have a tempo that is equal to the project's tempo in beats per minute and will automatically be a loop track if it is between the default durations of 0.5 seconds and 30 seconds. The Number of beats on the Stretch tab will be four times the number of measures of the loop region in the project (four beats per measure). The root note will be the project's default key, but this will have no bearing on the actual key of the media file itself.

In Step 8, you can make many final adjustments to the tempo and downbeat. Moving the Downbeat marker around in the Track Properties dialog will reposition the entire media file in the event and will help you set up the loop to begin on Beat 1. You can also adjust the tempo either manually or by dragging the orange measure markers, using a simple drum track as the metronome. Make sure that after you adjust the tempo, you again right-click the Track Header and select Use original tempo to set the project tempo to the new tempo of the loop.

As long as the project tempo is the same as the tempo assigned to the media file, there is no loss of quality. It doesn't matter if you guess at the tempo in the Beatmapper Wizard or Track Properties window; as long as the project and media files assigned tempo are the same, the file will not be stretched.

ACIDizing with One-Shots

Between all of the tempo changes and then matching the project tempo and adjusting the downbeat, the previous procedure can get frustrating when used on media files that do not have a very constant tempo or a distinctive beat. Another way to set the tempo is by changing the track to a One-Shot. In many ways, this is easier and less prone to error, since One-Shot tracks are always played back without distortion. Recall that One-Shot tracks do not have tempo or beat information, so they always play back at their default speed. By placing a simple drum beat in another track and then adjusting the tempo of the entire project, you can perhaps more easily figure out the tempo of a media file. And since the eventual goal is to create a short loop file from the original, it doesn't matter that no beat information is saved with the original. Press F8 on your keyboard to turn snapping off while dragging the event back and forth to line up the beats in the media file with the drum beat.

TIP

Slip trimming may be useful here. This is done by holding down the Alt key while dragging the middle of an event. This slides the media around inside the event without moving the event itself.

Finally, when the beats are synchronized between the media file and the drum track, mute the drum track (or solo the track with the loop material) and render the new loop file, making sure that Render loop region only is selected. Figure 9.9 shows a long One-Shot that has been carefully lined up to match the simple beat in the track below it. The tempo of the project was carefully adjusted to match the One-Shot by listening to the beat in the other track, which changed tempo with the project while the One-Shot did not. Notice also that the event does not need to be trimmed since the loop region is going to determine the material that will be rendered to the new media file.

In summary, when creating new looped media files using One-Shots, the technique is to modify the tempo of the entire project to match the tempo of the original media file and then Render the loop, which will automatically be ACIDized based on the project.

Figure 9.9
Determining the tempo of a One-Shot by altering the project tempo and comparing it to the media file. The simple drum loop acts as a metronome.

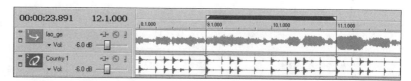

Once you have determined the tempo, you may want to change the track back to a Beatmapped track armed with this new tempo knowledge, which you can add to the Stretch tab in the Track Properties window. Click the Save button in that window to save the tempo information with the file.

Tempo, Beats, and Loops

Technically, Loop tracks do not have a tempo adjustment, but the Number of beats item on the Stretch tab in the Track Properties window can control the speed of playback in a rough way. Loop media files are recorded at a set tempo, however, and, as with other ACIDized media files, this information is saved with the file. The Save button in the Track Properties window does not save Number of beats or tempo information for loop files.

Tempo information in a file needs to be saved in a different way for loops. Since the Track Properties window for Loop tracks does not have a tempo item, there is no way to change a loop's tempo. Changing the Track type to Beatmapped, changing the tempo, and clicking the Save button will save the tempo information, but only as long as the media file is used in a Beatmapped track. As soon as you change the Track type to Loop, the original tempo of the loop will be used. This can allow you to have two separate tempos associated with a media file, one for Beatmapped and one for Loop.

CHAPTER 9

Loop tempo is saved only with a newly rendered file, where the tempo is determined by the project tempo. If you want to change the default tempo in the media file, you will need to render the loop to a new media file from a project with the tempo you want to use.

As previously mentioned, the Number of beats item can adjust the tempo of a loop in an indirect and rough way. The default number of beats is saved to the media file of a loop when the loop is rendered out of ACID. It is simply the number of measures times four. In a project with a tempo of 150 bpm, a loop that is created from a loop region of four measures will have a Number of beats entry of 16. If you change this to 8, ACID will play the file as if it had only eight beats and it will play back at twice the rate. If you used this media file in a project that had a tempo of 75 bpm (half of the original tempo) and you changed the Number of beats to 8 (playback at twice the speed), it would play back at the rate it was created.

Figure 9.10 shows the same media file used in three different tracks. Track 1 uses the default Number of beats (8) for a two-measure loop file. In the duplicated Track 2 (right-click the track header and select Duplicate track), the Number of beats was changed to 4. One occurrence of the loop now occupies only one measure and the file plays back twice as fast. Track 3 is another duplicate of Track 1, but the Number of beats is 16 in this case.

Figure 9.10
The same media file is
used in all three tracks,
with the Number of
beats in the Track
Properties window
being the only
difference.

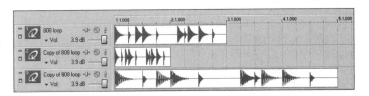

There is one special use for the Number of beats item, and that is in matching media files recorded in differing time signatures. While most commercial loop files are recorded in 4/4—that is, four beats in every measure (4/1) with a quarter note (1/4) getting a single beat—some loops are recorded in different time signatures. If you ever find the perfect loop, but find that it is recorded in 6/8, you may be able to force it to fit by changing the Number of beats. For example, in the loop 6-8_Cowbell.wav, the default Number of beats is 8. In a project composed of mostly 4/4 media files, the cowbell will not fall on the beat. If you change the Number of beats to 6 in the cowbell track, the beat will align with a 4/4 project. This will squeeze the media file and cause some distortion, but it may not be audible. Figure 9.11 shows this more clearly.

Figure 9.11
The top track contains a 4/4 reference file, with a drum hit on every beat. Tracks 2 and 3 are the same media file, with different Number of beats properties.

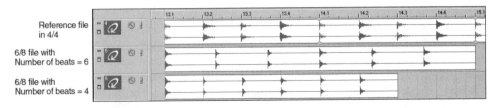

Determining Key

There is no easy way to determine the key of a media file. If you performed it yourself, you may already know the key. If you used a piece of sheet music, it is possible to figure out the key from the key signature. Guitar is one of the more natural instruments to use to identify key, since the chords played on the guitar are expressed in keys. Keep in mind that longer media files and recorded materials frequently have a number of key changes, which makes for interesting listening, but it defeats the purpose of setting a key for a media file. In this case, you'd want to make sure the media file is inserted into a One-Shot track or that the root note on the Stretch tab in the Track Properties window of Loop or Beatmapped tracks is set to Don't transpose.

The purpose of setting the key of a loop or Beatmapped file is so ACID can automatically pitch shift the track to fit the project key or follow project key changes (see Chapter 4). This is a very convenient feature, but it depends on accurate determination of the key as saved to a media file.

NOTE

As with tempo information in ACIDized media files, key information is extra user-entered data and is not determined in any way by the inherent audio aspects of the file, which cannot be automatically detected by ACID. A file that was recorded from a microphone of you playing the guitar at 100 bpm in the key of G can be ACIDized at 160 bpm in the key of D#. This is likely to result in the file being incorporated incorrectly into ACID projects.

If you don't know the key of a performance or a sampled media file, and you are sure it is short and doesn't contain any key changes, there are at least two ways you can determine the key of a loop with minimal trial-and-error stumbling. Keep in mind that while the root note of a loop and the key of the loop are equivalent concepts, the root note does not need to be used in the loop. You could write an entire symphony in the key of D and never play the actual note D at any time.

The first way to determine the key requires an ear that is not tone deaf and an instrument that can play a clean tone. An electronic instrument is best, since these are already in tune. Then determine the key of the loop by playing a note on the instrument while the media file is playing back and taking a guess at the key. This isn't hard, but it does require some practice. Unfortunately, there aren't any magic secrets to getting it right.

The other way is to find a few simple loops with clear tonal qualities that have key information saved with them. Simple solo parts without complex harmonies work best. Insert an ACIDized loop—most likely a loop from Sonic Foundry—into a project. Change the project's key to be the same as the media file's key. The media file's key can be seen in the Summary region at the bottom of the Explorer window or as the root note in the Track Properties window. The number after the key (for example, A3) should represent the octave of the note—but it always seems to be either octave 3 or 4 in ACID—from the lowest sub-bass to the highest piccolo. Figure 9.12 shows the various octaves. (A3 might be called A4 if the first octave is numbered Octave 1, as it sometimes is numbered.)

CHAPTER 9

Figure 9.12
Octave numbers on a
standard keyboard.

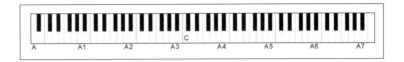

After changing the project to match the reference media file, insert the file that you want to
determine the key of into the project and create an event. Create a loop region and play back the
project continuously over the section of the event you want to use as a loop. Now adjust the
pitch of the reference event or track up and down using the + and − arrows on the numeric
keypad. You will not have to move more than eleven semitones up or down. When the tones
match, you have determined the key. This requires a pretty good ear, and there may be a number
of harmonies that don't match exactly but still sound quite good. Once you have matched the
key, add or subtract the number of half-steps (semitones) from the project key to calculate the
actual key. For example, if the project is in A and you need to pitch shift the reference loop +5,
then the key of the unknown loop is D. Use the project key pop-up menu to visually count this
out if you need to. You could change the project to this key and then render the loop to save the
key information to the media file, but, unlike tempo changes, saving key information to a loop is
simply a matter of changing the root note and then clicking the Save button at the top of the
Track Properties window. The octave is always 3, as in A3, with user-created loops.

Loop Limitations

All of this automatic pitch shifting and tempo adjusting by ACID is transparent to most users, as
it should be. You don't really need to be thinking about these things when you are in a creative
groove. But there are powerful calculations going on to make sure that as the tempo of a project
speeds up and the various loops keep up with the beat, the loops don't end up sounding like a
chipmunk band. This process of changing the tempo without changing the pitch is the key
technology that makes ACID work. Likewise, you can change the pitch or key of a loop without
changing the tempo.

Limiting the Limitations

As the heading to this section suggests, this magic has some real-world limits. All pitch and
tempo changes beyond the original key and tempo of an audio file results in some distortion to
the audio. There is no question about this. For small changes and in most typical ACID projects,
this distortion is completely inaudible. At some point, however, the effects of changing the
tempo without changing the pitch become noticeable. Beyond this point, the damage becomes
intolerable. In the end, it is a subjective call as to what is unacceptable, but there are some
general guidelines.

▶ ACID has a hard limit of +/−24 semitones (half steps) for pitch shifting. This is
   a four-octave range, which is about the range of the very best singers in the
   world. Since you can use a pitch shift in a project, track, and event, and these
   changes are all additive, technically you can pitch shift in a range of more than
   eight octaves, but only your dog will care about this ability.

▶ ACID projects are limited to a tempo range from 70 bpm to 200 bpm by default. Again, this is a huge range, suitable for most music genres. To change this to an even greater range (or more limited), from the Options menu, select Preferences. Then, on the Editing tab, change the Project tempo range.

▶ The type of music or audio is important. Vocals and the human voice are especially good at revealing distortion caused by stretching or pitch shifting. Clear and simple solo instruments without complex harmonics (for example, a flute) also do not tolerate large changes in tempo while ACID tries to maintain the pitch.

What does this distortion sound like? Distortions from pitch shifting are the most obvious and the least likely to be troublesome since you usually start getting an artificial sound from the pitch shift itself (such as "chipmunk" sounds) before the distortions from maintaining the tempo become obvious. More commonly, adjusting the tempo without causing pitch shifting must be approached more cautiously. The effect can range from simply sounding a little false to stuttering to strange echoes and flanging effects.

On the Other Hand…

…chipmunks are kind of fun. In most normal situations, you will not want to change the pitch and the tempo at the same time, but this is what would happen if ACID did not compensate for one or the other during processing. By disabling these features, you can transform loops or especially Beatmapped files into cartoonish songs performed by chipmunks. This is good for about a ten-minute diversion when you could be spending valuable time watching television instead. Insert a song recorded from a CD or a Beatmapped file into a track. If the file has not already been Beatmapped, you can quickly run through the Beatmapper Wizard to get a rough tempo, although, since the Wizard is usually used to prevent the pitch shifting, it isn't particularly important to get this 100 percent correct. In the Track Properties window, change the tempo to one-half (1/2) of the original tempo and play the track.

More Loops!

There are literally dozens of places where you can get more media files to use as loops. The rest of this chapter is devoted to various sources for more loops, both commercial loops for sale and loops available for free on the Web. In all cases, you need to carefully read the license agreements to determine if you can use the loops legally in your own projects. In almost all cases, when you purchase loops from a loop library, you are also purchasing the rights to use these loops as well. This is often described as royalty-free, which means you can use them without paying additional royalties. It may be more difficult to assess the licensing and royalty situation of loops that are available for download from the Web.

Get Media from the Web

You can browse for new loops for free right from within ACID. From the File menu, select Get Media from the Web (you must be connected to the Internet for this to work). ACID will first contact a Sonic Foundry server to search for providers and update the server information. Then the server will check for your registration information. If you chose not to provide contact information, you will be required to re-register. From Sonic Foundry's standpoint, Get Media from the Web is a value-added feature to ACID and a marketing tool to gather user information. There is nothing inherently evil about this, and Sonic Foundry very clearly and ethically states its privacy policy up front. You can elect to not be contacted by Sonic Foundry or anyone else and maintain your privacy, but you will need to enter contact information to use this service. And, boy, is it worth it. At last visit, there was well over 50 MB of free stuff, including MIDI DLS files (see the following MIDI chapter). So register and get ready to get some great loops that will certainly tempt you to buy a new library or two.

The window that opens with the "Members Only" Get Media site operates like any Web browser, except that it is organized to make downloads easier. Click on the various links to select the files you want to download, then click the Start button at the bottom of the page to retrieve all of the files on your list. These files will be downloaded and automatically extracted into the folder you selected on your local computer.

NOTE
While you are downloading using the Get Media feature, you will not be able to use that instance of ACID. To use ACID while downloading, you will need to run another instance of the program.

Browsing the Web

Although none of the sources presented here is guaranteed, and inclusion on this list does not imply an endorsement, at the time of this writing, the sites mentioned here were well maintained and appeared to offer high-quality loops. This is not a comprehensive list of loop sources but only a handful of places to get you started. Like any "favorites" list on the Internet, it is of only limited temporary value and you should try typing something like "loop sample audio library" into your favorite search engine to find more.

www.acidplanet.com/
www.apocalypse-sound.com/
www.crosswinds.net/%7Emcmu/mc.htm
www.digimpro.com/
www.djsamples.com/home/home.cfm
www.e-drummer.net/
www.flashkit.com/loops/index.shtml
www.fruityloops.com/
www.groundloops.com/
www.looperman.com/
www.modarchive.com/waveworld/
www.pocketfuel.com/
www.samplesearch.net/?top50
www.samplecity.net/
www.wavesamples.cjb.net/

10

The Secret Life of ACID MIDI

The addition of MIDI capabilities to the 3.0 version of an already formidable multimedia application is amazing. In typical Sonic Foundry style, the execution of this feature is solid and uncompromising. While ACID is not a tool to edit or create MIDI files and does not have the depth of tools that a dedicated MIDI editing application might have, the new MIDI features expand ACID's creative potential dramatically. In addition to the ability to include MIDI songs in your project, ACID 3.0 lets you change the instrumentation and perform other simple modifications as well as record your own MIDI tracks straight into the timeline. The surprising thing about all of this, especially considering the complexity of MIDI, is that the simplicity of ACID remains.

MIDI

MIDI stands for Music Instrument Digital Interface. It is a relatively simple and universal computer communication standard that allows synthesizers, sequencers, drum machines, electronic instruments, controllers, and computers to talk to one another. MIDI data is not audio data that can be used to create noise out of a speaker, unlike *.wav or other media files with audio data. Instead, it is a set of instructions that tell a MIDI instrument how to play. In the case of your computer, your sound card may act as a MIDI instrument or device. While MIDI is a fairly simple standard, the huge variety of devices and possible configurations can rapidly lead to confusion.

It is very important to understand the distinction between a MIDI device that creates sound out of your speakers and the actual source of the MIDI data itself. One of the easiest ways to identify this difference is to look at the size of a MIDI file versus the size of an audio file. Thirty seconds of MIDI data is only a very small fraction of the size of thirty seconds of audio data, no matter how highly compressed it is.

A simple example of a MIDI device is a MIDI keyboard plugged into your computer. The simplest MIDI keyboard is only a "dummy" device that outputs MIDI data such as the note played and how long the key is pressed. The keyboard does not actually make any music by itself, but sends this MIDI data to the sound card, where it is interpreted and then output to your speakers. Ultimately, the quality of the sound depends on the quality of the device that interprets the MIDI data and not on the device that generated it. Some keyboards do make sounds by themselves without being plugged into your computer. These synthesizers and pianos may be thought of as two MIDI devices in one: one to generate the MIDI data and one to interpret this data and output sounds. Many times, these devices will have two or more outputs, one or more for MIDI data and one for audio out. The sound that comes straight out of the keyboard into an amplifier will sound very different from the MIDI data as interpreted by your sound card.

In ACID, "MIDI" means MIDI data and not the sound produced by your MIDI instrument. If you have a high-quality keyboard with excellent audio output, you may want to record the audio signal into ACID, just as you would record any audio source (see Chapter 6). MIDI files, MIDI tracks, and recording MIDI data in ACID are MIDI data issues.

MIDI Standard

The first version of the MIDI standard was released in 1983 as a way to ensure that all electronic instruments (and now home computers) would speak the same language. While the protocol has been modified and extended a number of times in the intervening years, the basics remain the same.

MIDI Data

The stream of MIDI data from a MIDI keyboard or a MIDI file being played back in ACID contains information about the music to be produced by the MIDI playback device (your sound card synthesizer). For a single note, this information includes (among other things) the key of the note; how long it is played (duration); the instrument used (voice, patch); how hard the note is played (velocity); whether it is sustained with a sustain pedal; how it fades after the note is released; modulation; volume; and panning. As one example of MIDI data, the key or pitch of a note can be expressed as a numerical value from 000-127. This gives MIDI a total range of 128 semitones, or half-steps, which is considerably more than a standard 88-key piano keyboard. Figure 10.1 shows this range against a piano keyboard. The frequency of the sound is marked in Hertz (Hz) along the top of the diagram.

Figure 10.1
The total range of possible MIDI notes extends well beyond a standard keyboard and well below the threshold of human hearing.

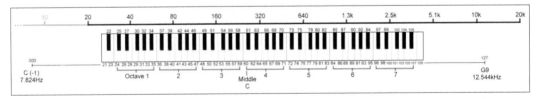

General MIDI

There are 128 instrument sounds (patches) in the MIDI standard. General MIDI (GM) specifies how that basic repertoire of 128 sounds is assigned to the various patch numbers. These may be numbered 1-128 or 0-127. These sounds can be broken up into sixteen family groups.

Table 10.1

General MIDI patch number assignments.

Program number	Instrument sound	Program number	Instrument sound	Program number	Instrument sound	Program number	Instrument sound
Piano		**Bass**		**Reed**		**Synth FX**	
1	Piano	33	Acoustic	65	Soprano Sax	97	Rain
2	Bright Piano	34	Fingered	66	Alto Sax	98	Soundtrack
3	Grand Piano	35	Picked	67	Tenor Sax	99	Crystal
4	Honky Tonk	36	Fretless	68	Baritone Sax	100	Atmosphere
5	Electric 1	37	Slap 1	69	Oboe	101	Brightness
6	Electric 2	38	Slap 2	70	English Horn	102	Goblins
7	Harpsichord	39	Synth Bass 1	71	Bassoon	103	Echoes
8	Clavichord	40	Synth Bass 2	72	Clarinet	104	Sci-Fi
Melodic Percussion		**Strings**		**Pipe**		**Ethnic**	
9	Celesta	41	Violin	73	Piccolo	105	Sitar
10	Glockenspiel	42	Viola	74	Flute	106	Banjo
11	Music Box	43	Cello	75	Recorder	107	Shamisen
12	Vibraphone	44	Contrabass	76	Pan Flute	108	Koto
13	Marimba	45	Tremolo Strings	77	Blown Bottle	109	Kalimba
14	Xylophone	46	Pizzicato	78	Shakuhachi	110	Bagpipe
15	Tubular Bells		Strings	79	Whistle	111	Fiddle
16	Dulcimer	47	Harp	80	Ocarina	112	Shenai
Organ		48	Timpani	**Synth Lead**		**Percussive**	
17	Drawbar			81	Square Wave	113	Tinker Bell
18	Percussive	**Ensemble**		82	Sawtooth Wave	114	Agogo
19	Rock	49	Strings	83	Calliope	115	Steel Drums
20	Church	50	Slow Strings	84	Chiff	116	Woodblock
21	Reed	51	Synth Strings 1	85	Charang	117	Taiko
22	Accordion	52	Synth Strings 2	86	Solo Vox	118	Melodic Toms
23	Harmonica	53	Choir Aahs	87	Fifths	119	Synth Drums
24	Tango Accordion	54	Voice Oohs		(sawtooth)	120	Reverse Cymbal
		55	Synth Vox	88	Bass + Lead		
		56	Orchestral Hit				
Guitar		**Brass**		**Pads**		**FX**	
25	Nylon	57	Trumpet	89	New Age	121	Guitar Fret
26	Steel	58	Trombone	90	Warm	122	Breathe
27	Jazz	59	Tuba	91	Polysynth	123	Seashore
28	Electric	60	Muted Trumpet	92	Choir (Vox)	124	Bird Tweet
29	Muted Electric	61	French Horns	93	Bowed Glass	125	Telephone
30	Overdriven	62	Brass	94	Metallic	126	Helicopter
31	Distorted	63	Synth Brass 1	95	Halo	127	Applause
32	Harmonic	64	Synth Brass 2	96	Sweep	128	Gunshot

The General MIDI standard was created so that generic Standard MIDI Files created on a sequencer or notation application may be played back on another device while preserving the integrity of the original selection. Another part of this standard is a separate set of percussion instrument sounds, usually assigned to Channel 10. This is a special instrument (patch), since each note on the keyboard may be assigned to a different instrument (for example, C= snare, D = woodblock, E = cymbal).

Different companies have expanded on the basic GM standard over the years—for example, Roland uses what it calls GS (General Standard) and Yamaha uses XG—but all basically function the same way and are largely compatible. All of these standards specify only how the instruments are organized and do not have anything to do with the quality of the sound or the type of sound synthesis.

MIDI Synthesis

The most important issue in sound card quality as it relates to MIDI is synthesis of the data into sound. Up until this point, the quality of your sound card has not mattered very much when working with ACID. Beyond a certain basic level, all sound cards play back and output audio files with fairly high fidelity. Of course, there may be important differences in the quality of the card itself, such as whether it outputs analog or digital signals and how electronically "quiet" it is, but essentially all cards play back media files the same way. Even consumer-level hardware outputs very high-quality sound. MIDI is a different story.

FM Synthesis

The quality of your sound card's MIDI is very important if you use it to synthesize MIDI data, as most people do. At the lowest quality levels, MIDI data can be interpreted by the FM synthesizer on your sound card. This device will probably sound a bit like a video game. Unless you are going for a Casio sound as Trio famously did with "Da Da Da" back in the early Eighties—or you want only artificial electronic-sounding instruments (perfect for techno or other electronica genres)—FM synthesis is limited. Most sound cards come with some sort of hardware-based FM synthesizer that may even be the default MIDI playback device. Since this is usually on the sound card itself, your computer does not need to process any information when playing back MIDI files, it only needs to send the MIDI data to the sound card. This frees up your CPU for more important tasks and is a real advantage. Many games use the hardware FM synthesizer on your sound card for just this reason.

Wavetable Synthesis

A step up in quality from FM synthesis is wavetable synthesis, which interprets MIDI data and then plays back this data using actual samples (not unlike *.wav files) from real instruments. This is a huge improvement over a basic FM synthesizer and may be all you ever need. Keep in mind that the quality of the sound from wavetable synthesis depends on the quality of the samples, so wavetable is not a magic way to get perfect MIDI. On a sub-$100 sound card, it is unlikely that the samples are going to be of the highest quality. On the high end, for example, professional-level electronic pianos often have extremely high-quality samples from real instruments that most of us would not be allowed to touch in real life.

Wavetable synthesis on a sound card is sometimes hardware based. This means that the MIDI instructions are sent to the card and played back and mixed on the card, which is where the instrument samples (wavetable) are stored. Generally speaking, this is good, since this means that the samples that make up the wavetable do not take up any memory (RAM) on your computer. Many popular sound cards load the wavetable into RAM, which can impede your computer's performance. Some sound cards allow you to replace the samples on the wavetable with other samples, either of your own creation or as created by professionals. Examples of this are Creative Labs and Ensoniq SoundFonts and the more general DLS (DownLoadable Sounds) standard.

Wavetable samples are similar to ACID loops and fall very near one another on a musical continuum. Samples typically used for MIDI applications are shorter in duration than most ACID loops and are most frequently only a single note. With the right software—say, Sound Forge and Creative Labs Vienna—you can edit *.wav files to be used as loops in ACID from SoundFont samples or convert ACID loops into SoundFont samples.

Software Synthesis

So far, the discussion of synthesis has focused on your sound card and what it can do in terms of MIDI. In the past, sound cards have been a critical part of the MIDI equation since computer memory (RAM) and CPU speed were at a premium and needed to be optimized. It was very important for the sound card to take care of as much of the MIDI processing as it could to free up the rest of your computer for other tasks. While we'd all like to maximize our computer's performance, it is not as important to free up RAM or CPU cycles anymore. Modern multimedia machines in the 21st century are quite powerful and are loaded with RAM. This has led to the possibility of using a software synthesizer to interpret MIDI data. As with any software on your computer, software synths get loaded into RAM and use your CPU to generate music. Perhaps surprisingly, many of the most popular sound cards with wavetable synthesis actually load the wavetable samples into RAM anyhow, although the actual wavetable synthesizer is on the sound card itself. The great advantage to this is that you do not need to be limited to your sound card's hardware. Most sound cards also come with some sort of software synthesizer. If you have a decent sound card but are unhappy with the MIDI playback, you might consider purchasing a good software MIDI synthesizer instead of buying new hardware. See the next section on the limitations of using a software synth with ACID.

A huge variety of software-based synthesizers are available, including software emulation of FM synthesis, ancient tube organs, classic arena rock synthesizers, some of the best modern synthesizers from famous manufacturers, and wavetable synthesis. Microsoft has a DirectX SoftSynth included with DirectX7 that is easily and extensively used in Windows applications, including ACID; it is optimized to use as few resources as possible. Ultimately, this SoftSynth uses your sound card to produce the actual sound.

Configuring MIDI in ACID

As mentioned, the quality of the MIDI output from ACID does not depend on ACID but on your sound card. Configuring ACID to use the correct MIDI device can be a complicated task. Since wavetable synthesis is often the highest-quality synthesis on a sound card, getting ACID to output wavetable samples properly is important. Unfortunately, wavetable synthesizers often use some of the same circuitry that the sound card needs to play back regular media files, and this can cause conflict. This section is going to discuss how to configure ACID MIDI tracks to get the highest quality and talks about some workarounds for a few potential problems.

Preferences

To begin configuring ACID for MIDI, from the Options menu, choose Preferences. In the Preferences dialog box, click the MIDI tab. The list at the top of the tab contains all of the possible MIDI devices that are currently available on your system. This list is identical to the devices listed in the Windows Multimedia Properties dialog, which can be accessed by clicking the Start button on the taskbar and selecting Control Panel. Then, in the Control Panel, double-click the Multimedia item and click the MIDI tab. You can add new instruments to the list in this dialog box, but that is usually automatically done when you install the software for a new device. The list of instruments in ACID can be made a subset of all instruments by selecting only preferred instruments (see Figure 10.2). Notice that the title of the list in ACID is "Make these devices available for MIDI track playback and Generate MIDI Clock." This means that you can route ACID MIDI tracks through these devices for playback; you cannot route tracks through any of these devices and render the track to an audio file (see the next section).

Figure 10.2
Select a subset of devices in ACID to make available for playback and MIDI Clock generation.

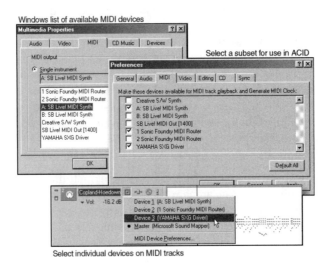

MIDI Playback—Track Routing

While there are a large number of ways to interpret and play back MIDI data on your computer using any number of hardware and software devices, there is only one way to use MIDI to render a project in ACID. On the Track Header for MIDI tracks, the track must be routed through the Master device, which is the DirectX SoftSynth that ACID uses internally to process MIDI data. Click the Device Selection button (the Bus Selection button on audio tracks—see Figure 10.2) to see the list of available devices. The specific device that is available is set up on the Audio tab in the Preferences dialog box (see Figure 10.2).

NOTE

MIDI tracks must be routed through the Master bus in order to be rendered with the project. All other devices are external to ACID.

ACID MIDI tracks need to use the Master bus (DirectX SoftSynth) to render projects. Other MIDI devices listed on the Bus Selector (see Figure 10.2) act as external devices and are used only for playback. All MIDI tracks in a project automatically use the same device; changing the device on one MIDI track changes all MIDI tracks. As one example, if you are using a Yamaha SXG software synthesizer, your project will sound as if the MIDI track was being mixed into the project. In reality, the audio tracks in the project are mixing in ACID, but the MIDI track is being processed by an external device (software, in this case) that is mixed with the output from ACID outside of ACID on the sound card. Therefore, when you render the project, the MIDI track is silent. There is a way around this problem, however.

Figure 10.3
The number of the external MIDI device is displayed on the Track Header.

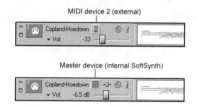

Track routing of MIDI devices also has an impact when using other applications simultaneously with ACID. Typically, only one application can use any particular device at a time. So, if you are using Cakewalk SONAR and it is using the B synthesizer on your sound card, you will be unable to use that synthesizer in ACID. Fortunately, most sound cards come standard with at least one hardware synthesizer and one software synthesizer. Installing additional software synthesizers is also another option. MIDI track routing is also important when generating MIDI Time Code and Clock, as discussed later in this chapter (see "Recording Audio Output from MIDI Playback").

MIDI Rendering—Track Routing

The most important aspect of using the Master device for MIDI is when you render projects, as discussed above. Since the Master device is internal to ACID and the other devices are external, tracks that use these devices for MIDI playback will not be able to take advantage of any FX or pitch shifting. Notice that the Master device track (bottom) in Figure 10.3 has an FX button, while the other track does not.

Rendering projects with MIDI tracks is exactly the same as rendering any other project and is discussed in detail in Chapter 12. Just to repeat: If you render a project and find that the MIDI track is silent, but the track previews when you play back the project, the problem is that you are not using the Master device for the MIDI tracks.

Working with MIDI

ACID 3.0 is not a MIDI editing or creation tool. Still, ACID deftly handles MIDI files—going beyond simply allowing you to include MIDI in your project—by matching the tempo and beat of the MIDI file to the project. Unlike audio files, tempo, beat, and measures are an inherent part of the MIDI file, making this a straightforward task.

Adding MIDI to ACID

Adding MIDI files (and, thus, MIDI data) to a project is as simple as adding any other type of media file to ACID, although the data itself is fundamentally different. To add a MIDI file (*.mid, *.smf, or *.rmi) to ACID, use the Explorer window to locate and preview the file, then double-click it or drag it to the timeline. A blank MIDI track is inserted into the timeline and you only need to paint or draw an event on the timeline to add the data (see Figure 10.4). MIDI events do not display waveform information as audio events do, since MIDI files are not composed of audio data. Instead, the short horizontal lines in the event roughly correspond to the duration of individual notes while the vertical position roughly indicates the tone or pitch of the notes. This is meant to provide visual cues that correspond to the contents of the event and, like waveforms, is very useful in eyeballing alignment of events in ACID. As with other types of files, the tempo and beat information inherent in the file is used to synchronize the MIDI data with the project and with other media in the project. Key (pitch) information is not a separate part of a MIDI file and cannot be detected by ACID.

Figure 10.4
A MIDI track and events as inserted into an ACID project.

Since MIDI files are often longer than just a few seconds, MIDI events are not usually looped, although they will loop if the events are made long enough. When you begin drawing a MIDI event on the timeline, no matter where you begin, the event will start drawing at the beginning of the event (as with all events). This can make finding short sections in the middle of a five-minute MIDI file difficult to find. One way to deal with this is to draw out the entire event and locate the parts you want, splitting the event where needed (press S on your keyboard). Also try using the Slip Trim technique, where you can move the media around within the event without changing the event boundaries: Press and hold the Alt key while dragging inside an event.

MIDI Track Properties

As with standard audio files in ACID, a number of variables can be changed in the Track Properties dialog box for MIDI files. In addition to pitch shifting and markers, you can also change the instruments used in a MIDI file from within ACID.

General Tab

The General tab looks and functions much like the General tab in all of the other track types.

▶ The **Reload** button allows you to reset any changes you've made to the MIDI track back to the defaults of the MIDI file by reloading it into the project. The **Replace** button lets you browse for another MIDI file to use in place of the current one. This is most useful when you have used a number of envelopes on the main timeline and don't want to have to redo them or when you have edited the MIDI file in an external application and saved it to a new name. The **Save** button saves the root note to the MIDI file, but it does not save any other information. Most of the changes made in the Track Properties dialog box are saved at the project level when you save the project.

▶ The Track type and other information about the MIDI file cannot be changed.

▶ **Pitch shift** allows you to adjust the key, or pitch, of the MIDI file without setting a root note on the Voices tab. The shift is measured in semitones, or half-steps, and is limited to $+/-24$. The changes made here are reflected on the Track Header.

▶ The **MIDI timeline** graphically displays the MIDI information. Individual horizontal lines represent individual voices or instruments. The length of the line shows the duration of individual notes. The up and down wiggle of the line corresponds to the pitch of the note, although this is only a rough visual indication and is not particularly accurate. ACID is not a MIDI editing application, and details in pitch are, therefore, not very important. You can create markers and regions on the timeline, but they can't be saved with the MIDI file by using the Save button at the top of the window. Instead, you will need to save this information with the project.

Figure 10.5
The General tab for
MIDI files is similar to
the one for audio files.

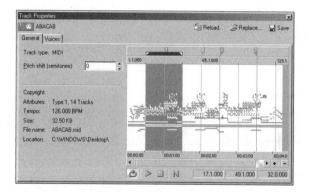

Voices Tab

While ACID is not a MIDI editing program, you can change the voices or instruments used in a MIDI file on the Voices tab. Here's how:

▶ The **Root note** functions the same as in other Track Properties dialog boxes. Most MIDI tracks will use Don't transpose as a root note, since MIDI events are usually longer and may contain internal key changes. If you would like a MIDI track to change key as the project does, set the root note of the MIDI file to be the same as the project key. This will ensure that the MIDI file will play back in the default key it was created in and will not be transposed initially. Transposition for MIDI files poses less of a distortion problem than with audio files. The root note can be saved to the MIDI file using the Save button at the top of the Track Properties window.

▶ A **Voice set** is the set of voices or instruments for MIDI. Windows and most sound cards come with a default set of sounds (usually 128—see Table 10.1), but you can get additional sets. Some voice sets might be grouped by genre (for example, a techno set) or may specialize in a particular instrument (for example, a piano voice set). The Voice set list in ACID allows you to select additional

CHAPTER 10

DownLoadable Sound sets (DLS) on your computer. As the name suggests, DLS files have a *.dls extension and can be downloaded from a number of sites on the Internet. Some examples of some DLS sets are the Roland GS or Yamaha XG sets. DLS sets use the DirectX SoftSynth for playback and thus can be mixed into ACID projects and rendered out using the Master device. Both DLS-1 and DLS-2 formats are supported in ACID, but your sound card may not support both. The difference between the two is not important in ACID. The default GS sound set (16 bit) is found here: C:\WINDOWS\SYSTEM32\DRIVERS\GM.DLS. The **Load** button allows you to add DLS files to the Voice set list.

TIP

The Get Media from the Web option on the File menu allows you to get free DLS sets from Sonic Foundry.

The Voice set list occupies the largest section of the Voices tab and allows you to change the voices that are played back in the MIDI file. Changes made to these options are not saved to the MIDI file, and the Save button does not make any of these changes permanent. The changes made here can be saved with the project, however.

▶ The **Channel** sets how the voice is routed in the MIDI device (in this case, the sound card). There are sixteen possible MIDI channels, and multiple voices can be set to a single channel. By and large, it doesn't matter what channel is selected for which program, but the drums have been traditionally placed in Channel 10. Many MIDI files will have multiple percussion voices all set to Channel 10.

▶ The **Program** is really the voice selected, and it is the most important control on the tab. Sometimes called a patch, voice, or instrument, the program can be selected by clicking the triangle (arrow) next to the instrument name on the list. This will drop down a rather long list (depending on the Voice set selected and the MIDI device used for output) that has all of the instrument names on it. To preview an instrument sound, click it once on the list. This selects that instrument and allows you to hear how it sounds in your project while it is playing back. To select an instrument (program) and close the list, double-click the entry.

This list may be subdivided into a number of banks (see Figure 10.6), each of which contains a different set of patches (programs). Anything on the list can be selected, regardless of the bank. The voices and banks that are available again depends on the Voice set and the MIDI output device selected.

Figure 10.6
Different Banks
contain different
sets of instruments.

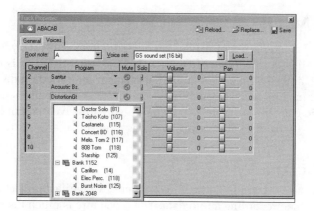

CHAPTER 10

▶ The **Mute** and **Solo** buttons function to mute and solo individual voices in the MIDI file. Multiple Solo buttons can be pushed at a single time, as can multiple Mute buttons, of course.

▶ The **Volume** and **Pan** sliders likewise function to adjust the volume and panning of individual voices, giving you more control over the mix of the MIDI file. The Pan sliders can be especially useful in creating a larger sense of space in a MIDI file, which are usually all bunched up in the middle.

NOTE

DLS sets are similar in many ways to the proprietary SoundFonts from Creative Labs and Ensoniq. SoundFonts can be converted to the DLS format with the right software (such as Audio Compositor or Awave Studio), but some quality may be lost as many SoundFonts use audio filters (for example, compression or low-pass filters to make the various notes in a set more uniform).

MIDI Tracks on the Timeline

MIDI tracks and events behave much the same as other tracks and events in ACID. The Track Header contains Mute and Solo buttons as well as a Multipurpose slider to control panning and volume. Tracks and events can be pitch shifted by right-clicking the track header or an envelope or by pressing the + or − keys on your keyboard's number pad. Unfortunately, MIDI tracks cannot take advantage of Volume or Pan Envelopes and, since MIDI tracks cannot be routed through a bus in the Mixer window, they cannot use FX envelopes, either. Besides these limitations, everything else is the same. See Chapter 2 for more information on working with tracks and events in general in ACID.

Recording MIDI

Just as you can record an audio performance into an audio track in ACID, you can also record a performance from a MIDI device into a MIDI track. In this case, MIDI data is recorded (note, duration, instrument, and so on) and not audio data. This is an important distinction, since audio data takes up much more space on your computer but can also be manipulated in different ways. Audio data, for example, can be modified with envelopes and routed through auxiliary busses, while MIDI data allows you to change the voices and instruments used.

Recording MIDI Data

Recording the performance data from a MIDI instrument live while a project is playing back is perhaps more simple than recording audio data. The procedure is much the same (see Chapter 6) and you don't have to worry about the many problems surrounding recording audio through a microphone, such as ambient noise and recording levels. To record MIDI data from a performance while an ACID project plays back:

1. Move the timeline cursor to the position where you want to start recording.
2. On the Transport bar, click the Record button or press Ctrl+R on your keyboard.
3. In the Record dialog, select the MIDI option Record type (see Figure 10.7). At this point you should be able to play your MIDI device, the meters should jump, and you should be able to hear the audio. If you can't hear anything, but the meters jump, see the following section on "Monitoring."
4. Click the Start button. The project begins playback and the recording starts.
5. Click the Stop button to end the recording.

A MIDI file is saved to your computer and a new track is inserted into the project with an event that contains the recording. The name of the file and the location where the file is saved can be set up in the Record dialog box in the File name and Record folder boxes. It is a pretty good idea to set up a folder dedicated to holding your recordings instead of using the default location where ACID was installed.

Figure 10.7
The Record dialog.

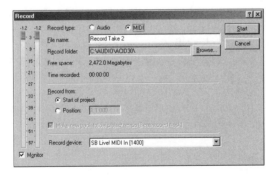

The files are automatically named and numbered according to a default scheme: Record Take 1.mid, Record Take 2.mid, etc. While the file name can be changed in the Record dialog, ACID defaults back to this numbering for every take. As with all tracks, the name of the track is taken from the name of the associated media file. If you alternately record both Audio and MIDI data, the file names will continue to increment (for example, Record Take 1.**mid**, Record Take 2.**wav**, Record Take 3.**mid**, etc.).

NOTE

Unlike audio recordings, MIDI data cannot be recorded into separate takes by turning on Loop playback mode while recording. This is because regions cannot be saved with the MIDI file but only with the project.

Monitoring MIDI Performances

When recording MIDI data, ACID is not recording audio data. Therefore, it is not necessary to hear what you are playing in order to record MIDI. The meters in the Record dialog box will still jump and data will still be recorded to a track even if you can't hear anything. Obviously, this makes performance difficult, so you should select a device to monitor your performance. From the Options menu, select Preferences, and then, in the Preferences dialog, go to the MIDI tab. On the MIDI Thru device for recording option, select a MIDI device. Only devices that are selected on the list at the top of the tab will be available, as shown in Figure 10.8. Some devices (for example, Sonic Foundry MIDI Router) cannot be used directly for playback. Some software synths will not respond quickly enough for accurate monitoring and will produce significantly delayed audio. In any case, what you hear is not what is being recorded: MIDI data is being recorded, so the actual device used to monitor the performance is simply a matter of personal preference.

Figure 10.8
The MIDI Thru device for recording is used to monitor MIDI performances.

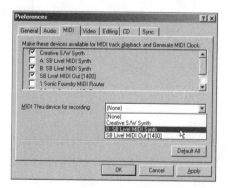

While you can turn the volume up too loud on a MIDI track and cause clipping, it is not possible to cause clipping on the meters in the Record dialog box by playing MIDI data too loudly.

Selecting an Instrument

The MIDI data recorded into ACID is recorded without a specific instrument selected. To change the voice or the instrument used in the track, open the Track Properties dialog box for the newly created track. Then go to the Voices tab and, under the Program data field, click the arrow and select a Bank and instrument (voice), as shown in Figure 10.9. This new instrument information is not saved with the MIDI file, even if you click the Save button at the top of the window. Instead, instrument information is project specific and will be saved with the project that contains the media file. To make this a permanent part of the MIDI file, you will need to use a MIDI file editing application.

Figure 10.9
Selecting an instrument (program) in the Track Properties dialog.

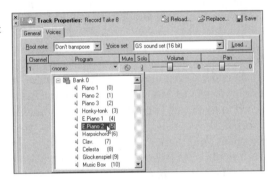

Recording Audio Output from MIDI playback

Selecting various MIDI devices in the Track Header for MIDI playback was discussed in the section on "Track Routing." While any MIDI device on your system, both hardware and software, can be used to play back MIDI data in ACID, you can render only the audio output from MIDI tracks that use the Master (internal DirectX SoftSynth) device. It may seem like a tease to be allowed to select from a large list of possible MIDI devices but not have the output rendered to the final media file. Remember that these alternate MIDI devices are to be considered as external devices. They should be thought of as synthesizers external to your computer that receive MIDI data from ACID and then send analog audio output back into your sound card's AUX port. As with all audio that comes into your sound card, the sound from these external devices can be recorded into an ACID track. This will record the output from these devices as an audio file, just as you would record any other audio source (see Chapter 6). The most important concept to remember is that you are not recording MIDI data (to be discussed later), but you are, instead, recording the analog audio signal from an external device. To do this:

1. Insert a MIDI file into a track and solo the track.

2. In the Track Header, select the MIDI device you want to use.

3. In your sound card's mixer, find the Record settings or Windows Record Control panel (see Chapter 6) and isolate the output from the MIDI device (see below). This will not be the MIDI output (which will be your sound card's default MIDI). This is the most difficult step, and it is discussed in more detail later.

4. In ACID, click the Record button.

5. In the Record dialog, make sure the Record type is Audio. Remember, you want to record the audio signal, not MIDI data.

6. Set the Record from to Start of project.

7. Click Start.

8. The project (with the MIDI track soloed) will play back using the MIDI device selected. Click Stop when finished. A new track will be inserted with a Beatmapped audio file of the MIDI track.

This only briefly reviews material covered in more detail in Chapter 6. Keep in mind that you are recording an audio signal. The hardest part is going to be figuring out how to isolate the audio from the MIDI device for recording (Step 3). This may require some trial and error, because every sound card is different. Here is an example using one of the popular SB Live! series of cards:

1. In the Windows Control Panel, double-click the Multimedia item and make sure Show volume control on the taskbar is selected on the Audio tab.

2. In the taskbar tray, double-click the Volume control (speaker icon).

3. In the Play Control dialog, from the Options menu, select Properties.

4. In the Properties dialog, select the Recording option.

5. Deselect all options except the Wave option (the Wave item should be the only one selected—see Figure 10.10).

6. Click OK.

Figure 10.10
The record mixer dialog box for an SB Live! Sound card in Windows.

You can leave the Record Control dialog box open while you record the MIDI track to an audio file in ACID to adjust the recording gain. For this sound card, the Wave option is any sound produced by the sound card that will be output to the speakers. In this case, the signal will be very clean since it will go from the sound card directly to the recorded audio file on your hard disk.

It is also possible to record the output from another application—for example, a specific MIDI playback or editing application—or record the audio data from a live performance as it is played back through another application. This is going to require some deft juggling of the various MIDI and Wave devices on your computer, making sure that the MIDI application and ACID use different devices for playback. When conflicts occur, ACID will most often gracefully display an error message saying that playback cannot occur since the device is already in use (see Figure 10.11). Click the Details button in that dialog box to see which device ACID is trying to use and then change either ACID or the other application. At times, unfortunately, one or both applications may crash or lock up as they both struggle to use the same device for playback and recording. You may be able to select the "What U Hear" option in the mixer for SB Live! cards to record the audio data you want.

Figure 10.11
A device conflict error message in ACID (but not a crash!)

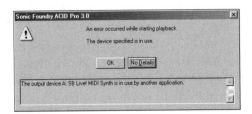

TIP

If you've been scouring this book looking for the best way to crash ACID (or any other MIDI application), this is it: Try to use the same MIDI device with two different applications at the same time. To avoid conflicts, be very cautious about setting up MIDI devices in applications you are going to run simultaneously. Most of the time, ACID will handle these conflicts gracefully with an error message, but they can sometimes cause your system to hang.

MIDI Triggers and Time Code

ACID can act as a MIDI device in a studio setup, both outputting MIDI Time Code (MTC) to other devices and accepting MIDI triggers from other devices and applications. The purpose of this is to synchronize ACID with your MIDI setup by allowing other devices to start ACID playback or to start and synchronize other devices from within ACID when you start playback of a project. The MIDI device or software application needs to be able to send and/or receive MTC, so simple dummy keyboards will not work. More complex synthesizers with sequencers, however, often have this capability. In professional MIDI studios, there is often a small box that is dedicated to generating timecode and synchronization and sometimes called a controller or a sync unit.

CHAPTER 10

MIDI Time Code (MTC) is a standard way of measuring time in MIDI and is not the same as a MIDI Clock. MIDI Clock is based upon musical beats from the start of a song, played at a specific tempo, and is therefore relative to time in the real world. Both MTC and MIDI Clock data can be used to trigger ACID and can be generated by ACID to trigger other devices and applications. MTC is not the same as timecode as used in video, although the two can be set to measure time the same way. For clarity, in this book, "timecode" is used to refer to the various types of SMPTE video timecode, and MIDI code is referred to as MTC or MIDI Timecode (also a standard from the Society of Motion Picture and Television Engineers—SMPTE, pronounced "simpty"), as it is in ACID. This is not a widely followed convention, however. In this discussion, a master device is the device or application that generates the MTC or MIDI Clock that is used to control the slave device, which is triggered and synchronized with the master.

MTC or MIDI Clock?

MIDI Clock is also a better choice for MIDI exclusive applications, such as MIDI editors and sequencers. MIDI Timecode, on the other hand, is more broadly targeted and can be used with everything from tape machines to video production equipment. In the end, the right choice is the one that works.

Generate or Trigger?

Should you generate MTC or trigger from MTC in ACID (you cannot trigger from MIDI Clock)? In other words, should ACID be the master device or the slave? Very broadly speaking, ACID seems to be better in the role of master, generating MTC or MIDI Clock to trigger and sync a slave application.

Generating MTC and MIDI Clock from ACID

Whether you choose MTC or MIDI Clock is largely a matter of what the slave application wants to use. In some situations—for example, when your project has tempo changes—the MIDI Clock may work better.

ACID can be configured to output or generate MTC to trigger and synchronize compliant external hardware devices and other MIDI software applications on your computer. Any ACID project can generate MTC regardless of whether you are using MIDI in the project. Although ACID's new MIDI features are pretty spiffy, ACID is not primarily a MIDI tool, so using ACID for the loop-based part of a larger project with a dedicated MIDI device or application is a very useful combination.

Configuring MTC Generation

MTC and MIDI Clock are generated in ACID using a MIDI device on your computer. Configuring ACID to generate code is a matter of selecting a device to use, much the same as you select a MIDI device for MIDI playback at the track level. To set up ACID to generate MTC:

1. From the Options menu, select Preferences.
2. Click the Sync tab.
3. Under the Generate MIDI Timecode settings option, select an Output device. This is going to be a MIDI device, hardware or software, on your sound card.

NOTE

Just as it is not possible to use the same MIDI device in ACID and another application at the same time, so it is also not possible to play back MIDI in ACID and generate MTC using the same device (see Figure 10.12). When you select a device to output MTC on the Sync tab, that device will be grayed out on the MIDI tab. MIDI Clock is slightly different and can be generated simultaneously with playback on the same device.

Figure 10.12
MIDI devices cannot be used for conflicting purposes.

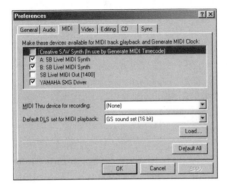

4. From the Frame rate list, select the format you want to use to measure time.

5. The frame rate does not speed up or slow down time, only how it is measured. These are all various standards that have been used for different purposes over the years. For example, movies are twenty-four frames per second (fps), while color television in the United States is 29.97 fps. In audio, 30 fps is probably the most frequently used standard. More important than which particular standard you choose is that both of your devices (ACID and the other application) are using the same standard. MTC and other relevant timecodes are measured in hours, minutes, seconds, and frames (hh:mm:ss:ff), with the number of frames in a second being the only difference.

Triggering Another Device with ACID

Once ACID is set up as the master device to generate the appropriate MTC, the next step is to configure the slave device that will be triggered and synchronized. For software applications, this will involve selecting a port to listen from for MTC and making sure the frame rates are the same. The process will be very much like setting up ACID to listen for MTC, so see the following section for more information on that process. Of particular interest will be the section on Sonic Foundry's Virtual MIDI Router, which allows you to select a port other than the default hardware MIDI port. Once the device is configured:

1. Cue the slave device or application to listen for MTC.

2. In ACID, from the Options menu, go to the Timecode item and select Generate MIDI Timecode or press F7.

3. Play back the ACID project.

4. ACID will immediately begin playback and will generate the MTC at the same time, using the output device or port specified in the Preferences dialog box. ACID's transport controls (Play and Stop) will be used to control the external devices.

Since there are many types of devices, both hardware and software, that can listen for and be triggered by MTC, it is not possible to tell you how to set up your specific device. In the case of another software application, however, the behavior is very likely to be similar to the way ACID listens for MTC: For more information, see the next section on how to trigger ACID playback using an external MTC device.

There is a specific example later in this chapter detailing how this all works between ACID and Cakewalk Pro Audio (now SONAR).

NOTE

While playback will begin almost immediately and be perfectly synchronized, there can be a 1 to 3 second delay between when you press Stop in ACID and when the slave device stops.

The time display at the upper left of the timeline can display the MTC and MIDI Clock being sent out from ACID from the chosen device. To view the MTC that is being generated by ACID, right-click the time display and select MIDI Timecode Out from the context menu (see Figure 10.13).

As you have noticed, configuring and generating MIDI Clock is a similar process. As with MTC, you will need to select an output device, but MIDI Clock is measured in terms of tempo, measures, and beats, so it is not necessary to select a format. MIDI Clock can be generated by a shared device used for playback.

Figure 10.13
ACID-generated MTC can be viewed on the time display. Notice that you can also enable generation here as well.

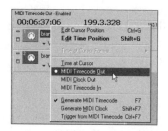

Triggering ACID with MTC

ACID can also be used as the slave device, receiving MTC from a master device and using that to cue project playback and synchronize with a master device. A master device might be another software application on your computer or an external sequencer or dedicated MTC generator. The process is basically the reverse of the above: configure ACID, enable (arm) ACID to listen for MTC, begin playback or generation of MTC from the master device. To configure ACID to accept MTC:

1. From the Options menu, select Preferences.
2. Click the Sync tab.
3. Under the Trigger from MIDI Timecode settings option, select an Input device. This is going to be a MIDI device, hardware or software, on your sound card.

Most consumer-level sound cards have only one hardware MIDI port and, therefore, only one default driver for MIDI input. This input driver can be shared between two applications running at the same time, so you can trigger and synchronize playback from two applications at the same time. It is not possible to use this port to communicate between two software applications, but you can install a software-based Virtual MIDI Router (VMR) to create another MIDI input port so you can use another software application to trigger ACID. Sonic Foundry has included its VMR on the ACID CD. Specific usage is discussed later in this chapter. Once you have configured the master device to generate MTC, make sure the frame rate of the device and ACID match and then:

1. Ready the master device for playback and generation of MTC.
2. In ACID, from the Options menu, go to the Timecode item and select Trigger From MIDI Timecode or press Ctrl+F7.
3. Right-click the time display and select MIDI Timecode In. The display will show a MIDI Timecode In–Waiting…message to verify that ACID is listening for MTC.
4. Begin generation of MTC from the external device or start playback of the master device.

When ACID is chasing MTC, the time display message will show MIDI Timecode In–Locked and all controls within ACID will be disabled. While ACID can generate MTC and MIDI Clock data, it can only be triggered by MTC. This is not unusual, and you may find many devices that can accept MIDI Clock data from another device but may not be triggered by it.

Advanced Sync Preferences

There are a number of advanced MTC generation and triggering options. These can be accessed by clicking the Advanced button on the Sync tab in the Preferences dialog box. This opens the Advanced Sync Preferences dialog box with three tabs, one for each of the three sync options. If you have not selected a device in the Preferences dialog, the corresponding tab will not be visible in this dialog. Many of these options will need to be adjusted only when you are having problems with devices incorrectly interacting with ACID, perhaps responding, but not quickly enough.

▶ The **MTC Input** tab corresponds to the Trigger from MIDI Timecode settings item and allows ACID to compensate for breaks, delays, and other irregularities that may occur when listening to MTC generated by a master device. Once ACID has been triggered and synchronized, it can continue at the same rate and stay more or less in sync without any additional input. If ACID is responding to trigger messages but is falling out of sync, these options may help. You can keep Free-wheel for timecode loss selected in almost all situations. If ACID remains waiting (listening) and is not triggered by the master device, these options will not solve the problem.

▶ The **MTC Output** tab corresponds to the Generate MIDI Timecode settings item and allows you to configure which messages are sent to the slave device. In most situations, it will be necessary to generate Full-frame messages only on start and stop of playback and record. In almost all situations, you should not use internal timer, as this can cause the applications to drift out of sync.

▶ The **MIDI Clock Output** tab corresponds to the Generate MIDI Clock settings. This tab configures the Song Position Pointer (SSP) and is specifically used to sync the timeline cursor. The optional item at the top of the tab can be selected to always send a start signal when playing back, even if playback starts in mid-song. This will always make the slave device start at the beginning of the song. If this is not selected (which I recommend) and you begin playback in ACID in mid-song, the slave device will begin playback from the current cursor position in ACID, allowing you to stop and play ACID and maintain control of the slave.

Virtual MIDI Router

Sonic Foundry's Virtual MIDI Router should be included on your ACID CD in the /extras/ folder, but it can also be downloaded (with your ACID serial number) from the Web site:

www.sonicfoundry.com/download/step2.asp?DID=317

To install this tiny (less than 10 KB) application/driver, you must install the VMR as a New Hardware device from the Windows Control Panel (see Figure 10.14). Detailed instructions can be found in the README file that is included with the driver and in ACID's online Help and Manual. The final step is to select the number of ports you want to make available, from one to four. If you only want to communicate between ACID and one other application, one virtual port is sufficient. You will need to restart Windows after installing the VMR driver. After restarting, the number of ports created by the VMR can be configured by going to the Windows Control Panel, selecting the Multimedia option, and then clicking the Devices tab. Under the MIDI Devices and Instruments option, you will find the Sonic Foundry MIDI Router. You will need to restart your computer before these changes will take effect.

Figure 10.14
Final configuration
of the Virtual MIDI
Router after installation.

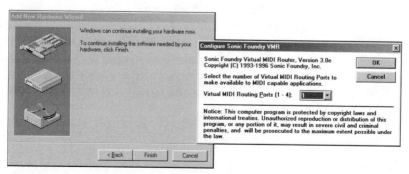

To use the VMR for syncing purposes, select a Sonic Foundry MIDI Router port (numbered 1-4) on the Sync tab in the Preferences dialog in ACID (see Figure 10.15) and set up the other application to listen or send over the same port.

Figure 10.15
ACID-generated MTC can be viewed on the time display. Notice that you can also enable generation here as well.

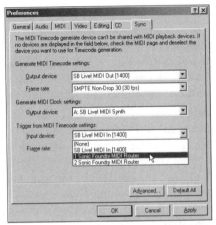

Syncing Example: SONAR to ACID

All of this talk of MTC, syncing, and virtual routing can seem rather complicated, and it is when you consider all of the potential devices that can be hooked together. As one real-world example, the following procedure shows you how to use ACID to trigger and sync Cakewalk SONAR (or Pro Audio 9) using MIDI Clock. In this case ACID is the master device and SONAR is the slave. If you have a choice, this seems to work better than the other way around. And, since SONAR is primarily a MIDI application, in this example, ACID is going to generate MIDI Clock, which SONAR also seems to prefer:

1. Run both ACID and SONAR.

2. Configure ACID to output MIDI Clock using 1 Sonic Foundry MIDI Router as an Output device for the Generate MIDI Clock settings on the Sync tab of the Preferences dialog box.

3. Right-click the time display and select MIDI Clock Out to view the generated clock. Press Shift+F7 on your keyboard to enable (arm) ACID. The time display will read "MIDI Clock Out–Enabled."

4. In SONAR, from the Options menu, select MIDI Devices. In the MIDI Ports dialog, on the Input Ports list, select 1 Sonic Foundry MIDI Router (single click it to highlight it) and click the OK button.

5. From the View menu, select Toolbars and make sure the Sync toolbar is selected and visible. Click the MIDI button and press Play. A message will appear in the lower left corner of the workspace reading, "Press ESCAPE to cancel... Waiting for MIDI Sync."

6. Press Play in ACID. ACID will begin playing and SONAR will immediately follow.

Every time you stop playback in ACID, you will need to re-arm SONAR to listen for MIDI Clock. SONAR will automatically sync playback beginning at any point in your ACID project. See Figure 10.16 for a summary of the various settings and what you should see when everything is properly configured and armed.

Figure 10.16
ACID as the master device triggering and syncing Cakewalk Pro Audio with MIDI Clock. SONAR works the same way, although the application has a different look.

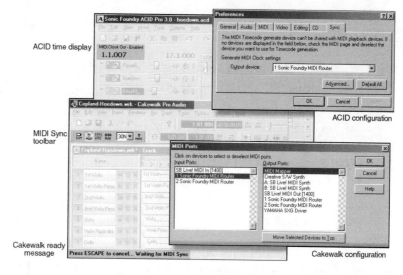

NOTE

SONAR seems to work better as the slave, with ACID as the master. You can crash your computer by assigning SONAR to output MTC and listen for MTC on the same port, especially if ACID is already using the port to output MTC.

FX and MIDI Tracks

One of the largest criticisms about MIDI sound is that it sounds very unnatural. This makes sense since it is computer generated, but advances in MIDI technology have made it more and more realistic. Perhaps the greatest advance in recent years has been the widespread use of wavetable synthesis, which uses real instruments to create the sound. MIDI authoring tools have also gotten better and better, even allowing the composer to add imperfections in timing to individual notes, simulating real human performers. Of course, controlling the quality of samples and the details of MIDI authoring are all well outside of ACID's domain.

MIDI files using even the best wavetable synthesis also tend to sound very clean and flat. This is because the samples need to be created to be used in the widest variety of situations. Almost all samples are, therefore, completely devoid of any sense of space or ambience. ACID FX plug-ins can be very useful in making an artificially perfect and balanced MIDI file sound more natural by adding this sort of space to the track.

NOTE

MIDI tracks must be routed through the Master device on the Track Header to use FX. Other devices are external to ACID and cannot be processed by ACID, but they will still work for playback.

The best plug-in for creating space is probably the Reverb FX. To add a Reverb plug-in to a MIDI track:

1. Make sure the MIDI track is using the Master device for playback.

2. Click the FX button on the MIDI track.

3. In the Audio Plug-in window, click the Edit Chain button.

4. In the Plug-In Chooser dialog, select a Reverb plug-in, click the Add button, then click the OK button.

5. The controls for the Reverb plug-in are visible in the Audio Plug-in window. Solo the MIDI track and adjust the Reverb. Then unsolo the track and finish adjusting the FX in relation to the project.

There is more detailed information on using FX in general in Chapter 8, where you can also find a detailed examination of the Reverb plug-ins. Be careful not to overdo the Reverb effect, which is easy to do since more space generally sounds better. At some point, however, the Reverb will begin to sound like, well, reverb and will be instantly perceived as artificial. You also need to carefully try to match the sense of space in the MIDI track with the other media files used in the project. While it is not technically an effect, panning individual voices 10 percent to 20 percent left and right in the Track Properties dialog box for a MIDI track can do wonders for a sense of space. MIDI files very often have all of the various voices bunched up in the middle, which adds to the artificial sound of the files.

Especially useful in improving the quality of MIDI in ACID are Equalization plug-ins. Any of these can be used to bring out the specific voices you want to emphasize, although keep in mind that you can also do this by increasing the volume of individual voices in the Track Properties dialog box. Boosting the bass frequencies a little can often add richness to MIDI tracks.

11
Video

One of the biggest new features in ACID 3.0 is the addition of a video track. This makes ACID an excellent tool for scoring a sound track. This is not just useful for creating music video-type productions but can be utilized in just about any video project, from sweetening the existing audio track to narrating a voiceover or adding sound effects. ACID is not a video-editing tool, however, and is, therefore, best used with projects that have finished video post-production. You could, of course, create music in ACID and then import it into an audio track in your video-editing software, but the advantage of being able to visually include a video track in your project makes synchronization and timing much easier. The powerful background tempo adjustments without pitch shifting mean that ACID can match the video content precisely and effortlessly. Video capabilities bring ACID from the realm of audio into the domain of true multimedia creation.

Working with Video

ACID is not a video-editing application but should be thought of instead primarily as a scoring tool. Because of this, ACID's video features are robust but simple. This section will introduce you to adding video to ACID projects and working with that video. In addition, we'll look at some of the more complex features that allow you to precisely synchronize video to audio, right down to matching action to tempo.

Adding Video

Adding video to ACID is much the same as adding audio and MIDI. First, browse for video media using ACID's Explorer window, then add a video track, and draw an event on the timeline. Unlike audio media files, video files cannot be previewed as you browse for them in the Explorer window. Here's what to do:

1. Browse for video media using the Explorer window.
2. Select video files (single-click) in the Explorer window. Only the audio will be previewed. You may turn on automatic previewing by clicking the Auto Preview button on the Explorer window toolbar.

3.   Double-click files to add the video to timeline.

4.   Draw an event in the newly created video track.

The video file is inserted into a video track at the top of the timeline with an event that automatically spans the entire duration of the file. Just below the video track, a One-Shot track is also created (see Figure 11.1). This track contains an event with the audio track from the video file, if one exists. Since the video files used in ACID will typically span the entire project (in fact, they usually will define the project), the audio track can be quite long. This means that you will likely have to wait a few seconds while a peak file (*.sfk) is built. Peak files contain the graphical information that is drawn as the waveform in events on the timeline. As discussed in Chapter 9, One-Shot events are not loaded into RAM, so the audio track is always accessed from the hard disk (as is the video).

Figure 11.1
A video track and its associated audio in a project.

The audio track is just like any other audio track in ACID, and the Track Type can be changed in the Track Properties window to Loop or Beatmapped. Since it is likely that you will want the audio component of the video file to remain in sync with the video, the Track Type should probably not be changed. If the tempo of the project changes, the duration of Beatmapped and Looped events also changes, but One-Shot events do not. The video track is unaffected by tempo changes as well.

To remove a video track, right-click anywhere in the video track and select Remove Video. This will not remove the corresponding audio track. You can also hide the video track from view without removing it from the project by right-clicking the video track and selecting Hide Video. The track will disappear, leaving the corresponding audio track untouched, but the video will remain a part of the project and the video can still be previewed in the Video window. The Show Video Track option restores the video track to the timeline.

Previewing Video

The Video window is the simplest window in ACID, having only a few buttons. The window is used only to preview the video from the timeline and cannot be used to preview video from the Explorer window. The Video window can be made visible from the View menu by clicking Video or by pressing Alt + 4 on your keyboard. The Video window can be set to any size and can be resized by dragging the edges.. The video inside the window is locked into specific aspect ratios relative to the original source video to prevent distortion and improve playback performance.

The top of the window has a simple toolbar that displays the name of the media file, a Copy button to grab a de-interlaced screen capture of the video, and an External Monitor button (explained shortly). The bottom of the window can display a status bar that shows the dimensions and frame rate of the original source media file as well as the dimensions of the video as it appears in the Video window and the actual frame rate as displayed. A few other options are available on the context menu, which is displayed by right-clicking anywhere in the window (see Figure 11.2). Selecting Display at Media Size will set the Display size to the size of the original file; this can result in only a portion of the video being visible if the Video window is smaller than the frame size of the media file.

Figure 11.2
The Video window and its associated context menu.

External Monitor

As of the year 2001, television monitors are fundamentally different from computer monitors. When color television was developed in the 1950s, a number of technical problems needed to be resolved. One issue was the difficulty with then-current technologies in achieving a frame rate that was fast enough to prevent image flickering. The solution was to divide every frame into two fields, one composed of all of the odd lines in the picture and another composed of all of the even numbered lines. These two fields were then combined, or interlaced, into a frame of video. That meant video at 30 frames per second (fps) would really be displayed at 60 fields per second. Due to problems with interference with the 60 Hz electric standard (among other things), the NTSC video standard in the United States is now 29.97 fps and is interlaced. On the other hand, computer monitors, developed only in the last fifteen or so years, are not interlaced and are referred to as progressive scanning. In addition, computer monitors typically display video using tens of millions of colors, while televisions are limited to about two million.

The problem is—and this is a significant problem—that you cannot be sure that what you see on a computer monitor is what your movie will look like on a television. Video that has not been modified with filters that change the color or hue, has not used effects, does not use computer-generated graphics or text, and has not had the speed changed (for example, slo-mo) will typically not have any problems. Otherwise, you will need to make sure that your titles are the right color on a television and that the interlacing is correct. Since all of these potential problems will have been introduced into the video in your primary video-editing program and not in ACID, there isn't much to say about this here. But the External Monitor option still allows you to preview video on your television, via an OHCI-compliant IEEE-1394 DV (FireWire) card and DV camcorder. This can be a nice way to preview video, since it frees up valuable screen real estate. Whether you can use an external monitor or not depends on your hardware and DV camcorder. This can be troublesome to set up, but Sonic Foundry has a number of documents online to assist you with getting this feature to work. In short:

1. Connect your camcorder to your IEEE-1394 DV card and turn it on in playback mode (VTR).

2. Connect the video out (RCA jack or S-VHS) from the camcorder to your television. You do not need to connect the audio cables, since audio is not sent through the DV card for preview purposes.

3. In ACID, click the External Monitor button.

There should be a short pause before the video is displayed on your television. You can hide or minimize the Video window in ACID to regain workspace area and use the television exclusively for previewing. Figure 11.3 summarizes the configuration.

Figure 11.3
A video track and
its associated audio
in a project.

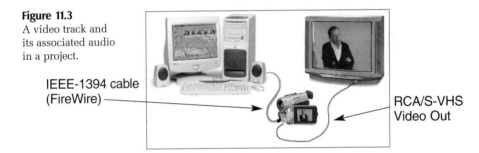

IEEE-1394 cable
(FireWire)

RCA/S-VHS
Video Out

From the Options menu, select Preferences and then, in the Preferences dialog box, go to the Video tab. From the External monitor device list, select the device that you want to use. Usually, the only DV device listed here will be OHCI Compliant IEEE 1394/DV. Since this is a hardware-dependent feature, only DV cards that meet this standard will work. When your camcorder is not connected and powered up, the Details window in the dialog will read Device Unavailable. You can use source media files that are not DV files; these will be converted to DV on the fly for previewing purposes.

In some cases, due to hardware issues, the video on the External Monitor might not be synchronized with the audio, which is obviously a critical issue in ACID. You should be very wary of this potential problem. If you notice that the video in the Video window in ACID is precisely synced with your audio, but the video on the external monitor is not, you can change the Sync offset to bring the video back in line.

Video Tracks

Only one video track and one video event are allowed in ACID. It is always the first track in the project and is indicated by a gray video icon. Unlike other tracks, the color cannot be altered and the name of the track cannot be changed. The size (height) of the track can be changed. The single video event cannot be split, but can be trimmed from either end and can be moved back and forth on the timeline. When you render the final video media file, areas of the project at the beginning or end that only have audio content will be rendered black in the video.

NOTE

Only one video track can be used in ACID at a time. The single event in the video track cannot be split, but it can be trimmed at either end.

Video tracks do not have any properties that can be displayed in the Track Properties dialog box. None of the audio controls (Volume slider, Mute button, and so on) on audio and MIDI tracks is available or necessary on a video track, and neither are any envelopes.

Video Events

The single video event that spans the duration of the media file can be dragged on the timeline and trimmed, but it cannot be split or changed like other events. The event displays some information about the file on it (see Figure 11.4). The pictures in the video event are derived from individual frames in the video, with the small triangles below the pictures marking the location of the frame on the timeline and the numbers on the picture identifying the frame number. The exact format of the numbers displayed can be changed to match the Time Ruler or to match the format of the media file, or they can be hidden all together by going to the Video tab in the Preferences dialog box.

Figure 11.4
Video events display numerical values identifying frame numbers in a number of formats.

Because of the many different types of media that can be used in ACID, time can be measured in a wide variety of ways. The right half of the time display always shows the measures.beats.milliseconds, as does the ruler at the top of the timeline. The left hand of the time display can be customized to fit your preferences. For example, when creating video projects for broadcast in the United States, you would want to use the NTSC video standard, which is SMPTE Drop (29.97 fps, video). To change the format displayed, right-click the time display or the Time Ruler below the timeline. Then, from the context menu, choose Time at Cursor Format and select the format. If the Time Ruler at the bottom of the timeline is not visible, from the View menu, select Time Ruler. Make sure Show Time Ruler is selected and has a check mark next to it.

Scrubbing

Scrubbing is the term used to describe shuttling back and forth over a video event to preview the contents of the file without playing the file back. This gives you more control over positioning the cursor for editing purposes. It is not particularly important for audio work, but it is highly useful in finding frames in video. Use the left and right arrow keys to move the timeline cursor and scrub the video. The Video window always displays the contents of the video at the cursor position, but the picture in the video event on the timeline also displays the contents of the video at the cursor position. As you move the cursor back and forth, notice that the triangle and frame number move with the cursor inside the picture in the event, and the contents of the frame change constantly. The amount of movement of each press of the arrow keys depends on the zoom level of the project. When zoomed out, each press may move a number of frames at a time, while at higher zoom levels, each press might advance or retreat one frame or less.

Zooming

The frame numbers and triangles beneath the pictorial representation of frames change with the zoom level in the project. Zooming in further will reveal more detail and eventually, at higher zoom levels, individual frames are marked by lines between the numbered frames. At even higher zoom levels, every frame is represented by a picture in the event and a frame number. As you can see in Figure 11.5, the Time Ruler will match the frame marks in the event if the time format selected is the same as the source video. This serves as a very quick way to convert absolute frame numbers into the more complex time formats, providing the event starts at time zero in the project. A mouse wheel is very useful for quickly zooming in and out, something which you may do even more when working with video.

Figure 11.5
The Time Ruler
and frame numbers
on the events can be
set to match.

Video events snap to the grid marks in a project, which demarcate measures and beats. At higher zoom levels, when individual frames can be resolved, video events also snap to frame boundaries. This behavior can be toggled on and off by pressing F8 on your keyboard.

Synchronizing Audio and Video

If the audio track of the video file falls out of sync with the video, due to trimming or movement of the video event, right-click the audio event and, from the context menu, select Synchronize with Video. This works only for the audio from the video file. If the file has remained a One-Shot (as it probably should), this will move the file back into sync. If the audio Track Type has been changed to Beatmapped, and the project tempo has changed, the audio file will be moved back in sync and the tempo will be changed to one that allows the audio to be exactly synced with the video for its duration, which is the original tempo of the project when the video event was inserted.

While the video event must remain whole, the audio event associated with the video can be split, trimmed, moved, and otherwise processed just as any other One-Shot. Each individual event can be moved independently and can, therefore, be moved out of sync. These individual events can be moved back into sync, individually, by right-clicking and selecting Synchronize with Video.

Marking Video Frames

Since video is composed of discrete pictures or frames, the exact time when a frame begins is marked with a triangle below the image representing the frame in the event. Lining up audio events with frame boundaries can be fairly important, and it is not all that hard to do. The problem is that at most reasonable zoom levels for working with audio, individual frames of video are not visible, so finding the exact two frames that divide one scene from another can be tricky. Markers are very useful here. You might want to initially zoom in and find the critical junctures in the video event, mark the frame boundaries with markers (press M on your keyboard), and then zoom out to work on the audio. As Figure 11.6 shows, when zoomed in far enough, individual frames are visible and numbered (all frame numbers increment by one). The cut between the two scenes is clearly visible, but this is such a high zoom level that working with audio is difficult. Notice that in the top image, the entire timeline encompasses only a few frames and spans only a fraction of a second. The bottom image is zoomed out to a level where beats and measures are visible.

NOTE

When dropping a marker on an exact frame boundary at a high zoom level, you may notice that it does not seem to be at the boundary after you zoom back out. Trust the marker and not the thumbnail representations on the video. Watch the Video preview window to verify this, because it always displays the exact frame at the cursor position. In this situation, the arrow keys are very useful for moving back and forth in the project a frame or so at a time.

Figure 11.6
Individual frames are numbered in the top example, while the bottom example is zoomed out further.

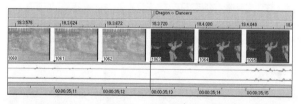

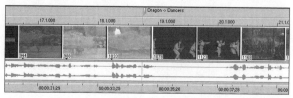

Matching Project Tempo to Video

Matching tempo to the action in a video can be very important. If you look again at the bottom image in Figure 11.6, you'll notice that the marker does not fall exactly on the beat but occurs just before Beat 4 of Measure 18 (18.4). This may or may not be close enough for your purposes, but let's say that you really wanted the cut between those two scenes to fall exactly on Beat 1 of Measure 19 (19.1) or even Measure 20 (20.1). You'll recall that changing the project tempo will change the duration of the project and thus shift the timing of every event as it relates to the video, which acts as a One-Shot and does not stretch or compress as a result of tempo variations. To adjust the tempo to the exact value you need to move that marker to 20.1, follow this procedure exactly. Any extraneous mouse clicks will mess this process up, so be careful and get ready to hit Ctrl+Z and start again:

1. Drop a marker at the scene change (as shown in Figure 11.7). Notice that the project tempo is 120.000 bpm.

2. Click the marker to move the cursor to the marker's position.

3. Drag the marker to the place on the timeline where you want the scene change to take place. In this example, we are going to drag the marker to the 20.1.000 position. Leave snapping turned on so that the marker will instantly snap to the 20.1 grid marker. Note that the timeline cursor remains at the marker's original position and does not move with it as it is dragged.

4. Right-click the marker and, from the context menu, select Adjust Tempo to Match Cursor to Marker.

Figure 11.7
Adjusting the tempo of a project to match the action in the video.

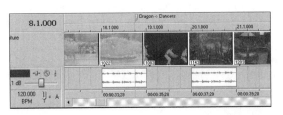

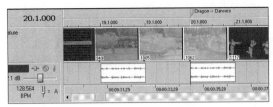

The entire project will shift relative to the video (and any other One-Shot tracks, such as the audio from the video file) as a result of a change in tempo. In this example, the tempo will speed up to 128.564, as you can see in Figure 11.7. If you zoom in on the marker position, it will still be exactly where it was before in the video and, thus, at exactly the same position relative to time in the real world. In relation to the project, looped or Beatmapped tracks, and events, however, it is in a completely different position. The tempo difference from 120 to 128 is not that great, but it is noticeable even though ACID will make sure the pitch of the events does not shift. Here we moved only a little over a measure in a project that lasts almost four minutes, but the change in tempo was still fairly significant. It is important to have the video and audio as closely synced as you can get it before using this process to make final adjustments. Also keep in mind that this shifts the entire project and you cannot use this to sync up multiple areas of the project. While the example uses a cut in the video as the synchronizing event, this is also very useful when synchronizing the project audio with the audio track from a video file.

Video Audio

In many ways, the audio track that was recorded along with the video on the camcorder requires special consideration in ACID. It is not a loop and should not be stretched or altered. It usually won't be beatmapped, often for the same reason. It will often be the longest audio event in the project and, as discussed previously, it often needs to remain in sync with the video.

As with all audio (and video, for that matter), the most important factors in getting good quality audio happen well before we get to post-production in ACID. Camcorder microphones are very high on the list of microphones that you do not want to use for recording audio. Any decent external microphone will eliminate a host of background noise problems, but this will require some research to get the right microphone for your application and camcorder. One common example would be a shotgun mic, which can be found for less than $100. Lapel mics are even cheaper and are great for interviews. Be careful with wireless mics, however, as they can be unpredictable and may receive interference, depending on your location. If your subjects are going to remain very close to the camcorder, a wired lapel mic is more reliable and cheaper. In any case, when using an external microphone (which not all camcorders will accept), get a pair of earphones to monitor the recording session. If possible (and it is not on most camcorders), turn off the automatic audio gain control, especially in interview situations, and adjust the gain yourself with a sound check before recording.

When recording a live concert, it would be best to avoid the entire microphone issue all together. In this case, bring along an additional recording device and hook directly into the soundboard. Camcorder microphones will be perfect for recording ambient crowd noise to mix into ACID later, but the sound from the band will be of the highest quality through the soundboard. Small DV audio recorders are ideal for this purpose, but any device that records digitally (such as an MD recorder or even a spare DV camcorder) or that records timecode on the tape will be very useful.

NOTE
Do your research before you attempt to hook anything up to a soundboard. Not only do you need to get the right size connection hardware, but you need to make sure that the signal coming out of the sound board matches what your recording device wants (for example, matching balanced or unbalanced signals). Just because the plug fits doesn't mean it will work.

In the end, you are going to need to sync this audio up with the video, and this may be difficult when using an analog tape machine, which may allow the tape to drift slightly because of variations in playback speed. Synchronizing audio to video from separate sources is simply a matter of finding a sharp and distinct noise (for example, a drum beat or hand clap) and lining

CHAPTER 11

up the waveforms on the timeline. Since ACID is not a video-editing application, this is the same process you would use in your video editor when using multiple cameras for a single shoot: Audio waveforms can be much easier to line up than trying to match video frames visually. Indeed, the clichéd Hollywood clapperboard is used not only to identify the scene and take before a shot but is even more important for synchronizing the audio. Even a simple handclap before starting the action is very useful for syncing up multiple cameras and audio later.

Fixing Poor Audio

Audio that is recorded using an onboard camcorder microphone is usually of very poor quality. This is not a condemnation of the technology or the quality of onboard microphones—which do a remarkable job of recording in low-level noise situations, are usually directional, may respond to match the zoom level of the camera, and sometimes have sophisticated noise reduction algorithms. The problem is that today's ultra compact camcorders are designed to make the camera easier to use and more portable. In the process, it has become impossible to get truly good quality audio from a camcorder without some kind of external microphone.

Camera motor noise is chief among the problems with a microphone that is in contact with or even inside the camcorder body. Additionally, in the course of designing camcorders that are easier to use, automatic gain (volume) controls mean that in quiet situations, camcorder microphones often get more and more sensitive. This can result in a breathing of the audio track, with the volume gradually getting louder when there is silence in the room and resulting in the background noise growing louder. Automatic gain control is a type of compression and acts very much like a Compression or Dynamics audio FX plug-in. To eliminate camera noise using the Track Noise Gate plug-in (as one example), do the following:

1. Click the FX button on the track with the camera noise.

2. In the Audio Plug-In window, click the Edit Chain button.

3. In the Plug-In Chooser, double-click the Track Noise Gate plug-in and click OK to close the dialog box.

4. Select an item on the Preset list and simultaneously play back the project to hear the changes in real time.

The Noise Gate plug-in will reduce all low-level noises below the Threshold level to zero, making these sections silent. The idea is to retain the content and eliminate the background (camera) noise, so you will need to play with the thresholds. There are a couple of other FX plug-ins types that are especially useful for camera noise:

▶ **Dynamics**—A number of dynamics plug-ins can be used to apply noise gates and compression to tracks. The entire process would be to first eliminate background noise with noise gate, then apply compression to reduce the peaks in the file, and finally increase the gain (volume) of the entire track. Without the compression, increasing the volume would cause clipping. Without the noise gate, the background noise would become too loud. See Chapter 8 for more information, especially on the Noise Gate plug-in and the Graphic Dynamics plug-in.

▶ **Equalization**—Camera noise is often isolated to a narrow range of frequencies or a couple of different, but narrow, frequency regions. Even the simplest of equalization plug-ins, such as Track EQ, can be used to isolate and eliminate camera noise. Again, see Chapter 8 for more information on using these plug-ins. The Multi-Band Dynamics plug-in allows you to apply dynamics to specific frequencies and is an excellent tool as well.

Ducking

Ducking is the term used to describe the process of temporarily lowering the volume of an audio track, usually to lower the volume of the music for a voiceover narration. The basic process is very simple and can be quickly accomplished with Volume envelopes in ACID.

As you might have guessed, this is not such an easy thing to do if you needed to duck the volume of a couple dozen tracks at the same time. Practically speaking, it is not feasible. Instead, you might want to wait until the very end of the project before adding the voiceover narration. Here's how:

1. Mute any tracks (such as the voiceover narration, if it is already inserted) that you don't want to duck under the voiceover.

2. From the Tools menu, select Render to New track. Enter a name and press the Save button. This will mix down all of the tracks to a single file and insert a new track into the timeline.

3. Delete (or mute) all of the tracks you mixed down so there is no duplication. You can select and mute (or delete) multiple tracks by holding down the Ctrl or Shift key while clicking on the track header.

4. Draw an event on the timeline that encompasses the duration of the media file and, in this case, the project.

5. Insert a volume envelope into the track; right-click anywhere in the track and, from the context menu, select Insert/Remove Envelope > Volume.

6. Double-click the envelope to add points (nodes). Each duck will require four points, as shown in Figure 11.8.

7. Drag the middle of the line (at the center of the four points) down to reduce the gain. The shorter segments between point one and two and between three and four serve as a brief fade-in and fade-out. These can be very short, often less than half a second.

Figure 11.8
Two sections of the mixed-down background music track (bottom) have been ducked down to allow the voiceover to be heard more clearly.

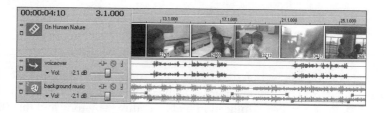

CHAPTER 11

Mixed-down tracks are inserted as Beatmapped tracks. As such, the track inherits the key and tempo of the project. If the project key or tempo is changed, the Beatmapped track will also change.

Rendering Video

While the fundamental procedure for creating video files is identical to creating audio files— File menu > Render As > (select a video format)—the actual rendering can be significantly more difficult. Video files tend to be much larger and may take much longer to render. For video that will go back out to your DV camcorder and television, the decision on format is easy: Render the video once in exactly the same format. For video that is intended for the Internet, an intranet, or other distribution on a computer (for example, CD-ROM), the choices are much more complex, because the files must be carefully compressed, balancing quality against file size.

Render Once

For video that is intended to go back out to your camcorder and television screen, file size and transmission are not issues. You must maintain absolutely 100 percent of the quality of the original, and that means that you do not want to re-render the video. The only way to do this is to use exactly the same settings in your original video. To find the proper render settings, select the file in the Explorer window and look in the Summary View (see Figure 11.9). If the Summary View is not visible, click the arrow next to the Views button and make sure Summary View is checked.

Figure 11.9
The Summary View at the bottom of the Explorer window displays the relevant video properties.

As shown in Figure 11.9, an NTSC-standard Digital Video (DV) file in the United States would have dimensions of 720×480 at 29.970 frames per second (fps). So rendering would occur like this:

1. From the File menu, select Render As.
2. From the Save as type list, select Video for Windows (*.avi).
3. From the Template list, select NTSC DV.
4. Enter a name and click the Save button.

Rendering should be relatively fast, roughly equal to the duration of the file. This is because the video is not actually being rendered but is being copied to a new file. If the rendering process takes a long time, it may be an indication that something is wrong and that the file is, indeed, being re-rendered. To check the settings, from the Render As dialog, click the Custom button, which opens the Custom Settings dialog. For DV, this is fairly easy, but the process may be more complex for other types of video. The list in Figure 11.10 shows two ASUS codecs which might be used to capture video from a non-DV camcorder (for example, Hi-8 or VHS-C). When rendering video from these sources, you would want to use that codec. This list is found in the Custom Settings dialog box, on the Video tab, in the Video format list. The particular codecs will change from machine to machine and will often depend on your hardware (in this case, an ASUS capture card). Despite the apparent wide variety of choices, there is only one choice to maintain the highest quality: Whatever the codec of the source material, that is the codec you should use on the Video format list.

Compression

Video that is destined for playback on your computer is much more complex to render. This is because this type of video needs to be compressed, reducing the file size and making video download times more realistic. Compression occurs in a number of different ways and always results in some loss of quality.

▶ **Frame size**—Full-frame-size video can typically be 640×480 pixels for video in the United States. Reducing the frames' size can dramatically decrease file size. Internet video should rarely be higher than 320×240, but it isn't a bad idea to maintain the aspect ratio. This means that 720×480 DV video might be reduced to 360×240 or 180×120.

▶ **Frame rate**—Full-frame-rate video in the U.S. is almost 30 frames per second (fps). Reducing this to 15 fps directly reduces the file size by a half.

▶ **Compression method**—Finally, there are a number of different computer algorithms that can be used to compress video. Programs used to compress video are known as a codecs because they perform COmpression and DECompression. Some are better than others, and some are better at specific applications. In addition, you need to understand who your viewers are, because they also need to have the same codec installed on their computers as well. Furthermore, streaming technologies frequently require special Web servers to distribute the files over the Internet properly, so you will need to verify that your Internet service provider (ISP) has the correct server installed. Specific compression methods are discussed in more detail in the following sections.

What Compresses Well

Not all video compresses equally well. Talking heads, such as on the evening news, and video with little action compress well. Fast-action sports, ocean waves, and trees with quivering leaves all compress poorly. Unfortunately for ACID, music videos, or anything with a lot of cuts and scene changes also tend to compress poorly. And what is considered good compression? Well, anything can be compressed, but the obvious goal is to have something that still looks good afterward. On the Internet, what "looks good" is highly subjective, and almost all video—even the very highest of quality using the latest 21st century codecs—still does not compare well with even the lowest-quality television broadcasts.

Compression of video can be done a number of ways, but it is most commonly done in two places: intraframe and interframe. Intraframe compression is done within single frames of video and is similar to the way a JPEG image (a very popular still image format on the Internet) is compressed. While an uncompressed picture (in, say, the BMP or TIFF formats) may identify every single pixel in an image with 100-percent fidelity and might take up 1 MB (1,000 KB) of hard disk space, the same picture saved as a JPEG might only be 20 KB. This is done by creating blocks of similar color. For example, where an uncompressed image represents four slightly different blue pixels with four pieces of information, a JPEG image might change all of those pixels to the same color of blue and represent the entire block with one piece of information. This does result in a loss of some quality and can sometimes be seen as blockiness in an image, especially along high-contrast lines.

The other way video is compressed is interframe or between frames. In this case, there can be a similar process of comparing blocks of color in a number of different frames and saving this information to a single piece of information, instead of many pieces for each frame. This is why video with little motion (little change between frames) compresses much better. Of course, this is a great simplification to this decidedly high-tech process, but even a basic understanding will help you to make better choices about video for the Internet.

ACID can save video in four basic formats: *.avi, *.mov, *.rm, and *.wmv. These formats do not define individual codecs and should not be confused with the actual codecs that are used for compression. In other words, it is not possible to say that *.mov files are better than *.wmv files, since each may use different underlying codecs or possibly even very similar codecs. There are situations where you might want to use one or the other, and the following sections should guide you a bit in making a decision.

Video for Windows (*.avi)

The *.avi file format is the Video for Windows general-purpose file format and can use a large number of codecs, some suitable for professional-quality productions and some suitable for highly compressed Internet transmission. Figure 11.10 shows a list of the possible codecs that might be available on a typical Windows PC, although the exact codecs will vary depending on what you have installed. This list is found by clicking the Custom button. Then, in the Custom Settings dialog, click the Video tab and then select a codec from the Video format list.

Figure 11.10
Select a video
codec from the
Video format list.

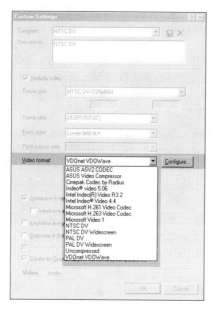

In most cases, the *.avi format is best used for video that is not intended for high compression, since Microsoft has a different format tailored for compression (*.wmv). Still, the older Cinepak and Indeo codecs yield fairly good quality video, although the file sizes are larger. These codecs are also widely available, even on older PCs, so compatibility is usually not a problem. Usually, *.avi files are used in capture and editing for video that is going to go back to television (see the previous Render Once section), although there is no reason why highly compressed codecs could not be used with the *.avi format (for example, VDOnet or the Microsoft H.263 Video Codec).

Most codecs on the Video format list for *.avi files will have a special configuration properties box that can be accessed by clicking the Configure button next to the Video format list.

Streaming

Streaming is the process of allowing you to watch a video as it is being downloaded. There is nothing magic about streaming video. Despite what you may have heard, it does not download any faster than anything else. To watch an entire video from beginning to end requires the same amount of time, streamed or not. Some streaming methods do allow you to view the middle or end of a video file without downloading the entire video, however. The concept behind choosing an appropriate stream is to create streaming video files that match the bandwidth of the viewers' connection to the video, either over an internal company intranet or over the Internet. For example, you might want to stream video at 256 Kbps for viewers with DSL connections. The idea is that the video stream data rate should not exceed the connection speed data rate, allowing the video to be transmitted and played back at the same time. Of course, the real world is a complicated place, consisting of ISPs, routers, and Internet congestion—among a million other variables—so selecting a proper data rate for streaming video is not easy.

CHAPTER 11

Properly streamed video also usually requires a server, such as a Windows Media Video server. This software server must be installed on the computer that is to be storing the accessible video file that people can download. This is usually at an ISP, although you could run it yourself on a computer connected to the Internet. While the compression codec and player are free of charge from Microsoft, the server is not. Your ISP may not offer this service at all or may charge to let you use it. Most likely, you will need to shop around for a company that specializes in streaming media service in order to properly stream your video.

This does not mean that you must stream streaming formats. As mentioned, streaming formats can produce some very highly compressed video files. These files can be put on any Web site or CD-ROM and anyone with the proper codec will be able to download and play them back; they just won't stream properly.

NOTE

Data rate is measured in bits per second (bps). Bits (b) are different from bytes (B), which are used to measure file size, where:

$$1 \text{ byte (B)} = 8 \text{ bits (b)}$$

So if you wanted to stream a one-minute, 1 MB (megabyte) video file in real time, the minimum data rate you would need to achieve would be:

$$(1,000,000 \text{ bytes} \times 8 \text{ bits/byte})/60 \text{ seconds} = 133 \text{ Kbps}$$

Remember: This is the minimum data rate. In the real world, you would certainly need a connection with a higher rate.

QuickTime (*.mov)

As *.avi is to Windows PCs, so QuickTime (*.mov) is to Macs. The QuickTime format is a very popular and widely accepted format that can use a huge variety of codecs, from uncompressed broadcast quality to the most highly compressed streaming Internet formats. In many ways it is more useful than *.avi, since QuickTime is commonly available on PCs everywhere, but it is not necessarily better or higher quality, since that depends on the codec used.

The Video tab in the Custom Settings dialog for the *.mov format contains all of the codec and compression variables.

▶ The *.mov format is, as its name suggests, primarily a movie or video format, but you can also create *.mov files that are audio only. The **Include video** option needs to be checked for all video projects.

▶ The **Frame size** and **Frame rate** options are standard variables. In most cases, you will want to keep the aspect ration of the frame size (for example, 640×480 source goes to 320×240 or 160×120) to prevent distortion. Standard frame sizes are available on the list, or you can select Custom frame size and enter your own settings.

▶ **Field order** is only important for video that is going back to a television set. Computer video should use None (progressive scan), and one of the other two options (most often Lower field first) should be used for television. Field order (interlacing) problems will manifest themselves only on a television monitor due to technological differences between television and computer monitors (although that is slowly changing). Jumpy or jittery video on a television may be an indication of field order problems. Your video capture card's manual should have information about the proper settings.

▶ The **Pixel aspect ratio** sets whether individual pixels are square (1.000) or rectangular (any other value). Most simply, computer video uses square pixels and television uses rectangular pixels (most often 0.909). Problems with the aspect ratio result in distorted video, although it is often very subtle.

▶ The **Video format** is the codec used to compress the video. As with the *.avi format, different codecs are available, depending on your computer system. Each codec has its own settings and variables that can be modified by clicking the Configure button. Some of the items on the Video format list for *.mov files in ACID are really still image formats (see Figure 11.11). When one of these are selected, QuickTime will save each frame of the movie in the selected format (for example, BMP), package them into a single file, and then save a *.sfl file along with the movie (*.mov). This small file contains instructions that tell the QuickTime player how to play the file back. Some of these still image formats are not designed with video in mind and will result in huge files that cannot be played back smoothly due to computer limitations. One example is the Windows uncompressed image file format *.bmp. A five-second, 320×240 *.mov file at 30 fps saved with the BMP format yields a file that is more than 34 MB. In contrast, the same file could very easily and nicely (although not losslessly) be compressed to a very high quality file of less that 1.5 MB. Some of the formats that may show up that are really intended for still images are BMP, Photo JPEG, Planar RGB, PNG, and TIFF. Some other formats will also produce very large file sizes and are designed for highest-quality video and not compressed video. You can also do Render Once (see the previous discussion) with *.mov format, although on Windows PCs, most capture cards will want an *.avi file.

CHAPTER 11

Figure 11.11
The Video format list in this dialog box identifies the codec and not the file format.

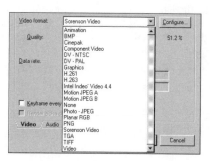

▶ The **Quality** slider can affect the quality for some formats and is usually an intraframe variable. It is rare for the quality to improve significantly above 80 percent for compressed files without dramatically increasing the file size.

▶ The **Data rate** is a way to control the size of the final movie regardless of the Video format, frame size, or frame rate. Only video formats designed for compression will be able to use this. It is possible to try the impossible by setting the Data rate to some low value and use an uncompressed codec with a large frame size and frame rate (for example, constraining 720×240 at 29.97 video to a 56 Kbps data rate). Practically speaking, the Data rate is useful when you have some idea of what final file size (data rate) you want at a particular and well-chosen frame size and frame rate. The Unconstrained option will create a file that uses the chosen codec's settings, while the Basic option will allow you to set a **Target rate** for the codec. Some codecs (but none of the ones visible in Figure 11.11) also allow a **Peak rate** variable, which will compress the file as best it can—often higher than the target rate but never exceeding the Peak rate.

▶ The **Keyframes every** option is used to determine which frames are saved at a higher quality and are used as references for the more highly compressed frames between them (see the discussion on Iframes under the *.wmv format). Higher numbers yield higher quality but also larger files.

▶ **Render alpha channel** allows you to set transparent areas in your video that allow background material to show through. This works only for uncompressed formats (such as *.TGA) and would need to be set up in your video editing or animation program.

The Audio tab is similar to many other audio tabs in ACID rendering. Details are presented in the next chapter. The last tab for the *.mov format is the Streaming tab. There are a few options here that are specific to streaming video from a QuickTime Streaming Server installed at your ISP. Contact your ISP for information on streaming the *.mov format and which options are available.

NOTE

This book details the latest and greatest. By the time you read it, however, there may very well be updates to these formats: Some may have new version numbers and others may even have completely different names (although the companies should still be around).

RealMedia (*.rm)

The RealMedia streaming video format is the most complex of the streaming formats that come with ACID. While this may make it a bit more intimidating at first glance, it also has the most flexibility. RealMedia servers are widely available at some ISPs, but you may not need a RealMedia Server running on the Web hosting machine to stream this format. Regardless, as with all other codecs, your viewers will need to have the RealMedia player installed on their computers to view these videos.

The Custom Settings dialog box, like the other formats, has a number of templates that can be selected if you don't want to deal with the many complex options available with this format. The **Encode Settings** tab is similar in function to the bit rate tabs in other streaming codecs.

▶ The **Target audience** is where you can select the specific bit rate of the stream for the entire file, video and audio included. Bit rate is explained at the beginning of the previous section on streaming.

▶ The **Audio format** basically adjusts whether the file is in stereo and the overall quality. The **Video quality** sets the overall video quality, but there are many more controls that are used to adjust the video on the various tabs. Neither of these gives you precise numerical control over the stream; click the Advanced button to define the settings for each preset.

▶ The **File type** is important depending on whether your ISP has a special RealServer. Most ISPs do not, and the ones that do will almost certainly charge for its use. The advantage to using a RealServer is that you can select multiple bit rates so your audience can choose a bit rate for streaming without you needing to render a number of different files at different bit rates. The Single Rate option is less flexible, but these files can be streamed off of your ISP's current Web server without any modification. This is a serious advantage of this format over some other streaming formats.

▶ Try to keep the aspect ratio of the resized video the same as the original video in the **Re-size video frames** option to prevent distortion. Select Custom from the list if none of the presets matches your needs. See the next bullet point for information on changing the frame rate.

▶ The **Advanced** button opens the Target Audience Settings–Video Clips dialog box, which allows you to define the numerical value for all of the presets. The **Audio** tab lets you set the precise numerical value for all of the presets on the Audio format list. Because you can select from eight Target Audiences and four presets for each under the Audio settings, there are quite a large number of scenarios you can plan. It is not possible to increase the bit rate of the four presets beyond the bit rate of the Target Audience selected. The **Video** tab is simpler and lets you select a bit rate (Target Audience) and the Max. Frame Rate in frames per second (fps). The **Target Bitrate** tab allows you to set the exact bit rate for each of the Target Audience options. The preset values are probably close to the proper values for each of the named presets, but you can enter any values you like here. For example, you could set the 28 K modem preset, which implies a roughly 28 Kbps stream, to encode 1,500 Kbps files, which is insane.

The **Video** tab in the Custom Settings dialog box determines how the codec encodes the video. Each of the four options is explained quite well within the dialog box itself. You should always use **Enable 2-Pass Encoding** for the final movie. Although this makes the rendering process significantly longer, squeezing every ounce of quality out of your video is critical. You may want to deselect this option when you are experimenting with finding the best settings, but make sure you turn 2-Pass back on again for the final render. **Enable Variable Bit Rate Encoding** is another highly recommended rendering option. As noted, this may increase the time it takes for the video to begin playing but usually only by ten seconds or less. The benefits can be significant, and most Internet users are tolerant of a few seconds of delay at this point. Instead of sending a constant stream at, say, 60 Kbps, variable bit rate encodes low-action/low movement sections of video using less bandwidth and higher-action/higher-movement areas with higher bit rates. The sum of the bit rates is still 60 Kbps, however.

The **Advanced Video** tab allows you to select the specific Video codec used to encode the video. All three codecs are basically different versions of the same codec, with RealVideo G2 being the oldest, RealVideo G2 with SVT being newer, and RealVideo 8 (which also uses SVT) the newest. Although the names of RealMedia products and codecs change RealOften, there is a continuous line of development here. (Note: Just before this book went to press, RealOne was released.) The only reason not to use the newest codec is if you are certain your audience is using the older RealPlayer G2, which is now called RealPlayer 8.

The next four options on this tab control the technical aspects of how the codec proceeds. **Inverse-Telecine** determines how the frame rate is reduced from full frame rate (29.92 fps) to the compressed frame rate (15 fps) and just determines which frames are deleted (every odd frame or every even frame). Since frames must be eliminated no matter whether this is checked or not, it is hard to say whether using a different method will make any difference in your project. Likewise with the **De-interlace** option. Video on a television is interlaced and video on a computer is not, so all video that you view on a computer is deinterlaced in one way or another. Try experimenting with this option if you find stair-step artifacts in the rendered video or see numerous fine horizontal lines. The **High quality resize** filter will improve how the video looks when the viewer resizes the video, almost always to a larger size (for example, when playing the 320×240 movie back at full screen). The **Noise filter** may be used to smooth or blur the video. While this may sound like a bad idea at first, smoothing the video actually makes it easier to encode and will usually result in a higher-quality final video that may appear sharper overall. The **VBR maximum startup latency** option sets a value to the longest amount of time a viewer will have to wait for Variable Bit Rate encoding (on the Video tab).

As the dialogs note, VBR encoding can require more time before video playback is initialized. If the player is not allowed enough time to process the stream before playback begins, VBR playback will not be successful. The delay in playback startup is especially noticeable if the video starts with a higher bit rate (more complex) video sequence.

By default, the **Maximum time between keyframes** is 10,000 ms. You may want to decrease this value in an attempt to improve the quality of your video, but compression keyframes take up more space (they have a higher bit rate). It is unlikely that you would want to increase the time between keyframes.

The **Summary** tab has a few final options. **Enable perfect play** sets up a buffer in memory that stores video as it is streamed, which can sometimes improve the performance of the stream. This option will not make a difference as you preview it on your source computer but only when streamed. The other two options, **Allow download** and **Allow recording**, let you decide whether you want to let your viewers save the streamed file to their computers for local playback or whether you want to require people to come to your Web site for playback. This can be a method of preventing people from stealing and distributing your video themselves, but it can also discourage people with slower connections from taking the time to download higher-quality versions of your video for playback locally (that is, not streamed). The **Media clip information** group box is optional artist and copyright information.

Windows Media Video (*.wmv)

The Windows Media Video (*.wmv) format is up to version 7 in this installation of ACID 3.0, but there will certainly be a version 8 out by the time you read this. While the latest and greatest is nice to have and will probably be available for download from Microsoft, you must consider compatibility issues. Just because you have the most recent incarnation of any format or codec does not mean your audience does, and many people resent having to download another application to view your video. The *.wmv format is a streaming media format, although it doesn't have to be used that way. Here's how to use the *.wmv format:

1. From the File menu, select Render As and, from the Save as type list, select Windows Media Video 7 (*.wmv).

2. Select a Template based on your viewer connection to the source. It is possible to target a number of connection speeds, but this is discussed later.

3. Click the Custom button.

4. Bitrate is the most critical factor in streaming video. The total bitrate is the audio bitrate plus the video bitrate together. No matter what you select on the other tabs, the final file will have a bitrate that is equal to the one selected on this tab. It is possible to select audio bitrates that are higher than the total bitrate on the Bitrate tab.

5. Set the balance of bitrates between the Audio tab and Video. There is no way to do this except to experiment.

Finding proper bitrates and balancing the audio and video are not easy, because you are always going to ruin your crystal-clear video and your elegantly mixed audio. The trick is to determine the best possible acceptable quality for your target data rate. Audio takes up much less bandwidth than video and, since this is ACID, after all, you should be able to get pretty decent sound. One other unfortunate aspect of this process is that this experimentation takes a lot of time in rendering. Rendering compressed video is a slow process and there is no way around this.

The Video tab has a number of additional options on it to fine-tune the encoding of the visual portion of your file. While all of these controls are very important, their effects can be subtle:

▶ **Format** basically asks you to select a codec. MPEG-4 is an excellent video standard that can be used, either in a more general form (ISO MPEG-4) or in Microsoft's variant. The other two formats are proprietary Windows Media 7 formats, one for video in general and one that is optimized for screen captures of the Windows desktop and applications in action.

▶ **Frames/Second** is the frame rate and is not subtle at all. U.S. television is almost 30 fps, movies are typically 24 fps, and low-quality television cartoons are usually 15 fps. Frame rate is critical to the smoothness of the video, but lower frame rates dramatically and directly reduce file size.

▶ **Second/IFrame** is a subtle and complex variable that has no easy answer. IFrames are the Information frames (like keyframes) used by the codec. Keyframes are frames that are saved at high quality and thus take up more space in a file. The intermediate frames are derived from the keyframes that surround it. In the simplest case, you could have every odd frame be an IFrame and every even frame be an interpolated frame. Every intermediate frame would then take up virtually no memory and would not be saved in the file, but they would instead be rendered on the fly based on the surrounding keyframes (IFrames) and an amalgamation of the two. In practice, there are a number of intermediate frames between every pair of Iframes, and the rendering calculations can be quite complex. More pragmatically still, lower values (fewer seconds between IFrames) in this box means higher quality, since this is measured in the number of seconds between IFrames. Most other codecs measure keyframes in terms of Iframes/second, instead of the other way around.

▶ **Override default compression buffer** can be used to accommodate slower computers (but not slower Internet connections). This type of compression is very CPU intensive, and setting a value here can increase playback performance.

▶ **Image size** is another straightforward variable that sets the dimensions of the movie. I don't know why Microsoft suggests types of movies with the sizes (for example, Animation or Presentation small), but you should try to maintain the aspect ratio of the original or risk distortion. Select the Custom item from the list and manually enter the size you need.

▶ **Quality** is the basic keyframe quality of the compressed file. Again, this is a very subtle variable that is constrained by the bitrate and so may not be important. There are few advantages to increasing the quality above 80 percent, yet 0 percent does not seem to harm the video.

On the Bitrate tab, you can select a number of different target bitrates for the final file. The size of the file will need to be large enough for the higher bit rate, but all of the selected bitrates will be available on the Windows Media Video Server.

Video Editing?

While ACID 3.0 can handle finished video very nicely, it is not a video-editing application. If you double-click a video event in ACID, or right-click a video track and select Edit Video, a promotional message pops up advertising Sonic Foundry's video-editing applications (see Figure 11.12).

Figure 11.12
A promotional message advertising Sonic Foundry's video-editing applications.

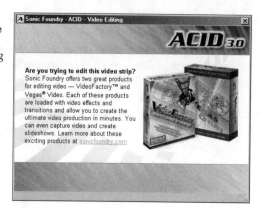

In addition to VideoFactory and Vegas, there are a host of applications from many companies available to edit video on your computer—but at the point where you are using ACID to score a project, the video editing should probably already be finished. One advantage to using Sonic Foundry video-editing software is that the audio is not an afterthought in these products. As discussed in the last chapter, you can use ACID's MTC and MIDI Clock features to synchronize and trigger these video-editing applications, adding a new dimension in flexibility to video scoring. As shown in Figure 11.13, by linking Vegas and ACID, you can edit video simultaneously with the musical sound track in ACID, using Vegas' Preview window to monitor the timing and synchronization. Here's how:

1. Run both Vegas and ACID.

2. Configure ACID to output MIDI Timecode (MTC: ACID and Vegas both chase MTC and not MIDI Clock). This is done from Options > Preferences > Sync tab. In the Generate MIDI Timecode settings option, select one of the Sonic Foundry MIDI Routers. See the previous chapter for details.

3. Configure Vegas to chase MIDI Timecode. Going through the same menus as the last step, select the same device you selected for the Trigger from MIDI Timecode settings on the Sync tab. Place the Video Preview window in a location that will not be covered by ACID once ACID has the focus (see Figure 11.13).

4. Enable (arm) Vegas to listen for MTC: Go to Options > Timecode > Chase to MIDI Timecode, or (as in ACID) press Ctrl + F7 on your keyboard. Vegas' time display will show MTC Input Waiting…

CHAPTER 11

5. Enable ACID to generate MTC: Go to Options > Timecode > Generate MIDI Timecode, or (as in Vegas) press F7 on your keyboard. ACID's time display will show MIDI Timecode Out–Enabled.

6. Play back ACID; Vegas will chase ACID and the time display will read MTC Input Locked.

Depending on the complexity of your project, the combination of using a professional-grade video editing application in synchronization with ACID can tax your computer. Complex sections of your video project, especially areas with lots of overlay graphics and titles, may not preview at the full-frame rate when working this way. This is a good way to fine tune both the video and audio, although it is a bit clumsy and hard on your computer. Following the philosophy of "Render Once" for video, you may want to work with both applications, render the ACID project first, and then insert the audio from ACID into the video application. It is usually better to render audio twice (once in ACID and once in the video app) because you can render audio uncompressed. Video on a computer is almost always compressed in some way, and preventing recompression is critical.

Figure 11.13

Synchronizing ACID with Vegas video editor for expanded possibilities.

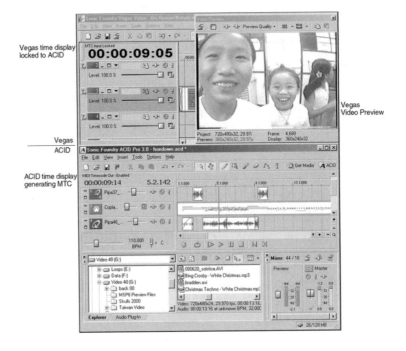

12
Publishing

Publishing your music breaks down into two separate but interrelated steps: rendering and distributing. Rendering is the process of saving your music to an audio file that can be played back independently of ACID. Distributing is a matter of selecting a destination for your music, whether streaming it over the Internet or burning an audio CD. This chapter is a varied one and covers everything from file formats and codecs to streaming media and copyright laws.

Rendering

ACID projects (*.acd) contain all of the information about loops, timing, envelopes, and effects necessary to create a song, but they are not audio files in and of themselves. These project files need to be saved to an audio file format before they can be listened to by the general public. This process of saving to one of these formats is known as rendering. Rendering is also the verb used to describe the creation of audio files, video files, and 3D computer animations, among other things. Rendering in ACID is a fairly simple process—on the surface:

1. From the file menu, select Render As.
2. In the Render As dialog, enter a name for the file.
3. From the Save as type list, select a file format.
4. Click the Save button.

At first glance, this really couldn't be much more simple, but watch the third step: It's a long one. How to select the proper file format occupies a large portion of this chapter. For each file format, there are many controls and settings that must be adjusted. In most situations, you can achieve excellent results by selecting a Template that matches what you want to do with your music file. In some situations, you may want to fine tune the settings of the format to get the best results. The many complex and sometimes confusing controls fill the rest of the chapter.

Miscellaneous Rendering Options

Besides the particular details of each file format and codec discussed later, there are a few ACID-specific rendering options.

▶ The **Render loop region only** option lets you render a portion of the entire project. This might be done to create a new loop file or as a test of a smaller section of the project.

▶ **Save project markers in media file** saves all orange project markers with the rendered file. Project markers are used only for reference purposes and do not change the audio characteristics of a file. These markers are proprietary to Sonic Foundry and can be seen only by ACID (in the Track Properties window) and other Sonic Foundry products.

▶ The **Save each track as a separate file** option does exactly that. There are a number of reasons why you might want to render individual tracks or busses to separate files; primary among them is to send your creation to a post-production facility for professional mixing and/or mastering. You can add up to twenty-six (A-Z) busses in ACID and assign one or more tracks to each, as detailed in Chapter 2. Before rendering these busses to individual files, you might want to create a separate folder on your computer to contain them. To render the busses, select the Save each track as a separate file option in the Render as dialog box. Each track will be rendered one at a time to a media file that spans the length of the project, even if it is 90 percent silence. This means that if you have a ten-track project, the total combined file size will be ten times as large as a normal render and it will take ten times as long to complete. The files will be saved as Track ## trackname.wav (or whatever extension you have chosen).

Digital Audio

All audio files on a computer are digital. Regardless of the format or encoding used to convert an analog audio source to digital, some information is going to be lost in the digitization (quantization) process. This loss may be inaudible on a subjective level and may even be considered theoretically undetectable by humans, but there is an inherent loss of information nonetheless. There are three major variables that influence quality and file size: sample rate, bit-depth, and the number of channels.

Sample Rate

Sample rate is measured in cycles per second (Hz). This parameter identifies how many pieces of information are collected for every second of audio. An 11,000 Hz (11 kHz) sample rate would have 11,000 pieces of information in a second. Higher sample rates are better, but the quality—or fidelity—of the digital file to the original analog source depends on the frequency of the audio. Higher frequency audio is, by definition, composed of more audio waves per second and thus requires higher sample rates for quality digital audio. In other words, lower-pitched audio can be digitized at lower sample rates and still retain a fair degree of fidelity. Figure 12.1 shows an example of how a continuous wave of analog audio might be digitized into discrete pieces of information (quanta). The top image is how the waveform might appear over time. Notice that the waves on the left side of the graph are slightly closer together, representing higher-frequency sound waves. The middle graph is a simulated digitization of the waves and does a poor job with the higher-frequency waves. Actually, it doesn't do a very good job with any of the waves, but this is just an illustration. The bottom graph has a sample rate that is double, or twice, the middle graph. It gets much closer to representing the original wave. In the real world, sound waves are much more complex and varied, especially for music and other rich sources.

Figure 12.1
A continuous analog audio signal and how it might appear once digitized. The bottom graph represents a sample rate twice the middle graph.

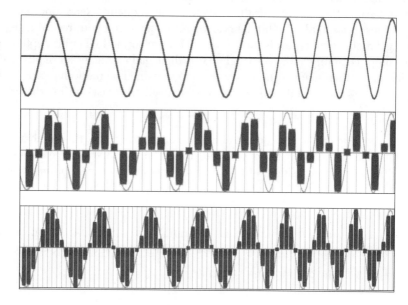

Bit Depth

The second variable that determines quality is the bit depth. Bit depth determines how much information is used to describe each sample. More information per sample yields higher-quality audio at the expense of larger file sizes and, together with the sample rate, bit depth dictates the quality of digital audio. For one second of uncompressed CD-quality audio:

$$(44,100\text{Hz} \times 16\text{-bit}) \times 2 \text{ stereo channels} = 1,411,200 \text{ bits}$$

or, since there are eight bits in a byte:

$$(1,411,200 \text{ bits}/8) = {\sim}176,400 \text{ bytes}$$

For a number of reasons (including the actual size of a byte), this is only an estimate. The file created has a small amount of additional information saved in the header, so the actual number is slightly larger.

Since the dawn of CD audio, 44.1 kHz, 16-bit digital audio has been considered perfect. From the previous discussion, it is easy to see that this is an exaggeration. When CD audio was new, the argument went that this level of digital quality was fairly above anything a human being could discriminate, and this is probably more or less true. Modern computers, camcorders, DAT machines, and studios can now exceed this quality level, as can ACID. In fact, ACID can save and play back 24-bit audio with a 192 kHz sample rate. Whether any human being could ever

CHAPTER 12

possibly detect the difference between one of these files and a standard CD audio file is debatable, although audiophiles will insist that the difference is not only detectable but that the gap between is as wide as the Grand Canyon. Whether the difference is minor or not, it cannot be denied that more information is saved with the higher bit depth and sample rate digital audio and that this is undoubtedly a good thing.

Keep in mind that there is no point in converting 44.1 kHz, 16-bit audio files to a "higher-quality" format, because this will not result in any increase in quality. Recording source material at the highest possible sample and bitrate is a good idea, provided your recording equipment supports the target digital quality levels. Rendering ACID projects to higher bit depth is also not a bad idea. Since projects modify audio files and mix media together, higher bit depths will result in greater fidelity in the final render. There is nothing to be gained by rendering projects at a higher bit depth—say, 24 bit—and then down converting to 16 bit for CD audio or Internet distribution.

Channels

The final setting that is common to almost all audio formats is the number of channels. The channels can be mono or stereo, with stereo files being twice as large as mono files. Mono should be seriously considered for voice and other non-musical applications.

Audio File Formats

The final song can be rendered (saved) to a number of file formats. It isn't really a matter of one being better than another, but your choice of a file format should be based on three factors:

▶ The destination of the file

▶ Whether it needs to be compressed

▶ Your audience and the software they have

The rest of this discussion refers to some of the most common formats, but you may have more or less, depending on the software installed on your computer.

For files that will remain on your computer, you should select a lossless file format. This means that the file will retain 100 percent of the quality and will not be compressed. Any file format on the Save as type list that you can save to can also be played back on your computer: *.aif, *.sfa, *.pca, *.w64, and *.wav formats are all appropriate selections.

Compressed file formats are for use when you need to create smaller files for transmission on the Internet or for spacesaving reasons on your computer. All compressed file formats result in some reduction in quality, although this reduction can be very minor to inaudible. The balance between file size and quality is a delicate one that requires some experimentation and experience to execute properly. Some compressed audio formats are *.mp3, *.ogg, *.rm, and *.wma. An additional consideration for compressed files that are destined to be distributed over the Internet is whether the format can be streamed.

NOTE

While file formats are recognizable by the file extension (such as *.wav, *.txt or *.html), audio and video file formats may also be wrappers around the real format (or codec) of a file. For example, a *.wav file might use the PCM (uncompressed) format or the MPEG Layer-3 format. See the section on codecs for more information.

▶ **Macintosh AIFF** (*.aif) is the standard audio file format for Macintosh computers, just as *.wav is for Windows. It is a lossless file format that preserves the quality of your audio, but it creates rather large files.

▶ **QuickTime** (*.mov) is primarily a video format, but it can be used for audio-only files as well. This format allows you to select a number of different codecs for compression, meaning that this format supports uncompressed and compressed audio.

▶ **MP3 Audio** (*.mp3) is a very popular format that produces well-compressed files that retain a good degree of quality. There are many settings that can be used to adjust the balance of file size against quality. Since this is such a widely used format, it is a good choice for songs distributed to a general audience over the Internet.

▶ **OggVorbis** (*.ogg) is another relatively new compressed media file format that is appropriate for audio delivered over the Internet. It is an open-standard audio format that can be freely used by anyone. Most other codecs, notably *.mp3, require some type of payment for their use (in most cases, you automatically pay when you buy software like ACID). OggVorbis yields high compression ratios, maintains good quality, and supports streaming. This is an excellent format, but, at the time of this writing, it is not as widely distributed as the *.mp3 or *.wma formats.

▶ **Sonic Foundry Audio** (*.sfa) is a proprietary format from Sonic Foundry that will be available only on computers that have software from Sonic Foundry installed on them. Like some other formats, you can select a number of codecs for compression, meaning that *.sfa files can be compressed or uncompressed, using any codec available for *.wav format files.

▶ **Sonic Foundry Perfect Clarity Audio** (*.pca) is another proprietary format from Sonic Foundry. This is a newer and more advanced format that compresses files losslessly. This means that the file size of a *.pca file is considerably smaller than standard uncompressed file formats while retaining 100 percent of the original file quality. For audio files that will remain on your computer, this is an excellent choice, since you can save disk space without sacrificing quality. Use caution when distributing *.pca files to others, because they won't be able to use them unless they have Sonic Foundry software installed. The amount of lossless compression depends on the complexity of the project and the source media used, but it can typically result in a file-size savings of 30 percent or so.

CHAPTER 12

► **RealMedia** (*.rm) is a compressed file format that is suitable for distribution on the Internet. A direct competitor to the *.wma format, RealMedia files are very highly compressed, retain good quality, and are designed to be streamed over the Internet. Listeners will need to download the latest version of the RealMedia Player (available as a free download) to listen to *.rm files, but this is a major format that is widely distributed. This format does not necessarily need a server to stream—see the section on using RealMedia format under "Streaming."

► **Sonic Foundry Wave64** (*.w64) is similar to the *.sfa format and allows compressed or uncompressed audio. The advantage to using this format is that it allows you to create much longer files than the standard Windows *.wav format, which is limited to creating files of less than two gigabytes (2 GB), which is more than three hours and twenty minutes (3:20:00) of CD-quality audio. As with other Sonic Foundry proprietary formats, *.w64 files cannot be played back with most applications other than Sonic Foundry programs.

► **Microsoft Wave** (*.wav) is the standard audio format for Windows PCs, just as the *.aif format is the standard for audio on Macs. Like the *.mov format, the *.wav format is not defined by the codec used to achieve compression but instead acts as a wrapper for a media file and allows you to select from a wide variety of codecs and compression methods.

► **Windows Media Audio** (*.wma) is the default format for highly compressed audio from Microsoft. The latest version (7) offers quality that is at least as good as the other highly compressed formats (*.rm, *.ogg, *.mp3) and can be streamed. It is also very nearly universally available on Windows PCs, thanks to Microsoft's controversial bundling practices. You will still need to make sure your audience has the most up-to-date player, especially if you follow new releases from Microsoft and update to version 8 when it comes out.

Compression

As hinted at in the previous discussion of file formats, the real decision about how to render your final song boils down to compression. The first question is: Do you need compression? If yes, then the second question is: What kind? Audio compression is considerably easier than video compression, and the choices you have are really between a number of compression methods that all produce quite good results. While this may seem like a fairly complicated topic at first, always keep in mind that you can almost always get away with picking a compression method and selecting a template without a second thought.

Lossless Audio

The conversion from analog to digital automatically results in some information being lost (lossy), so there are no digital audio formats that are lossless when compared to an analog signal. Within the realm of digital audio, however, some formats are considered lossless—that is, no audio information is lost when saving to a lossless format. For example, if you are using a 44.1 kHz, 16-bit source file in ACID and you render using a lossless format, the rendered file will be identical to the original. This does not mean information won't be lost when mixing files together, however, but this loss is due to mixing and overlap of the audio and not to the process of rendering the file. As the previous calculations show, one second of lossless audio at 44.1 kHz, 16-bit directly yields a file of about 176 KB.

Lossless means no loss of audio information. It is possible in many situations to eliminate unnecessary data from a computer audio file without losing audio information. This means that an audio file can be compressed in size while still maintaining 100 percent of the original file's audio quality. The Sonic Foundry Perfect Clarity Audio (*.pca) format is an example of a lossless yet size-compressed file format.

Compressed Audio

While all audio loses some quality when converted to digital from analog, compressed audio uses sophisticated algorithms to create smaller files while retaining much of the quality of the original. Most compression methods claim that the loss in quality is minimal, but the art of compression is balancing file size against quality. Every codec or compression method works in a different way. Some are targeted to compress spoken audio and some are better at music. Finding the best compression method for your particular audio requires some research and experimentation.

NOTE

Compression of file size is distinct from dynamic compression of audio, which is the process of reducing the dynamic range. This is discussed in depth in Chapter 8.

Most often compression results in a loss of quality in the stereo image or the spatial depth, dynamic range, and frequency range of the audio. Compression methods are developed using the principles of psychoacoustics, which is the study of how humans perceive sound. The goal is to remove information from the audio file that cannot be perceived by the human ear and brain. Of course, any science that involves perception and the human brain is bound to cover a lot of territory, which leaves plenty of room for discussion about which compression methods are the best. Again, the best compression method for your audio depends on what type of audio you are compressing (for example, spoken words vs. music), how much compression you need, and what sounds good to your ears. Compression is dealt with in more detail in the section, "Codecs and Compression."

Down Converting

Source audio of a higher quality (bit depth and sample rate) can be rendered to a lower-quality format. For example, it is possible, and may even be necessary, to convert 24-bit, 192 kHz audio to CD-quality 16-bit, 44.1 kHz audio, or even further down for Internet audio. This will result in smaller and, thus, more portable files. The process of down converting or down sampling is distinct from what a codec does in compressing a file. Combining careful down converting with a good compression codec is the key to minimizing audio file size.

Down converting automatically results in some loss of quality and has the same problems inherent in converting analog audio to digital. Some type of down conversion occurs for some files when you use source media files in ACID that are of a higher quality than the final rendered file. At times, this can introduce audible artifacts into the file that may be minimized and covered using the Dither plug-in, which is discussed in detail in Chapter 8.

Codecs and Compression

Audio (and video) files may be compressed when rendered to minimize file size. The files will then need to be decompressed when played back. This COmpression/DECompression process is done by the codec. Any codec that is used to compress a file also needs to be installed on any computer that you want to use for playback. Most file formats also define how the file is encoded (for example, *.jpg files use JPEG encoding), but this is not necessarily the case with audio and video files, where the file format can be distinct from the codec. The *.wav file format does not define how the file is compressed, and, in this case, the file format and the encoding format do not need to be the same. Indeed the *.wav file format can use PCM (uncompressed) encoding or even MPEG Layer-3 encoding, using any number of different codecs (see Figure 12.2). The *.wav file format merely serves as a wrapper around the file, telling Windows about the file and how it is to be played back. Using a Windows PC does not guarantee that you will be able to play back all files of the *.wav format, since some may be encoded with codecs that are not installed on your computer.

Figure 12.2
The *.wav format
can use any number
of codecs to encode
and possibly compress
audio.

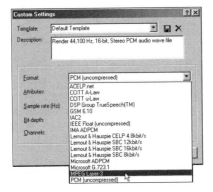

Confusion can arise because of the language used in the dialog boxes when rendering audio files. As Figure 12.2 shows, the *.wav file format Custom Settings dialog box allows you to select a format from a list. This is just a list of codecs and should not be confused with the file format. You can check which audio codecs are installed on your computer by going to the Windows Control Panel, clicking the Multimedia option, and, in the Multimedia Properties dialog box, clicking the Devices tab. By expanding the Audio Compression Codecs tree, as shown in Figure 12.3, you can view which codecs are installed on your computer. You'll notice that the list in Figure 12.2 is similar to, but not the same as, the list in Figure 12.3. For example, the single Lernout & Hauspie CODECs item listed in the Control Panel implies multiple codecs, which indeed show up in ACID's Format list as four individual codecs. The Indeo audio software codec does not show up in ACID as an independent codec at all, since it is only used to encode the audio associated with Indeo video files.

Figure 12.3

All of the audio codecs
installed in Windows
in the Control Panel.
Many more codecs may
be available in ACID
beyond this Windows-
registered list.

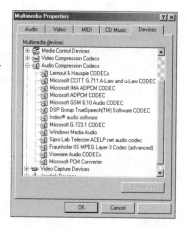

As mentioned, sometimes a file format is defined by a specific codec, or encoding, format. The popular MP3 format defines a file format (*.mp3) which is, in turn, defined by the MPEG Layer-3 encoding used to compress the audio. This MPEG Layer-3 standard for encoding comes from the Motion Picture Engineering Group, which precisely defines how the encoding works and the internal structure of what the file actually looks like. It does not define how this encoding is to be accomplished, however, and there are a number of different codecs available to perform the actual compression. There is, for example, the Fraunhofer reference standard codec, to name just one. While the quality of the files produced by different codecs is a constant source of debate, the final file must still conform to the MPEG Layer-3 standard.

There really are far too many codecs to list and explain individually here. Some codecs were previously explained in the file formats section, since some file formats are defined by the codec they use. A few of the more popular codecs are defined as follows:

▶ **PCM** (uncompressed) stands for pulse code modulation and is a standard lossless format. It is widely used by many formats, notably the Windows *.wav format.

▶ **ADPCM** (adaptive differential pulse code modulation) is a very popular audio compression system, widely used in telephony, HDTV, and many other applications. It is also a common codec used for compressed Windows *.wav files. Not all applications can read ADPCM encoded *.wav files, but most can. While ADPCM files are usually significantly smaller than PCM files, they are still not usually compressed as much as other Internet targeted codecs.

▶ Many of the codecs listed in the Windows Control Panel are used primarily for compression of voice data. For example, μ-Law (mu-) is used for digital telephony in North America and Japan, while A-Law is used in Europe. Other voice codecs include ACELP.net and DSP Group TrueSpeech. **Voice codecs** are not especially well suited to compression of music, but they work very well for the frequencies of speech. Variations on these codecs can be found in both the *.wav and *.mov formats.

This is just a small sample to give you some idea of what is available. A more substantial discussion of a few of the more important codecs follows in the "Streaming" section of this chapter.

CHAPTER 12

Quality and Data Rate

Higher data rates yield higher-quality audio. As discussed earlier, quality can be directly measured in terms of sample rate (cycles per second or Hz) and bit depth. CD-quality audio has a data rate of:

(44,100 Hz $\times$ 16-bit) $\times$ 2 stereo channels = 1,411,200 bits/s

or

1.4 Mbps

This is a pretty high rate for transmission across the Internet, but remember that this is uncompressed audio. There are a couple of ways to get the data rate down. One would be to lower the sample rate.

NOTE

Data rate is measured in bits per second (bps). Bits (b) are different from bytes (B), which are used to measure file size, where:

1 byte (B) = 8 bits (b)

So if you wanted to stream a one-minute, 500 KB audio file in real time, the minimum data rate you would need:

(500,000 bytes $\times$ 8 bits/byte)/60 seconds = 67 Kbps

FM radio is said to be equivalent in quality to a 22 kHz sample rate with 16-bit depth. Plugging this into our equation, we get:

(22,050Hz $\times$ 16-bit) $\times$ 2 stereo channels = 705,600 bits/s or 700 Kbps

This is still far too high for even a fast Internet connection, but this is still uncompressed audio. This is where the compression codecs come into play. One of the most widely used music formats is undoubtedly the *.mp3 format. If you select MP3 Audio (*.mp3) in the Render As dialog and then select the 64 Kbps, FM Radio Quality Audio from the template list, you will end up with what is claimed to be FM radio-quality audio at 22 kHz and 16-bit stereo audio. The calculation above shows that this stream would normally be 700 Kbps uncompressed. This gives a compression ratio of about 11:1 over uncompressed *.wav files, which is quite good, but it is not 22:1, as is suggested in the dialog. This is because the compression ratios listed are always measured against how compressed the audio is when compared to the original CD-quality standard.

So, we get 2:1 compression by lowering the sample rate (44 kHz > 22 kHz) and another 11:1 compression from the MP3 codec. Where does this major 11:1 compression come from? This is the heart of any compression format and is where the differences between the various formats will emerge. It is also where audible artifacts creep into the signal. Claiming that the audio is equivalent to FM radio is a bit disingenuous, since a broadcast FM radio signal is not digitally compressed. This is not to pick on the MP3 format—all compressed formats claim compression that is equivalent to CD-quality or FM-quality and so on, but these references refer only to the sample rate, bit depth, and the arithmetic—not to the actual what-you-hear quality.

Compression Artifacts

All compression codecs introduce some type of artifact into the audio (which would not be heard in FM radio). Whether these artifacts are audible or not depends on how good your hearing is and whether you work for the marketing department at a company that makes codecs. Some types of artifacts are more noticeable than others, and some codecs are more prone to certain types of artifacts than others. Some codecs are better at some data rates and worse at others. Some codecs are better at music, and some are better at voice. It is likely that some are better at encoding classical music with large dynamic ranges, while others do a better job on loud-and-always-loud rock music. In the end, deciding which codec produces the highest-quality output is a very subjective argument that depends on your personal preferences and particular audio application. In any case, compression artifacts can be heard as:

▶ Warbling or swishing, as if hearing music underwater

▶ Echoes, pre-echoes, flanging, and phasing, especially in the higher frequencies

▶ Tinny, metallic artifacts, including chirping and ringing, again in the higher frequency ranges

▶ Excessive sibilance and plosives on vocal parts, noise bursts, and pops

▶ Loss of high frequencies

▶ Loss of stereo separation, space, and reverb

While this sounds like a nightmare of artifacts that would completely ruin a song, these are infrequent and are designed to be difficult to hear. Unfortunately, they are more noticeable once you know what to listen for, as you now do. Sorry. These artifacts are truly a small price to pay when you consider the amazing 20:1 compression ratios (and higher) that you can get out of most codecs while still maintaining a decent level of quality. Just be happy that audio artifacts are much less apparent to the human ear than video artifacts are to the eye, which is why getting quality video over the Internet is extremely challenging. Of course, higher levels of quality in a codec will eliminate most, if not all, of these artifacts. See the section on Sonic Foundry's Perfect Clarity Audio (*.pca) format under "Audio File Formats" for more information on lossless compression.

Media Destination

Regardless of whether you choose a lossless or a compressed file format, any files that you intend to make available to listeners using another computer need to employ a format that is compatible with their software. The following is a summary of recommendations on which formats and codec are appropriate for which destinations:

▶ Material that will remain on your computer or be backed up to CR-ROMs as archives need to maintain 100 percent of the quality and can use Sonic Foundry's *.pca format. Since archives are for your use only, compatibility is not important, but quality is. Files using this format can be 70 percent as large as other lossless file formats, giving you some degree of space savings without compromising quality.

▶ Music destined for the Internet needs to be compressed for portability but must also use a format that is widely distributed. For example, if you use the popular *.mp3 format, you can be reasonably sure that your audience can play these files back. You might also consider using a streaming format, although streaming involves a host of other considerations beyond simply getting the file as small as possible (see "Streaming" later in this chapter).

▶ When burning audio CDs for playback on standalone audio CD players, you will need to select a file format that can be accepted by your CD-writing software. The *.wav format is the most widely accepted format, but many other standard formats may also work. Consult your audio CD-burning software for more information.

Publishing

Publishing your songs either on the Internet or on a record label is the absolute final step in song creation. While signing a contract with EMI Classics may be the most formal way of publishing your music, the Internet and home audio CD creation have made independent publishing of music for the masses a reality.

ACIDplanet

ACIDplanet is an online community developed and run by Sonic Foundry to promote ACID. It offers a place where users can exchange ideas and inspiration and, of course, publish music. The ultimate motivation for the site may be marketing ACID, but don't let that dissuade you from taking advantage of this wonderful resource. There are always songs to listen to, arguments to engage in, free loops to download, and re-mix contests to enter. There is no better place to submit your ACID songs to critical review and get serious people to listen to and comment on your creations. Did I mention free loops?

Publishing to ACIDplanet

The first step to getting started with ACIDplanet is to register with the site. This involves standard username and password procedures for security purposes, but you can also sign up for occasional newsletters and promotional messages from Sonic Foundry. These messages are infrequent and always involve special discounts and introductions to loop series, usually with pointers to getting a few free samples from the new libraries.

To configure ACID for ACIDplanet, connect to the Internet and, from the File menu in ACID, select Publish setup. A small dialog box will open (see Figure 12.4) as ACID attempts to contact the ACIDplanet Web site. If this is your first time, a registration Web page will start up. Once you have created an account, all changes to your account, artist profile, and song uploading can be done from the Publish Setup Web page.

Figure 12.4
ACID first attempts to make contact with the ACIDplanet Web site.

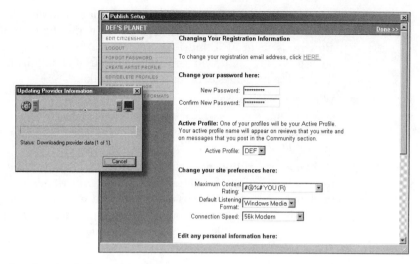

Songs can be rendered and uploaded to ACIDplanet in one easy operation by selecting Publish from the File menu. Once your account has been activated on ACIDplanet, this will start up a series of simple dialog boxes that will walk you through rendering to the *.mp3, *.rm, or *.wma format and then automatically upload the song when finished. You can also select files other than the current project, provided they are already encoded in a compatible format. Figure 12.5 shows the first dialog box in this series.

Figure 12.5
The publishing of an unrendered project begins with the selection of a streaming file format.

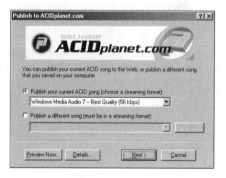

Lounge

It is tough to find true gems created with ACID in the Lounge due to the large number of songs posted here every day. The rating system doesn't always end up working all that well, since groups of people often collaborate to fix the ratings for each other. Stuffing the ballot box is part and parcel of this thing we call the Internet, and none of this is unique to ACIDplanet. The diamonds you'll eventually find in the rough make sticking around worthwhile. Of all the material in this book, the following is by far the most subjective, but this is how I get around the Lounge:

▶ Spend some time on the site. You won't need to browse around for more than an hour to start getting a feel for who's who. Go to the Community forum and see which posters are offering good, well-intentioned advice, then go and find their songs. Earnest folks don't always produce the finest art, but finding people who are serious about ACID music is important. After a while, you'll have a few favorite names you'll wait for new releases from. Send them an e-mail and ask them for some names of other people they like.

▶ While you can't always trust the reviews, look for specific, intelligent comments about a song, such as, "Nice equalization on the slap bass line." Be skeptical of all capital letter reviews and excesses of exclamation marks like "AW3S0M3 d00d!!!!!"

▶ The other half of this interaction is getting reviews of your songs. Again, it helps to have thick skin, and you will need to sort out who is serious and who is not on the site, but most citizens are earnest and will offer thoughtful critiques that are rarely without some encouraging compliments. ACID citizens want to like your music and will look for good qualities as well as things that could be better. To get people to review your work, you should spend some time reviewing other people's work.

8PACKS

Free loops, often designed to work together as a song. Enough said.

Contests

ACID Remix Contests are an extremely fun use for ACID beyond standard song creation from scratch. There are a few prizes offered every month or so, including loop libraries and software from Sonic Foundry. There's also a chance that someone might recognize your work, and this could be the first step on the road to fame. Loop Packs and starter project files are provided for songs in a number of genres from today's top artists. These are good practice and great fun, but be careful you don't spend too much time with these contests at the cost of your own creative projects.

Community

As with all online virtual communities, the free nature of this forum means that you need to wade through a lot of crud to get to the good stuff. It won't take more than a week of casual article perusal to begin to recognize the names of a few regulars that consistently post worthwhile advice. At the same time, you will also start to identify participants who rarely contribute anything but noise. It isn't hard to winnow the wheat from the chaff in this forum.

APRadio

If you find the free-for-all of the Lounge overwhelming, check out AP Radio, which acts as a type of Internet radio station, streaming songs submitted by ACIDplanet citizens. This can be a good way to hear a variety of songs without having to make the selections yourself.

On the Web

Including links to media files created with ACID on a Web page is as simple as providing a link to the file. This can be done by hand or with a WYSIWYG Web page-editing program. On the other hand, it is also possible to embed media files and players into sophisticated dynamic pages that respond to the media file and its contents. Although advanced scripting techniques are beyond the scope of this book, the next few sections should give you a few ideas about what can be done with multimedia on the Web.

Simple Web page

The easiest way to put media into a Web page is to provide a hyperlink to it in the HTML document. This can be as simple as:

```
<A href="my_song.rm">My Song</A>
```

While a text hyperlink may be a bit boring, it is nonetheless simple and effective. When the user clicks on the link, the appropriate player will load and play back the file in its own user interface outside the Web page. This will work for just about any file format.

Embedded Media

A more interesting and less obtrusive way of putting media files on your Web page is to embed the media player into the Web page. This means that the player and whatever controls you want to make available are actually visible as a part of your HTML layout. There are a number of ways this can be done for each of the various players (such as OggVorbis, Windows Media, RealMedia, or QuickTime), but in its simplest form, it couldn't be easier:

```
<EMBED SRC="my_song.mov" VOLUME="50" HEIGHT="60" WIDTH="144">
```

The embedded player has a few attributes describing the initial VOLUME as well as the HEIGHT and WIDTH of the player. The player can be made invisible by not setting a HEIGHT or WIDTH attribute. Figure 12.6 shows what a hyperlink to a media file would look like as well as a QuickTime player embedded with the code above.

Figure 12.6
A hyperlink and
an embedded media
player.

Different players accept and may require different parameters and may allow you to create your own play buttons, sliders, and frames (skins) or set the file to loop continuously. The simple example presented above will start playing automatically when the page loads, but scripting can be used to interact with the media, playing back or pausing in response to user input.

CHAPTER 12

NOTE

Embedded media with an invisible player allow you to create background music for a Web page. I find this very annoying: You should never force your viewers to download giant rich-media files. One excellent use of embedded media is for music that is a part of a presentation or slide show. If it is just background music to My Home Page, think twice before embedding that file!

Command Markers

Command markers are special temporal markers that allow a limited set of commands to be executed at a certain point of an audio file embedded in a Web page. This could include synchronized lyrics in a Web page or the opening of a Web page based on song playback. To add Command markers to a project, move the timeline cursor to the position where you want to add a Command marker and press C on your keyboard (or, from the Insert menu, select Command). Command markers appear as light blue markers above the timeline and main marker bar. The Command Properties dialog box, as shown in Figure 12.7, lets you decide what Command action is taken and when it occurs. For example, the URL Command opens the Web page specified in the Parameter box at the time noted in the Position box (Comments are optional).

Figure 12.7
Commands are added by pressing C on your keyboard.

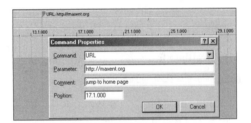

Command markers are supported only for RealMedia (*.rm) files and Windows Media (*.wmv and *.wma) files. Some commands are particular only to the Windows Media format and begin with a WM- prefix. Some commands only make sense for video presentations. The following table lists the commands, what they do, and what parameters are acceptable. Some of these commands interact with the Web browser and the HTML document that contains the media file. While the Command marker itself is fairly simple, the interactions can be quite sophisticated and may require some pretty serious scripting (JavaScript).

Table 12.1
Command marker reference for interactive streaming.

Command	Description	Parameter Example
URL	Jumps to the specified URL	www.sonicfoundry.com
TEXT	Displays text in the captioning area of the Windows Media Player located below the video display area. You enter the text that will display during playback.	Your text here!
WMClosedCaption	Displays the entered text in the captioning window defined with scripting.	Closed Captioned for the hearing impaired.
WMTextBodytext	Displays the entered text in the text window that is defined with scripting.	This is some narrative text in the body of the HTML document, like the lyrics to a song, for example.
WMTextHeadline	Displays the entered text in the headline window that is defined with scripting.	My Great Song Title
Title	Displays the entered text on the RealPlayer's title bar.	Rodrigue et Chimène
Author	Author information displayed when listener right-clicks RealPlayer and selects About This Presentation.	Claude Debussy
Copyright	Copyright information displayed when listener right-clicks RealPlayer and selects About This Presentation.	Copyright © 1890 - 1892
HotSpotPlay*	Video only. Plays the video specified when the HotSpot is clicked.	Duration (Dimensions) "LABEL" FILENAME.rm
MM:SS (LEFT, TOP, RIGHT, BOTTOM) "LABEL" FILENAME	00:10 (0, 0, 40, 25) "Play another file" next_video.rm	
HotSpotBrowse (video only)	HotSpot click navigates to new Web page in browser (RealMedia only).	
MM:SS (LEFT, TOP, RIGHT, BOTTOM) "LABEL" URL	00:10 (0, 0, 40, 25) "Go to ACIDplanet"	http:\\acidplanet.com
HotSpotSeek (video only)	Video only. HotSpot click jumps to new location in video (RealMedia only).	
MM:SS (LEFT, TOP, RIGHT, BOTTOM) "LABEL" MM:SS	00:10 (0, 0, 40, 25) "Go to exciting conclusion" 05:17	

* In all of these Commands, only the last one is required: If no duration is specified, it is assumed to encompass the entire duration of the file; if no dimensions are specified, the entire frame is Hot.

CHAPTER 12

Streaming

Streaming refers to the technology of allowing listeners to play back a file as it is being downloaded. This means that the user does not need to wait for the entire file to download before beginning to listen. It is not some magical format that allows faster downloads or smaller file sizes, and the listener will still need to download the entire file in order to listen to the entire song. Streaming can occur only if the download time for the file over the entire connection, from server to client to everything in between, is less than the total playback time of the file. Many compressed audio formats can be primitively streamed over any Web connection.

NOTE

A number of formats allow the listener to play back the audio file while it is being downloaded without a special streaming server.

More advanced streaming properties may require a server to properly stream. The server controls how the stream is being sent and may be able to compensate for network traffic problems, allow variable bit-rate playback, and let the listener randomly access different parts of the file (instead of listening in a linear fashion). Streaming media servers are sold by a number of streaming format companies and must be installed on the sending computer. This means that you may need to find an ISP that specializes in streaming media to distribute your media or work with your local ISP to get the proper server software installed.

A stream is a stream of data from a server to a client. While standard audio files on your computer are measured by size in KB or MB, streaming media files are measured in terms of data rate, or bits per second, such as Kbps (1,000 bps) or Mbps (1,000,000 bps). This terminology is used for any data rate and is more commonly used to describe Internet connections. For example, a 56K modem can send and receive data at 56 Kbps, while a DSL connection might support 100 Kbps. Just because a device can handle data rates that high doesn't mean you will be able to stream data that fast in the real world. Internet traffic, server loading, routing, brown outs, and just about anything else can cause your connection to the Internet to be much slower than what might be possible.

Streaming Formats

Audio is not nearly as complex to stream as video is, primarily because the data rate for audio can be dramatically lower than video while still maintaining a relatively high level of quality. Because of this greater simplicity, streamed audio does not always necessarily need a server to stream. For example, although the MP3 format is not designed explicitly as a streaming format, in many situations you can play back *.mp3 files as they are downloading, which is the essential definition of streaming. In other cases, and especially with video, a special server is required to stream audio. Streaming media servers also offer the possibility of more sophisticated streaming advantages, such as variable bitrate and multiple bitrates, as detailed ahead.

MP3 Audio (*.mp3)

MPEG Layer-3 audio encoding is very popular and widespread, provides good compression, and maintains high quality. It can be streamed as-is off any general purpose Web server in that the file can be played back as it is downloaded. It does not allow random access. The following summarizes some of the controls found in the Custom Settings dialog box for the MP3 format:

▶ The **Quality** slider sets how carefully the encoder works. Dragging the slider to the right will make the encoding process take more time, but it is recommended that you always take the time to encode at the Highest quality level.

▶ The **VBR Quality** slider is used to determine how Variable Bit-Rate (VBR) encoding works. VBR means that sections of the music that are easier to encode use lower bit-rates and more complex sections of music use higher bitrates, with the average bitrate being the chosen one. This controls VBR within the file and does not affect the streaming attributes of the file.

▶ The **ID3 Settings** tab allows you to add artist and copyright information to the file.

QuickTime (*.mov)

QuickTime is a do-all format that acts as a wrapper for everything from uncompressed lossless quality to streaming media. Since the particular properties of the *.mov file are determined by the codec chosen, it is difficult to discuss the variables in creating streaming QuickTime files. Many of the codecs available in the Audio format list can be streamed, although some are simply not appropriate for Internet streaming (for example, the 64-bit Floating codec). IMA 4:1, MACE 6:1, and Qdesign Music 2 codecs are all excellent choices for streaming. These codecs can be selected from the Audio format list on the Audio tab of the Custom Settings dialog box for the *.mov format. Unfortunately, there are not many audio templates available for this format.

To create a *.mov file that is properly wrapped for streaming, go to the Streaming tab in the Custom settings dialog and select the Prepare for streaming option (see Figure 12.8). On the Optimization list, the Fast start and Fast start with compressed header options create a file that can play while it is being downloaded, but it does not, technically, stream. The largest disadvantage is that the file cannot be randomly accessed, meaning that the listener cannot skip ahead in the song.

CHAPTER 12

Figure 12.8
The Prepare for streaming option must be selected to create streaming media files.

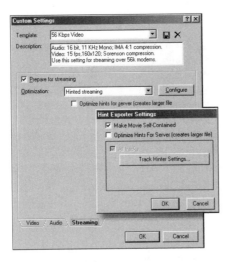

True streaming via a QuickTime Streaming Server must use the Hinted streaming option from the Optimization list. When rendered, this creates a hint track that tells the server exactly how the streaming will be accomplished. Click the Configure button and make sure the Make Movie Self-Contained option is selected. Do not adjust the Track Hinter Settings unless you know about the particulars of packet sizes, etc. on your server. For audio-only files, once the Optimization is set to Hinted streaming, everything else will be fine with default settings.

OggVorbis (*.ogg)

The OggVorbis dialog box contains relatively simple controls for setting up streaming. The quality and compression of this codec is very high and offers VBR encoding, which acts much like MP3 VBR encoding. While OggVorbis does not require a server to stream, there is a free streaming server (icecast) available for Windows32 and some Unix platforms that improves streaming performance. Ask you ISP if it would be willing to take the time to install and configure this server on its machines.

RealMedia (*.rm)

The RealMedia dialog box is the most complicated of any of the formats, which also means that it offers the most flexible set of controls:

▶ The **Target audience** group box sets up the broad category of bitrates that you want to make available. Multiple Target audience selections can be made when streaming off a RealServer (see below).

▶ The **Audio format** allows you to select a preset bitrate identified by a name. This controls how the codec compresses the audio and minimizes artifacts for the type of audio selected, maximizing the quality for that type. The dialog box operates in a slightly different way than others. On the Encode Settings tab, the Target audience check boxes are really just a way to select preset values, which are, in turn, determined by clicking the Advanced button. For example, the actual bitrates for the Single ISDN check box option can be set on the Target Audience Settings tab (see Figure 12.9), which appears when the Advanced button is clicked. The default bitrate range is from 32 Kbps to 44 Kbps, but you can select any bitrate you like. Each of the options in the Audio Settings group box shows up back on the Encode Settings tab on the Audio format list. This flexibility allows you to create preset bitrates that are completely unrealistic for the name of the Target audience (for example, you can create a 176 Kbps preset that can be selected for a 28K modem).

Figure 12.9
The Advanced button allows you to configure the bitrates for the presets on the Audio format list.

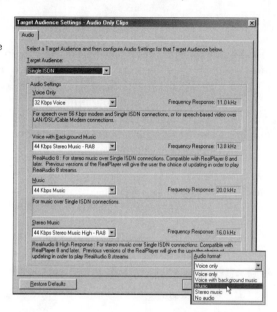

▶ The **File type** lets you select whether your file is streamed using a special-purpose RealServer. RealMedia files do not necessarily need a RealServer to stream, in which case you should select the Single Rate option. If your ISP has a RealServer installed, select the SureStream™ option, which allows a number of advanced streaming options. One significant advantage is that you can select multiple Target audiences rendered to a single file. Listeners can then select the speed of their connection for streaming. SureStream on a RealServer also offers other advantages over simply streaming off a normal Web server, such as error correction and variable bitrate control.

▶ The **Summary** tab allows you to add artist and copyright information to the file.

Windows Media Audio (*.wma)

The *.wma format from Microsoft is a direct competitor to the other highly compressed formats in terms of quality. Excellent results can be achieved with any of these formats, but the *.wma format has one (some say unfair) advantage over the others in that it is distributed by Microsoft. At this point, it does not have market dominance, but you can be certain that many of your listeners will already have the software to playback *.wma files on their computer.

This format has relatively simple controls and a solid list of templates to choose from in the Custom Settings dialog box. There are two codecs to choose from, although the ACELP.net codec is useful only for very highly compressed voice data.

CHAPTER 12

As with other formats, *.wma files do not need to be placed on a special server to allow downloading or even playback of media before the file is finished downloading. In order to properly stream, however, you will need to use the Windows Media Services server installed on your ISP's Web server.

Audio CDs

One of the best ways to distribute your songs is on an audio CD. There is no format that is more universally accessible and allows your music to be played back at 100 percent quality on a proper audio system. This is also a cost-effective solution as well. CD writers are now easily available for under $150 and are often standard equipment on new PCs. Blank discs have fallen well below one dollar and can be purchased in bulk for around thirty cents a piece. If you have been looking for an excuse to buy a CD writer (CD-R), ACID is it, and now is the time.

NOTE
Audio CDs are formatted in a very specific way (Red Book Standard). CDs formatted as data CDs are distinct from audio CDs, although data CDs are still a great way to back up ACID songs and projects.

Setting Up ACID for CD-Burning

Before you can write an audio CD (called burning), ACID must be configured to recognize your CD-writing hardware. From the Options menu, select Preferences and click the CD tab. In the Write drive box, select your CD writer from the list. In the Write speed box, select Max. Unless you have problems with CD writing errors, the driver used to do the writing will automatically select the fastest possible writing speed. Some older CD writers and their drivers may cause problems and you may have to set the Write speed manually in this box.

Burning Songs to a CD

Burning a single song to a CD is simple and does not require you to render the song first. From the Tools menu, select Create CD. This opens a dialog box with only a few buttons and a little information. Click the Add Audio button to render the song and write it to the disc. Depending on the speed of your CD writer, this should take only a minute or so for each song. The progress will be displayed along the bottom of the dialog box, as shown in Figure 12.10. The Write Buffer displays, as a percentage, the data that is in RAM and ready to be written to the disc. With older CD writers, this value could dip dangerously low and, if it reached zero, would ruin the disc. The buffer is likely to become low only if something goes wrong and either ACID is not able to render data quickly enough or your hard disk drive has problems. Typically, the buffer will remain above 90 percent for the entire process. Although there is a Cancel button in the dialog box that can be used at any time, after the burn has started, you should click Cancel only as a last resort in case of a program lockup or crash—the Cancel button is good only for creating coasters once the writing process has begun.

Figure 12.10
The Create CD
dialog box.

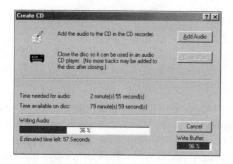

There are some issues with burning songs one at a time to a CD. Your CD writer needs to support writing to disc without closing the disc. Closing means the disc is finished, whether you have burned only one minute or sixty, and it cannot be written to again. Some older computer CD-ROM units and nearly all standalone audio CD players require a disc to be closed in order to play it. With most CD writers, however, there should be no conflicts with ACID, and you can write projects one at a time to the disc as you finish the song. Then, when the disc is full, select Create CD again, but this time click the Close Disc button. After about a minute, the disc will be closed so you can play it in any audio CD or DVD player.

Dedicated CD Burning Software

ACID's CD-burning capabilities are undoubtedly convenient, but they are also limited. There are a number of CD-burning applications available from other manufacturers that provide more features and options, including setting the delay time between songs. It is likely that a simple audio CD-burning software program was included with your CD-writing hardware. There isn't anything about ACID that interacts directly with these programs. Your only concern is that you render media files that are of the right format and have the right attributes. Most frequently, this means 44.1 kHz, 16-bit PCM (uncompressed) Wave (*.wav) files.

Copyright

Intellectual property in this age of effortless digital reproduction is a difficult issue at best. Technically, anything you create is your property and has an implied copyright from the moment you save it in any medium. Music CDs are obviously copyrighted whether they have an explicit copyright statement or not, but so are all songs that are posted to ACIDplanet and even songs simply saved to your hard disk. In the Project Properties dialog for many formats is a field for entering and saving copyright information using the © symbol, which can be added using the Windows Character Mapper or by pressing Alt+0169 on your keyboard. I suppose using this gives you some degree of additional protection, but it is pretty farfetched to believe that a stolen song court case would hinge on whether copyright information was saved with the song. Instead, a copyright notice is most useful in helping people who want to use your song to contact you.

NOTE

According to the U.S. Copyright Office: "Under the present copyright law, which became effective Jan. 1, 1978, a work is automatically protected by copyright when it is created."

This automatic copyright is not the same as registering (and paying for) an official copyright from the appropriate government agency. The name of this agency will vary from country to country, and international copyright law is a hot issue that will be very lucrative to attorneys for many years to come. In the United States, you'd go to the U.S. Copyright Office:

Copyright Office
Library of Congress
101 Independence Avenue, S.E
Washington, D.C. 20559-6000
(202) 707-3000

Or, better still:

www.loc.gov/copyright

There is extensive information on this excellent and well-organized Web site; start with "Information Circulars" under the "Publications" heading. The Forms item under the same heading has any form you need in *.pdf format. Just download the proper form, print it out, fill it out, and send it back. There are two forms that may be applicable to ACID projects:

▶ **Form SR** (Sound Recording) is used for sound recordings and is the most obvious form to use for ACID productions. This is used to copyright a particular performance of a song ("Phonorecords"). Registering the sound recording would allow others to cover their own version of the song and possibly make remixes. It is also possible to copyright the musical composition of a song ("Copies") with this form, although it is difficult to tell what could be copyrighted in the case of ACID projects, since the intent is to copyright sheet music. Perhaps ACID projects can someday be copyrighted along with the rendered song? Pragmatically, even writing out just the melody on staff paper is enough.

Of particular interest to ACID users on this form is Space 6: Derivative Works, which may be used to include information about the particular loops and samples used in your project. Loops from commercial loop libraries almost always give you blanket permission in the license to use the loops in your own creations, so this is not really a legal issue, but it would certainly be appropriate to list those loops in this space, even though it may not be required. You should not register a melody or bass line from a loop file as your own musical composition, however. So one example of the complete process might be to register the actual sound recording as rendered out of ACID, list the drum and bass parts created from Sonic Foundry loop files in Space 6, and also register your original vocal performance as a musical composition, including the melody and/or lyrics.

▶ **Form PA** (Performing Arts) can be used for music, songs, and lyrics, either as sheet music or as sound recordings. Form PA can be used to copyright the song as an idea and as a performance. In other words, a written play would be copyrighted using this form, but not necessarily a particular performance of the play. In musical terms, you could use a sound recording to register the intellectual property of a song without registering the particular performance on the sound recording. It seems like this form would also work for ACID songs, but Form SR is probably better. Form PA will definitely need to be used to copyright video productions.

The cost for filing one form is $30 (at least until June 30, 2002). This does not mean that you need to spend $30 for each song you register. In fact, one widely known trick is to register a bunch of songs on a single form as a single work. It could be that this is intended for multi-movement symphonies or possibly for albums, but the process of registering a Compilation of Sound Recordings or a Published Collection of songs is actively encouraged by the Copyright Office (see Circulars 50 and 56). By including all of your songs in a Published Collection, you can legally protect yourself for a minimal amount of money. Plus, in a few weeks, you'll get an official copyright certificate in the mail, suitable for framing.

13

Loose Ends

This last chapter wraps up all of the loose ends and gives you some tips to maximize your computer and ACID for audio production. Tips on managing the huge volume of media files you may collect, optimizing your computer, and configuring ACID's preferences are all covered.

Loop Management

Loop libraries are typically sold on CD-ROM. While it is perfectly acceptable to leave the loop files on the original disks, CD-ROM drives are much slower than hard disk drives. In addition, octopussing CDs in and out of the CD drive is not a very convenient way to access your loops. For these reasons, it is highly recommended that you transfer all of your loop files from CD-ROM to your hard disk. Multimedia files take up a large amount of space, however, so this could be a strain on your limited resources. The advantages are significant, and with drive prices falling to well under two cents per megabyte, buying an additional hard drive is a very easy and inexpensive upgrade. And you can never have too much space.

Reorganizing the loops on your hard drive is also a good idea. A typical loop CD from Sonic Foundry might be organized such that loop files are buried a level or two into the tree. For example, a library named Techno Basics might have loops organized like this:

> CD:\Loops\Bass\Bass01.wav.

On your hard drive, you might want to create a Loops folder (D:\Loops\) and then organize individual libraries by name:

> D:\Loops\Techno_Basics\Loops\Bass\Bass01.wav.

As you can see, the Loops subfolder below the Techno-Basics folder is redundant—we already know this is a loops folder. It is not that big of a deal, but you can save yourself a mouse click by moving all of the loops out of the loops folder and into the root for that particular library, as shown in Figure 13.1. It may seem that this saves you only a single click, which is true, but when multiplied by the hundreds and hundreds of times you will browse through your loops, the timesavings will be significant.

Figure 13.1
Renaming folders
for loop libraries on
your hard drive can
save time.

The Favorites folder in the ACID Explorer window is also an amazingly simple and useful tool. Select any folder and click the Add to Favorites button to add the entire folder to the ACID Favorites folder. Adding drum rolls and fills to the Favorites folder is a good example since these types of loops can be found in a number of different libraries and it can be hard to remember which library has the particular roll you need.

Some loop libraries organize large sections of loops by number (for example, bass01.wav, bass02.wav, bass03.wav, etc.). It would be very difficult, and not particularly useful, for the library's creator to name all of these loops. Instead, you can rename loops as you audibly browse through them using ACID's Explorer window. There are a few considerations, however:

▶ Loop media files can be renamed in ACID as they would be in Windows Explorer: single click, pause, and single click again; or right-click and, from the context menu, select Rename.

▶ Files on CD-ROM obviously cannot be renamed. Files that have been copied from a CD-ROM to your hard disk may have their Attributes (permissions) set to Read-only, which means they cannot be changed. To change the permissions, right-click a file and, from the context menu, select Properties. Then, on the General tab in the Attributes section, deselect the Read-only check box. You can do this to all files within a single folder by pressing Ctrl + A to select all.

▶ Renaming loops will make other projects that already use these loops unable to find them. When these projects are opened after renaming, an error message will prompt you to relocate these files. In this situation, careful renaming that retains the original name will allow you to easily relink to these files. For example, if you find that bass42.wav reminds you of a Bootsy Collins riff, you might rename the file to bass42_bootsy.wav or bootsy_bass42.wav. Either way, you can more easily find the file by name in the future while still keeping the root of the original name.

CHAPTER 13

RAM

With the exception of Beatmapped media files, all audio media files are loaded into RAM when inserted into tracks in an ACID project. This allows ACID to preview the project in real time without waiting for your hard drive. The total amount of RAM used is displayed in the lower-right corner of the application. This meter displays only the amount of space the media in the project is occupying in relation to the total amount of RAM on your computer; it does not reflect memory that is being used by ACID itself, by Windows, or by any other programs that may be running. It is, therefore, difficult to estimate exactly how much space is available for loops in RAM. As you might have guessed, more RAM is generally better for computing speed, but it is especially useful for multimedia applications. While the minimum recommended amount of RAM for ACID is only 64 MB, 128 MB is ideal, and it is unlikely that you would need more than that. If your projects are typically occupying 30 MB to 40 MB of RAM, 256 MB of RAM is not going to be any faster than 128 MB, depending on what else you are running in conjunction with ACID.

By default, ACID will remove media files from RAM when you switch to another application while using ACID or when you minimize ACID. As an example, Figure 13.2 shows what events on the ACID timeline look like when you switch to Windows Notepad. The waveform on the events disappears and the events display the message, "Media Offline. " Besides freeing up RAM, this allows files to be renamed or otherwise modified by other programs outside of ACID. These changes can change the project, so you may be prompted to reload the media file when you return to ACID.

Figure 13.2
The [Media Offline]
message is displayed
when ACID is not the
active application.

To change this behavior and leave media files in RAM, from the Options menu, select Preferences and, on the General tab, make sure you've selected Close media files when ACID is not the active application.

Processor Speed

Processor, or CPU, speed is, of course, an important part of your computer's performance. Multimedia applications such as ACID can often benefit from faster processor speeds. There are two areas where CPU speed affects ACID: project previewing and project rendering. Since previewing a project in real time is critical to using ACID, this area is more important than rendering times. The minimum requirements for ACID are very conservative, and ACID needs only relatively slow processor speeds (greater than 300 MHz) to work properly. The more loops you use in a project, the more processing power required. In addition, special effects (FX plug-ins) can be especially CPU-intensive and can quickly cause problems. These will manifest themselves in stuttering and crackling playback. As noted previously, most modern PCs will not have any problems due to CPU speed whatsoever, and most sporadic stutters and pauses will actually be caused by other applications running at the same time or even by Windows itself. The difference between these two problems can be observed; applications outside of ACID will cause random, sporadic, and widely spaced stutters, regardless of the project, while problems with ACID will usually be more frequent and isolated to particularly complex projects or sections of projects.

NOTE

Some stuttering and performance problems may be caused by more complex factors involving the interaction of the various parts of your computer. One of the first places you should start to troubleshoot these sorts of problems is on the Audio tab of the Preferences dialog box.

Rendering speed is also processor dependent, although a typical render to any uncompressed format should take only a few tens of seconds. More complex and highly compressed formats may require significantly longer rendering times, sometimes measured in minutes instead of seconds.

Preferences

The Preferences dialog box (click the Options menu and select Preferences) contains a host of options to customize and optimize ACID. Most of these options are covered in the relevant sections of this book:

General tab

Each of the following options can be selected or checked in the dialog box. Items that are selected by default are marked with an "**x**" on the following list.

▶ **x Automatically open last project on startup**—The last project you were working on when you closed ACID is reopened upon startup. Deselect this option if you want ACID to start a new, untitled, unsaved, and blank project every time it is run.

▶ **x Show logo splash screen on startup**—This controls whether the ACID 3.0 title screen is displayed during loading. Deselecting this option keeps this from being displayed but does not decrease loading time.

▶ **x Use Net Notify to stay informed about Sonic Foundry products**—This option allows Sonic Foundry to automatically inform you of product updates and patches. It works only when you are connected to the Internet while using ACID.

▶ **x Draw contents of events**—This controls whether the waveforms are drawn inside events on the timeline. Deselecting this can speed up the performance of ACID when scrolling or zooming on the timeline, but it will not improve playback or rendering.

CHAPTER 13

▶ **x Create undos for FX parameter changes**—FX plug-ins can be considered as separate applications from ACID and operate somewhat independently. Undos (Ctrl + Z) for both ACID and FX plug-ins use up memory (RAM). If you are running short of RAM, you can deselect this option to recover a small amount.

▶ **x Confirm media file deletion when still in use**—This option warns you only if you attempt to delete media files in the ACID Explorer window when they are currently being used in a project. Deleting files that are in use will result in tracks and events that have no corresponding media file. You can switch the media file used by a track and events in the Track Properties window.

▶ **x Close media files when ACID is not the active application**—This option frees up RAM when switching to other applications. See Figure 13.2.

▶ **x Enable multimedia keyboard support**—Multimedia keyboards are simply keyboards that have special additional hot keys used to control the playback of media files. When this option is selected, these hot keys can also be used to control playback in ACID.

▶ **Automatically render large Wave files as Wave64**—The Wave64 file format (*.w64) is a proprietary format from Sonic Foundry that allows much larger files than the standard Windows *.wav format, which is limited to creating files of less than two gigabytes (2 GB), which is more than three hours and twenty minutes (3:20:00) of CD-quality audio. This is a useful option to select if you are doing very long mixes at higher bitrates and sample rates. As with other Sonic Foundry proprietary formats, *.w64 files cannot be played back with most applications other than Sonic Foundry applications.

▶ **Prompt for region and marker names if not playing**—This will automatically create a text box with a flashing cursor to name markers and regions as they are added. This does not happen when dropping markers on the fly during playback.

▶ **x Create project file backups on save (.acd-bak)**—This option automatically creates a file with the same name but with a different file extension in the same folder every time you save. This file can serve as a backup in case the original is damaged or accidentally deleted. These backup files can be opened with the File menu Open command.

▶ **Preserve pitch for new Beatmapped tracks when tempo changes**—Tempo changes speed up and slow down Beatmapped and Loop files. By default, the pitch of Beatmapped tracks changes slightly in response to tempo changes. Selecting this option changes this behavior but requires more processing power and, in some cases, can result in distortions in these tracks.

▶ **x Automatically start the Beatmapper Wizard for long files**—This option automatically starts the Beatmapper Wizard for long files, as defined by the Open files as loops if between (seconds) option on the Audio tab in the Preferences dialog. For example, by default, "long files" are considered to be files more than 30 seconds long.

Audio tab

The Audio tab is used to configure your sound card(s) and drivers. Many performance problems can be solved here, although the default values should work in almost all situations.

▶ **Audio device type** allows you to select the software drivers ACID uses to interact with Windows and, ultimately, your sound card. The Microsoft Sound Mapper option leaves all driver decisions to Windows, while the Windows Classic Wave Driver option may allow you to select from a number of drivers listed in the Default audio playback device option.

▶ The **Default audio playback device list** will be active (not grayed out) only if the Windows Classic Wave Driver option is selected above. Individual pieces of hardware (sound cards) may have multiple possible software drivers, but this list is more typically used to select drivers from systems with multiple sound cards.

▶ **Playback buffering** is set to 0.25 seconds by default and should be adjusted only if playback is skipping or stuttering. Increasing the buffer may solve problems associated with the sound card only.

▶ The **Open files as loops if between (seconds)** option simply defines what audio files ACID considers to be loops and what files it considers potential Beatmapped files or One-Shots. By default, any media file with a duration of between 0.5 seconds and 30 seconds is opened into loop tracks, with shorter files being opened into One-Shot tracks, and longer files being opened into Beatmapped tracks. On the General tab, select the Automatically start the Beatmapper Wizard for long files option to run the Wizard for files defined by this range.

▶ The **Quick fade edit edges of audio events** option prevents clicks and pops that may occur when audio events are cut or split. By default, this option is set to 10 ms. Quick fade edges can be seen as blue curved fade envelopes on event edges if you zoom in on the timeline far enough, as shown in Figure 13.3.

Figure 13.3
Quick fade edges are visible on the split on the top event. The bottom event starts at the beginning of the media file and does not need a quick fade edge.

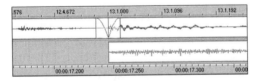

MIDI tab

This tab controls which MIDI devices will be available on the track header for MIDI tracks for playback. More information on using this tab in conjunction with MIDI tracks is detailed in Chapter 10.

▶ The first item allows you to select which devices (hardware and/or software synthesizers) are used for **MIDI playback** and **time code generation**. Selected items will show up on the device list in the track header for MIDI tracks. Although you can select from a number of devices for playback, only the default Master bus (DirectX SoftSynth) will allow you to render projects with MIDI files.

▶ The **MIDI thru device for recording** is the device (such as a MIDI keyboard connected to the MIDI In port) that is used to record MIDI performances as MIDI data to a *.mid file and into a MIDI track and event in ACID.

▶ **Default DLS set for MIDI playback** allows you to select a different DownLoadable Sound set. Click the Load button to browse for and select different sets. See Chapter 10 on MIDI for more information.

Video tab

The Video tab is primarily used to configure DV FireWire cards to output a video signal to a television monitor for preview purposes. The reason for doing this and how to configure this feature is discussed in Chapter 11.

▶ Thumbnail images of video can be labeled numerically in events on the timeline. Select how frames are numbered from the list, if at all.

▶ The next option allows you to select an OHCI-compliant IEEE-1394 device to route a DV video signal through your camcorder and out to a television set. When an OHCI device is selected, additional information is displayed in the Details box.

▶ A couple of additional options become available when an OHCI-compliant device is selected, as shown at the bottom of Figure 13.4. The first option selects the television standard you want to use, such as NTSC DV for North America. Since only the video stream is sent over the IEEE-1394 cable to your television, synchronization can sometimes be problematic. If you are experiencing synchronization problems between the audio from your sound card and the video as it appears on your television, you can adjust the Sync offset (frames) to fix it.

Figure 13.4
Additional options become visible when an OHCI-compatible IEEE-1394 device is selected.

Editing tab

The Editing tab sets some of the more general features of how ACID works. There are only three simple options:

▶ The **default Project tempo range** is set from 70 bpm to 200 bpm, which is a very broad range of possible tempos, from slow ballads to trip hop. These limits control what tempos are available on the Project Tempo button at the bottom of the track header. Since radical tempo differences between a project and the media files it uses can cause distortions, this limited range is a pragmatic consideration only. There is no reason why you should limit yourself to this tempo range if you use loops appropriate to your selected tempo.

▶ The **Editing application section** allows you to set a number of outside editing applications for modifying media files. Some examples might be Sound Forge or Cool Edit Pro. These applications will show up on the Tools menu as, for example, Edit in Cool Edit Pro. To add applications to the list, click the Browse button and locate the *.exe file that runs the chosen program. The Name item is for you to change as you see fit; the default Name will be the *.exe file name.

▶ **Check for Sonic Foundry Editors** is selected by default and allows ACID to automatically detect and list other Sonic Foundry applications on the Tools menu.

CD tab

The CD tab is used to configure both the burning of ACID projects to CD-R and the extraction (ripping) of tracks from audio CDs to media files on your hard disk.

▶ The **Write drive** allows you to select the CD-R device you use to burn CDs.

▶ Select the **Write speed** that works best with your CD-R drive. Select Max to allow your CD-R's software drivers to automatically set the write speed.

▶ **Audio extract optimization** can be left at Full unless you are experiencing problems with the *.wav files ripped from your CDs. CD tracks can be ripped by selecting Extract Audio from CD from the Tools menu.

▶ **Automatically save extracted CD tracks** is not checked by default. Extracted audio tracks are saved to a file on your computer and inserted into beatmapped tracks in ACID.

Sync tab

The Sync tab is used to configure MIDI Time Code synchronization between ACID and other MTC -capable applications. This topic is dealt with in more detail in Chapter 8.

▶ The **Generate MIDI Timecode** settings option sets up ACID to send MTC to another application to allow ACID to trigger that application. The Output device allows you to select the hardware and software combination used to generate MTC. Only devices that are not selected on the MIDI tab are available. The Frame rate determines the format of the MTC and needs to be matched in the receiving application.

▶ The **Generate MIDI Clock** settings option configures a MIDI Clock signal to be created by ACID (instead of MTC, as previously detailed). The Output device allows you to select the hardware and software combination used to generate the MIDI Clock and can be different from the MTC device.

▶ The **Trigger from MIDI Timecode** settings allows ACID to listen for and respond to MTC as sent from another application. The Input device sets the hardware and software driver that ACID will listen to, and the Frame rate sets the format of the MTC and needs to be matched to the sending application.

CHAPTER 13

Appendix
Shortcuts

The following is a comprehensive list of shortcuts and keyboard accelerations available in ACID. While it is not necessary (nor even possible for normal humans) to memorize this entire list, you should always remember that ACID utilizes keyboard shortcuts extensively. If you find yourself using the mouse to push buttons or navigating the same set of menus and submenus again and again, it is probably a good guess that there is some type of shortcut associated with these actions.

Mouse Wheel

Press these keys while using the wheel:	In order to:
None (default behavior)	Zoom in and out on the project
Shift	Horizontal scroll
Ctrl	Vertical scroll
Ctrl+Shift	Move timeline cursor one grid line
Ctrl+Shift+Alt	Move timeline cursor one video frame at a time (only with video in a project)
Press (and release) mouse wheel button	Auto scroll (click mouse button to stop)

Marker Bar

Press these keys:	In order to:
K	Insert Key change
T	Insert Tempo change
M	Insert Marker
R	Insert Region
C	Insert Command marker
1-9 (not on number pad)	Jump to the specified marker or region

Keyboard Navigation*

Press these keys:	In order to:
W or Ctrl+Home	Go to start of project
E or Ctrl+End	Go to end of project
Home	Go to start of selection area (loop region)
End	Go to end of selection area (loop region)
Page Down	Move right (forward) through project by Grid space
Page Up	Move left (back) through project by Grid space
Ctrl+G	Go to (and enter measure number)
\	Center project on position of timeline cursor
1-9 (not number pad)	Jump to marker
Left or Right Arrow	Move timeline cursor back or forward
Alt+Left or Right Arrow	Move timeline cursor one video frame at a time
Ctrl+Left or Right Arrow	Jump to previous or next marker
Ctrl+Alt+Left or Right Arrow	Jump to previous or next event edge (or fade edge) in selected track

These shortcuts allow you to navigate the timeline without using the mouse. Many of these shortcuts also work in the Chopper and Track Properties windows.

Keyboard Selection*

Press these keys:	In order to:
Shift+W or Ctrl+Home	Select to start of project
Shift+E or Ctrl+End	Select to end of project
Shift+Home	Select to start of selection area (loop region)
Shift+End	Select to end of selection area (loop region)
Shift+Page Down	Select right (forward) through project by Grid space
Shift+Page Up	Select left (back) through project by Grid space
Shift+1-9 (not number pad)	Select to marker
Shift+Left or Right Arrow	Expand selection back or forward
Shift+Alt +Left or Right Arrow	Expand selection one video frame at a time
Shift+Ctrl+Left or Right Arrow	Select to previous or next marker

Shift+Ctrl+Alt+Left or Right Arrow	Select to previous or next event edge (or fade edge)
I and O -or- [and]	Create a selection area at any time (on-the-fly during playback): press I or [(In) to start and O or] (Out) to end.
Ctrl+A	Select All
Ctrl+Shift+A	De-select All
Ctrl+Shift+ Drag Mouse	Create (draw or drag) a selection area (regardless of edit tool selected)
Backspace	Recover previous selection areas

As with Keyboard Navigation, these shortcuts allow you to make selections on the timeline without using the mouse. Almost all of these shortcuts are the same as the Keyboard Navigation shortcuts with the addition of the Shift key. Many of these shortcuts also work in the Chopper and Track Properties windows.

Playback (Transport) Controls

Press these keys:	In order to:
Spacebar	Play (Start or Stop playback)
Shift+Spacebar	Play from start
Enter	Pause
Ctrl+Home	Go to Start
Ctrl+End	Go to End
L	Toggle Loop playback
Ctrl+R	Record

Editing Commands

Press these keys:	In order to:
F5	Refresh loop waveforms
F7	Generate MIDI timecode
Shift+F7	Generate MIDI clock
Ctrl+F7	Trigger from MIDI timecode
F8	Toggle Snapping on and off
Shift+F8	Snap to Markers
Ctrl+F8	Snap to Grid
L	Toggle Loop playback mode
Ctrl+L	Ripple edit mode

Appendix

D	Change edit tool
Ctrl+D	Change to Draw tool
V	Insert or Show/Hide Volume envelopes
Shift+V	Remove Volume envelope
P	Insert or Show/Hide Pan envelopes
Shift+P	Remove Pan envelope
` (on ~ tilde key)	Minimize all track height (toggle)
Ctrl+Shift+Up or Down Arrows	Change track height
Up or Down Arrows	Zoom In or Out
Ctrl+Up or Down Arrows	Zoom In (jump to high zoom) or Out (to full project)
4 or 6 on the Number Pad	Move Selected event Left (back) or Right (forward) on the timeline in small intervals (regardless of snapping)
Ctrl+4 or 6 on the Number Pad	Move event Left or Right one Grid space
Alt+Drag inside of event	Moves the media around inside of an event (the event itself remains stationary)
Alt+Drag edge of event	Changes the size of the event, but the media inside remains stationary relative to the dragged edge
Ctrl+Alt+Drag inside of event	Move the event while leaving the media stationary relative to the project

Chopper Commands*

Press these keys:	In order to:
A or /	Add media from cursor
Shift+A or /	Add media to cursor
, or . (comma or period)	Shift selection area left or right
Ctrl+, or . (comma or period) (forward)	Move timeline cursor left (back) or right
N	Link Arrow to selection
; (semicolon)	Halve selection
' (apostrophe)	Double selection

Many Keyboard Navigation and Selection shortcuts also work in the Chopper window, in addition to some playback (transport) controls and zoom shortcuts.

Standard Windows Commands

Press these keys:	In order to:
F1	Help
Shift+F1, then click on an object	Context Sensitive or What's This? Help
Shift+F10 or Windows Command key	Context Sensitive menu
Shift+click two events	Select both events and all events between them
Ctrl+click multiple events	Select all clicked events (but not events between them)
Ctrl+Z	Undo (or Alt+Backspace)
Ctrl+Y	Redo (or Ctrl+Shift+Z)
Ctrl+C	Copy (or Ctrl+Insert)
Ctrl+X	Cut (Shift+Delete)
Ctrl+V	Paste from Clipboard (Shift+Insert)
Ctrl+B	Repeat paste from Clipboard
Ctrl+N	New project
Ctrl+O	Open project
Ctrl+S	Save project

Appendix

Index

INDEX

D

INDEX

F

INDEX

INDEX

INDEX

W

INDEX

Save $100s on Loops for ACID™

with Sonic Foundry's New Loop Subscription Series. Get the hottest new loop libraries first – twelve months a year. This premier new service puts a new loop library in your hands every month before they are released to the general public.

Call for price.

Save 25% on Vegas® Audio

Get Sonic Foundry's award-winning digital audio mutitrack editor and save 25%. To take advantage of this offer, place Vegas Audio in your shopping basket and enter this code: 8510. The discount will be applied as you check out.

Expires December 31, 2002

Save 25% on Sound Forge®

Get Sonic Foundry's award-winning, industry-standard, two-track digital audio editor and save 25%. To take advantage of this offer, place Sound Forge® in your shopping basket and enter this code: 8511. The discount will be applied as you check out.

Expires December 31, 2002

Electronic Musician

Mail in the attached card today to receive your

3 free issues

of **Electronic Musician**!

Courtesy of **Muska & Lipman**
and **Electronic Musician**.